KA POʻE KAHIKO
The People of Old

Ka Poʻe Kahiko

THE PEOPLE OF OLD

By Samuel Manaiakalani Kamakau

Translated from the Newspaper Ke Au ʻOkoʻa
By Mary Kawena Pukui

Arranged and edited
By Dorothy B. Barrère

Illustrated by *Joseph Feher*

Bernice P. Bishop Museum Special Publication 51

BISHOP MUSEUM PRESS
Honolulu

Previous printings of this book have been made possible through partial financial support from the University of Hawaii Committee for the Preservation and Study of Hawaiian Language, Art and Culture; the Jane Winne publication fund; and the Institute of Museum Services, a Federal agency in the Department of Health, Education and Welfare, which offers operating and program support to the nation's museums. To each of these, the Board of Directors of Bishop Museum wishes to express its appreciation.

W. Donald Duckworth, Director, Bishop Museum

© 1991 by Bishop Museum. All rights reserved
First published 1964 by Bishop Museum
Reprinted 1968, 1974, 1979, 1987, 1991, and 2000 by Bishop Museum
Paperback edition 1992
Printed in the United States of America by Thomson-Shore, Dexter, Michigan

    The paper used in this publication meets the minimum requirements of American National Standard for Information Sciences–Permanence of Paper for Printed Library Materials, ANSI Z39.48-1984.

ISBN 0-930897-81-1 Paperback edition
ISBN 0-910240-32-9 Clothbound edition
Library of Congress Catalog Card No. 66-5392

FOREWORD

In 1931 Bishop Museum sponsored the systematic translation of all of Samuel Kamakau's articles on Hawaiian history and culture that had appeared in the weekly newspapers *Ku'oko'a* and *Ke Au 'Oko'a* from October 20, 1866, to February 2, 1871. Two manuscripts resulted; one, containing his historical material, was published in 1961 by The Kamehameha Schools, under the title *Ruling Chiefs of Hawaii*. It is prefaced by a review of the life of Kamakau. The other manuscript contains Kamakau's account of the material and social culture of the Hawaiians before and during the early period of acculturation to Western ways, and is in the library of the Museum.

As in the case of the history series, the culture series was translated piecemeal by a group of Hawaiian scholars and the translations were gone over by Mary Kawena Pukui, the main contributor, and Martha Warren Beckwith, Professor of Folklore, Vassar College. Their work was completed in 1934 and is a completely literal translation, worded and annotated by Miss Beckwith. The present volume is a revision of the portion of their translation that deals primarily with the customs and beliefs of "the people of old," *ka po'e kahiko*.

Kamakau wrote at a time when his people still retained much knowledge of the changing culture, and many of his allusions and half-explanations, easily comprehensible to them, appear tantalizingly indefinite and incomplete today. This revision seeks to clarify most of those obscurities—by the insertion of bracketed editorial comment and by a more precise and interpretive rendition of Kamakau's words. It would have been impossible to do this without the background of personal experiences and the accumulated knowledge of Mary Kawena Pukui. With her to guide and instruct in an understanding of the cultural background, the present editor has sought to present Kamakau's meaning without incorporating interpretations not based on his actual words. The material has been rearranged to provide a continuity of thought, with the original newspaper sources footnoted. Many of Miss Beckwith's valuable notes appended to the literal translation have been included, and references given to other source materials for comparison and evaluation.

Almost all of the topics covered by Kamakau are expositions of aspects of the old culture. However, Kamakau was an ardent, vehement, and highly vocal Christian convert, and his own well-founded knowledge of the traditions of his people concerning their gods and their creation myths led him into willful interpretations and equations in his zeal to show a comparable background of belief between the Hawaiian and Christian concepts of god and man. He reiterates the theme of a supreme god, Kane, who with Ku and Lono becomes a threefold god, and who creates heaven and earth and "the things that fill them both," including the "first man," Hulihonua (or Kanehulihonua), and the "first woman," Keakahulilani. He alters the Hawaiian concept, similar to the Tahitian, of a nether region presided over by Milu, and displaces Milu with Manu'a, a "Satan" who rules over an underworld with strata comparable to the hells of the Christian teachings of his time.

David Malo, in the classic work *Hawaiian Antiquities,* gave a broad outline of the ancient culture; John Ii's personal experiences, recounted in *Fragments of Hawaiian History,* revealed the functioning of that culture. *Ka Po'e Kahiko* now adds those details which give new depth and meaning to these two works. The three are a composite picture of Hawaiian beliefs and customs as they were in the ancient days and in the transitional period of acculturation to introduced thoughts and concepts.

DOROTHY B. BARRÈRE

Honolulu, Hawaii
February, 1964

CONTENTS

Foreword	vii
Part One: The Society	1
Notes to Part One	21
Part Two: The Family and the 'Aumakua	23
Notes to Part Two	44
Part Three: The Spirit World	45
Note to Part Three	60
Part Four: Kaku'ai—Transfiguration	61
Notes to Part Four	91
Part Five: 'Oihana Lapa'au—Medical Practices	93
Notes to Part Five	114
Part Six: O ka 'Ana'ana a me ka Hana 'Ino—Magic and Sorcery	117
Notes to Part Six	140
Appendix I: Glossary	143
Literature Cited	149
Index	151

PART ONE

PART ONE

The Society

KA PO'E KAHIKO

A MAN CALLED Hulihonua and a woman called Keakahulilani are said to have been the first man and the first woman in the very ancient past, and are believed by the Hawaiians to have been their earliest ancestors. It is not clear from the tradition whether the ancient ancestors lived in Hawaii as ruling chiefs. Perhaps because there were not many people, family quarrels did not grow up. The parents were masters over their own family groups. For the 28 generations from Hulihonua to Wakea, no man was made chief over another. During the 25 generations from Wakea to Kapawa, various noted deeds are mentioned in the traditions and well-known stories. Kapawa was the first chief to be set up as a ruling chief. This was at Waialua, Oahu; and from then on, the group of Hawaiian Islands became established as chief-ruled kingdoms—Maui from the time of Heleipawa, son of Kapawa, and Kauai from the time of Luanu'u.[1]

In the time of Heleipawa, records began to be kept of the chiefs; of the day of birth, the land where each was born, the places where the placenta (*'a'a*) and its navel string (*ewe*) were deposited, the place where the navel cord (*piko*) was cut, the famous deeds of each, and the burial place where each was laid. These places became famous as burial places of the bodies of chiefs who had ruled well. Chiefs who did evil were known, and when they died, their bodies were cast away, apart from the chiefs who had ruled well. There were two kingdoms noted for this keeping of records, and so the chiefs of Oahu and Maui are well known through the traditions and chants of the people of old, *ka po'e kahiko*.

Oahu was the place where the first man was made.[2] There the ancient ancestors lived, and from there they spread out over the whole group of islands—from Hawaii to Kauai. However, in the settling down (*ho'onohonoho*) of the ancestors after Wakea and his wife Papa, the kahuna orders were made separate, to be over the families. The separation began with the priesthood order of Lihau'ula, the first

3

child of Kahikoluamea and older brother of Wakea. This order, the *papa kahuna pule,* was the first to be selected out (*wae*) and so the kahuna orders were kept separate throughout the entire race in the following generations. It was several hundred years afterward, when men became numerous, that a government by chiefs was established, and the race lived under kings (*Mo'i*), as is found in the traditions of the first chiefs of Hawaii.

The pedigrees (*ku'auhau*) of the chiefs in the line of succession (*mo'o ku'auhau*) from ancient times down to those of Kamehameha I are not the same. As their descendants spread out, the ranks ('*ano*) of the chiefs lessened. Sometimes the hereditary chief lost his land, and the kingdom was taken by force and snatched away by a warrior, and the name of "chief" was given to him because of his prowess. He then attached himself to the chiefly genealogies, even though his father may have been of no great rank (*noanoa*), and his mother a chiefess. Therefore, the chiefs were not of like ranks, and the islands came under the rules of different chiefs who were not all of high chiefly status (*kulana*)—not from generations of chiefs. One might be an *ali'i kapu,* a "sacred" chief of highest rank, another an *ali'i noanoa,* a chief of no particular rank, or an *ali'i ho'opilipili,* a chief who had "grafted" himself onto a chiefly genealogy. Or one might be an *ali'i lepo popolo,* a "lowborn" chief, as the people of Hawaii island commonly say about their chief 'Umi-a-Liloa.

THE DEGREES OF CHIEFS

1. NI'AUPI'O.—This chief was of very high rank.[3] If both the father and the mother were *ni'aupi'o* chiefs, and their chiefly kapus were equal, neither need remove his kapa in deference to the royal kapu of the other, and they would be equally warm in their regard for each other. The children born from their loins were *ali'i kapu,* sacred chiefs.

2. PI'O.—If a son and a daughter were born to *ni'aupi'o* chiefs, and they returned (*ho'i*) and lived together, the sister marrying her brother, and the brother his sister, this wondrous marriage (*ho'ao*) of theirs was called a *ho'ao pi'o,* an arched marriage; a *ho'ao kapu,* a sacred marriage; a *ho'ao weliweli,* a revered marriage; a *ho'ao kapu ali'i,* a marriage of chiefly kapu. No divine law (*kanawai akua*) would arise between them. The children born of these two were gods, fire, heat, and raging blazes, and they conversed with chiefs and retainers only at night.

For examples of *ni'aupi'o* and *pi'o* chiefs, there were Kamahana, the husband, and Lonokahikini, his wife with *pi'o kapu,* whose children Kapueookalani, Kaneoneo, and Nalanipipi'o were called *pi'o* chiefs and *ni'aupi'o* chiefs.[4] Also, there were the *ni'aupi'o* chiefs Kamehameha-nui and his sister Kalola-nui, who "returned and formed an arch" (*ho'i a'e no laua pipi'o*), and to them was born Kalanikauiokikilo, a *pi'o* chiefess. She lived with Kaneoneo, and to them were born Kalani-'omaiheuila and Kalanianoano [Kalanionaona], who was born nearly dead.

3. NAHA.—A *naha* chief had a mother of *ni'aupi'o* rank and two fathers ('*elua makuakane*)[5] of *ni'aupi'o* rank. They both had married the one woman, and one

chief had had a son by her, and the other had had a daughter; when these two returned and married each other (*ho'i hou a'e laua nonoho ho'ao*), it was a *naha* mating (*moe naha*). Thus it was when Kalola-nui, the *ni'aupi'o* chiefess, mated with Kalani'opu'u, a *ni'aupi'o* chief, and had Kiwala-'o, a son, and then lived with Keaoua (Keoua-kupu-a-pa-i-ka-lani or Keoua-kalani-nui-ahi-lapalapa), a *ni'aupi'o* chief, and had Keku'iapoiwa Liliha [Keku'iapoiwa III], a daughter; Kiwala-'o and Keku'iapoiwa lived together; it was a *naha* mating. Keopuolani was born, and from Keopuolani came Kamehameha III, his older brother Liholiho, and his sister Nahi'ena'ena.

Naha chiefs were kapu chiefs, but their kapus were not equal to those of a *pi'o* chief. Although born of the same mother, the *naha* chief did not call his *pi'o* sibling (*hoahanau*) "brother" or "sister"; the *pi'o* sibling was like a god.

4. WOHI.—The *wohi* chief was one whose father was a *ni'aupi'o, pi'o,* or *naha* chief and whose mother was a close relative (*pili hoahanau*) of his father, her parents being junior siblings to his parents (*kaikaina hoahanau na na makua*) in the family of the high chief, the *ali'i nui*. Or his mother might be the *ni'aupi'o, pi'o,* or *naha* chief, and his father the close relative from their parental generation, they being "second pedigree" chiefs (*mau ali'i kuhaulua*) in the family of the high chief [that is, children of the high chief by later unions with chiefesses]. The children born to them were *wohi* chiefs. The *wohi* chief was not of the same status as the *naha* chief, but there was a minor decree (*he wahi kulana kanawai iki*) that eased the *wohi* from the kapu of the *naha* chiefs and the *ni'aupi'o* chiefs while their name chants were being uttered. But if he transgressed the kapus of the *pi'o* chiefs, or of the gods, he would be burned in fire.

Kiwala-'o had the *ni'aupi'o* kapu, Kamehameha I the *wohi* kapu, Liholiho the *naha* and the *ni'aupi'o* kapus, and Kekuaokalani the *wohi* kapu.[6]

5. LO.—The chiefs of Lihue, Wahiawa, and Halemano on Oahu were called *Lo* chiefs, *po'e Lo Ali'i* ["people from whom to obtain a chief"], because they preserved their chiefly kapus. The men had kapus, and the women had kapus, and when they joined their kapus and children were born, the children preserved their kapus. They lived in the mountains (*i kuahiwi*); and if the kingdom was without a chief, there in the mountains could be found a high chief (*ali'i nui*) for the kingdom. Or if a chief was without a wife, there one could be found—one from chiefly ancestors. Kauakahi'ailani, Ma'ilikukahi, Kalona, Piliwale, Kukaniloko, Pa'akakanilea [Pa'akanilea], Ka'akauualani, Ka'au, Lale, Paoakalani, Pakapakakuaua, Nononui, Kokoloea, and a great many others were *Lo* chiefs.

6. PAPA.—The mother was a *ni'aupi'o, pi'o,* or *naha* chiefess, with the *kapu moe* (the "prostrating" kapu), or some other chiefly kapu, but the father did not have equally high rank, although he was a "lesser chief," a *kaukauali'i*, of a chiefly family. Their child would be a *papa* chief, and sometimes a *wohi* through the mother. He would have a lesser kapu than his mother, and a higher one than his father; he would be a *papa* chief, or sometimes a *wohi* chief.

7. LOKEA.—The father was a *ni'aupi'o,* a *pi'o,* or a *naha* chief, and the mother was of a chiefly family, related to him through her parents, who were younger

relatives (*mau kaikaina hoahanau*) of his parents; the children born to the two would be *lokea* or *wohi* chiefs.

8. LA'AU ALI'I (LA'AULI).—The father was of the family of the high chief, and the mother also [that is, they were children of the high chief by his secondary matings], and they had equal kapus; their children were called *la'auli* chiefs, and *kuhaulua*, "second pedigree," chiefs. They were indeed chiefs, belonging to the line (*lalani*) of the high chief.

9. KAUKAU.—The father belonged to the family of the high chief and was a chief of the second pedigree, a *kuhaulua,* and the mother was of a family of *kaukau* chiefs. Or the mother might have been the *kuhaulua* chiefess in the family of the high chief, and the father from a *kaukau* chief's family. Their children were *kaukau* chiefs (*kaukauali'i*) and belonged to the family of the high chief. They were known to be of the lineage of the chief, and they were chiefs with rank, *kaukauali'i.*

10. ALI'I NOANOA.—The people of Hawaii are accustomed to calling the *noanoa* chiefs *noa* chiefs, as David Malo has written in his *Mo'olelo Hawaii,* because that was what the people called them in the ancient days, we are told. If a *ni'aupi'o*, or *pi'o*, or *naha* chief, perhaps, lived with a country woman without rank (*wahine noanoa*)—not a *kauwa*, an outcast, but just a beautiful country woman without rank from birth—the child born to them would be a *noanoa*, because the mother was without rank. Or, if the mother were a chiefess and the father without rank, their child would be called an *ali'i noanoa,* a *noanoa* chief. People of Hawaii call *noanoa* chiefs *po'e ali'i 'ole* ("people who are not chiefs"). That is why they called the Hawaii chief, 'Umi-a-Liloa, a *lepo popolo* chief—because his mother was without rank, a *noanoa*. She was Akahiakuleana, who lived at the cape of 'O'okala, which extends from Kau'ula to Kealakaha in Hamakua, Hawaii.

11. ALI'I MAKA'AINANA.—There were many chiefs born in the countryside from fathers and mothers who were high chiefs. Some from among the *ni'aupi'o*, *pi'o*, and *naha* chiefs lived in the country, keeping secret their chiefly kapus and living like ordinary people "under clumps of grass" (*malalo o ke opu weuweu*), perhaps because their ancestors had been taken captive, or perhaps because they knew of the abundance of food in the country. Thus chiefly families were amongst the *maka'ainana,* the people.

In the pedigrees of the children who were taken to be companions (*aikane*) in the household of a chief, it might be found that one was the child of some high chief and a very close relative of the rulers of the kingdom. In such a way ruling chiefs were connected with the people. Some of the people (*maka'ainana*) who lived in the country were of the same blood as the rulers of the kingdoms and were related to them—to Keawe, ruler of Hawaii; to Kamalalawalu, ruler of Maui; to Kane'alai, ruler of Molokai; to Kakuhihewa, ruler of Oahu; to Manokalanipo, ruler of Kauai; or to Puwalu, ruler of Niihau. Such descendants are living among us today.*

---

* *Ke Au 'Oko'a,* October 27, 1870.

KAHUNA ORDERS

PAPA KAHUNA PULE.—The priesthood, *papa kahuna pule,* was of the *papa ali'i* chiefly class. There were many priests of this class and their families [relatives] who entered into the priesthood orders of the high chiefs or of the ruling chiefs, such as Ka'opulupulu, Manewa, Kanewahine, Kaleopu'upu'u, Kikaha, and He'ea, the chiefly kahunas of Oahu. So it was of those of Kauai, Maui, and Hawaii.

Kamehameha I maintained two priesthood orders—the order of Holoa'e, which had come down from Pa'ao, and the order of Kuali'i. Holoa'e had been the *kahuna nui,* high priest, in the hereditary line of kahunas (*mo'o kahuna*) from Pa'ao, and Hewahewa became the *kahuna nui* of the order of Holoa'e in Kamehameha's old age. The kapus, or rituals, of these orders were very high; and there were two gods of these orders. The ritual (kapu) for the order of Holoa'e was that of the god Kunuiakea, the *kapu 'ohi'ako.* The visible symbols of Kunuiakea, the great unseen god in the dark clouds of heaven, were Kuka'ilimoku, Kuho'one'enu'u, Kukeolo'ewa, and Kukalani'ehu. Kuaiwa and Holoialena were the kahunas of the order of Kuali'i, and there were many chiefs who belonged to this order—Ulumaheihei Hoapili, Kuakahela *ma,* Lonomauki *ma,* and others. Their rituals were those of the god Lonoika'ouali'i, the *kapu lama* and the *kapu loulu,* which were heiau rituals. Lonoika'ouali'i was the visible symbol of the god Lononuiakea, and it was called Lonoikamakahiki. The real man Lonoikamakahiki was different from the god, but he too was covered (*uhi*) with bird feathers on the head and had a *ka'upu** bird for an ensign (*lepa*), as a flag of privilege (*hae no ka lanakila*).

PAPA KAULA: ORDER OF PROPHETS.—There were many prophets, *kaula,* in the ancient days, and their main work was to foretell (*wanana*) the important events which were to take place in the future, and the outcome (*ho'oko*) of those things which were to happen. They foretold an overthrow of the government, the death of a ruler, the times when good or evil chiefs would rise up in the kingdom, when there would be an increase of the race, and the sources of the blessings which would be obtained. The prophets were independent people, and were inspired by the spirit of a god (*he po'e i uluhia i ka 'uhane o ke akua*). They spoke (*ho'oko;* literally "fulfilled") the words of the god without fear before chiefs and men. Even though they might die, they spoke out fearlessly.

Luhaukapawa is said to have been the first prophet, and there were: Mahea; Naula [Niula?]; Luaho'omoe, a prophet and priest (*he kaula a he kahuna*); Ka'akakai; Anahua; Mo'i, another prophet and priest; the women prophets, Nu'a, Nu'akea, Kapa'uanu'akea, and Lanikepue; and Mo'opuakea; Maka'alawa; Kilohi; Kiu; Lanikaula; Makuakaumana; Ma; and many others. The last prophet was Kapihe, who uttered his final prophecy near the end of the reign of Kamehameha I, saying, *E hui ana na moku, e hiolo ana na kapu akua, e iho mai ana ko ka lani, a e pi'i aku ana ko ka honua* ("The islands will be united, the kapus of the gods overthrown, those of the heavens [the chiefs] will be brought low, and those of the earth [the common people] will be raised up").

---

* See Appendix I for scientific names of plants and animals mentioned by Kamakau.

OTHER KAHUNA ORDERS.—There were many other orders of kahunas, such as the *papa hulihonua,* those who knew the configurations of the earth ["land experts"]: *papa kuhikuhi pu'uone,* those who knew how to locate sites; *papa kilokilo lani,* those who could read the signs, or omens, in the sky; the *kilo hoku,* those who studied the stars; the *kilo 'opua,* those who studied and read the omens in clouds; the *kilo honua,* those who read the signs in the earth; the *papa ku'ialua,* the experts in *lua* fighting; the *papa lonomakaihe,* the experts in spear throwing; and many other classes besides.

THE CLASSES OF PEOPLE

PAPA KANAKA: MANKIND.—Mankind as a class, *papa kanaka,* comprised the multitudes (*pu'ali kanaka*), the populace (*hu*), and the people in general (*maka-'ainana*). *Maka'ainana* might be called "reddened men" (*weo kanaka*), "mere commoners" (*pakanaka*), "sacrifices" (*heana kanaka*), "trash" (*la'ola'o kanaka*), "cloaks of skin" (*ahu'ili kanaka*), "humble commoners" (*manaku kanaka*), "kindling wood" (*pulupulu kanaka*), or "commoners" (*palule*). Among the *maka'ainana* were chiefly people (*po'e ali'i*), those of some chiefly rank (*po'e kaukauali'i*), men of property (*ko'iko'i*) or prominence (*hanohano*), and children who were brought up as "favorites" (*keiki punahele*) by their parents. All the classes of chiefs belonged to the *papa kanaka,* as well as the priests, prophets, those who studied the earth, and those who read omens. When the *papa ali'i* class lacked a chief or chiefess to be the ruler, one could be found among this class, and also priests, prophets, chiefs, petty chiefs, favorites, intimate friends, adopted children, attendants, and "pets." Of the *maka'ainana* it was said that, in the end, the well-being (*pono*) of the kingdom was in their hands.

PAPA KAUWA: OUTCASTS.—There were three kinds of *kauwa* [that is, three usages of the word]. A chief or a retainer might call himself a *kauwa* in order to humble himself before his superior (*haku*) or his ruler although he was not really a *kauwa;* or a server of the chief, related to him by birth, might be called a *kauwa,* such as the *kauwa hana,* who worked for the chief, a *kauwa lawelawe,* one who carried his belongings, a *kauwa iwikuamo'o,* who took care of his personal affairs, a *kauwa kua kahili,* who bore his *kahili,* a *kauwa hale kapa,* who took care of his tapa storehouse, or a *kauwa lomilomi,* one who massaged him. The real *kauwa* were born outcasts from their ancestors' time. They were a people much despised, and were called *kauwa kuapa'a,* "load-carrying outcasts," *kauwa laepuni,* "outcasts with tattooed foreheads," *kauwa makawela,* "red-eyed outcasts," or *kauwa 'ainoa,* "free-eating [godless] outcasts."

Chiefs who took a mate from among the *kauwa* because of beauty of person inflicted a lasting scar of disgrace on their descendants in this time. Rulers, chiefs, and people despised the *kauwa;* it was not proper to eat with them, or welcome them into the house, or sleep near them. When their masters (*haku*) died, *kauwa* were laid alive (*ho'omoe ola*) in their burial places with them; and *kauwa* were drowned by having their heads held under water (*lumaluma'i ola 'ia*) in the sea or in fresh water [as sacrificial atonement for the infraction of a kapu by their masters].

Occasionally some *kauwa laepuni* lived independently of their hereditary masters (*haku kanu*) in another place, or on another land, and kept secret their *kauwa* names. People of some prominence might take them as mates because of their handsomeness, and good-looking children would be born who in turn would be taken as mates by chiefs. Thus a future generation might ascend to be ruling chiefs; and in the end, descendants of *kauwa* might be chiefs. In comparing (*ho'omo'omo'o*) the ancestors of the *kauwa* and their masters, if a *kauwa* was found among a master's ancestors, the master's chiefly rank would fall low. He would be laid at the feet of his lord, and his eyes would be scooped out. *Kauwa laepuni, kauwa makawela, kauwa laepe'a, kauwa 'ainoa,* and *kauwa 'aumakua* not only belonged to rulers, they belonged to chiefs, and to people in general, the *maka'ainana*. They were a *kauwa* people, outcast and untouchable, from their ancestors on down.

The *kauwa* of Oahu became "lost in the shuffle" (*huikau*) when Kahahana and the Oahu chiefs died and Kahekili and his Maui chiefs took over the kingdom in 1783, and again when Kamehameha and his Hawaii chiefs took the kingdom in 1795. The *kauwa* hid themselves until the time when the *kapu akua*, the gods' kapus, were overthrown, and the kingdom became a "free-eating" one, *ke aupuni 'ainoa* [one without gods]. That released the *kauwa*. They continued to hide their shameful blemish (*'alina hilahila*), but they could not wash out their tainted blood. Their descendants are among the chiefs of this day. By mixing here, mixing there, the blood of lords has become mixed with the blood of *kauwa*, and there is nothing that can cleanse it (*'a'ole mea nana i huikala*).

KAPUS OF THE CHIEFS

In the ancient days there were many chiefly kapus [royal privileges], and they were in the hands of chiefs. They were apportioned according to the status (*kulana*) of the chiefs, and it was thus that the proper kapus belonged to each chief. Not by having the name of ruler, *inoa Mo'i*, or rising up over a district did a chief get the high chiefly privilege (*kapu ali'i ki'eki'e*), nor could he assume a chiefly kapu if he became a district chief. He could not assume a higher chiefly kapu than that originally given him.

The Kauai chiefess Kahamalu'ihi, also called Kalua-i-Ho'ohila, was the ancient source of the exalted kapu, the *kapu puhi kanaka*, the privilege to "burn" men, and the decrees (*kanawai*) Kaihehe'e and Lumaluma'i, which meted out death by drowning for violations of their kapus. Kualono'ehu was the chief who was sent to get this kapu. It was not assumed by just any sacred chief, that is, any *ni'aupi'o* or *naha* chief—they received the "squatting" kapu, the *kapu a noho*. It was Kuali'i Kunuiakea Kuikealaikauaokalani who received the *kapu moe*, the *kapu puhi kanaka*, and the *kanawai* Kaihehe'e and Lumaluma'i. They were his from the time he was in the womb of Mahuluanuiokalani.[7]

In the womb was obtained the rank of each chief—the *ni'aupi'o*, the *pi'o*, the *naha*, the *wohi*, the *kuhaulua*, or the *papa* chief—and by the rank of each chief was known which *kanawai* and which kapus belonged to him. Of the *ni'aupi'o*, the *pi'o*, and the *naha* chiefs, the kapus of the *ni'aupi'o* and the *naha* were equal, but were lesser than the kapu of the *pi'o* chief, and the kapus of the *wohi* and the *kuhaulua* were beneath their feet. The *kanawai* of the kapus of the *ni'aupi'o, pi'o,* and *naha* chiefs was the decree of death by burning (*puhi*) for those who defiled their kapus. If a man went to the house of the high chief and his shadow fell on the house, or if perhaps a *wohi* or a *kuhaulua* or a *papa* chief was walking along with the high chief and his shadow fell upon this *pi'o, ni'aupi'o,* or *naha* chief, he could not escape the fire. Chiefs and men were put to death (*ua pau*) if they used (*pili*) the mat, the tapas, the pillow, the malo, or anything else that belonged to the high chief. Because of the great many kapus of the *pi'o* and *naha* chiefs, it was not right for them to go out in the daytime; at night was the proper time for them to associate with other chiefs and people, when no shadow could be cast upon them. At night was the time when gifts of food, pigs, and valuables were brought to them.

Some kapu chiefs, when they went to the back districts, or to a place where they were not known, hid their chiefly ranks and went just as strangers (*kanaka e*). They did this so that the people (*maka'ainana*) would not die because of infractions of their kapus or their sacred *kanawai*. The ordinary people in the ancient days did not ever see the chiefs because of their kapus; and when the chiefs went into the country, they would not be recognized and would be sent to fetch water, or to fish, and were called by country names. The chiefs themselves were afraid of the consequences of their kapus; that is why they hid themselves in the back districts. The chiefs had many kapus, and those of the highest rank were called by the name of a god, or by the name of "heaven" (*lani*), where the gods lived.

The kapu of a god was superior to the kapu of a chief, but the kapus of the *ni'aupi'o* and *pi'o* chiefs were equal to the gods'. The violators of their kapus need not be offered to the gods (*'a'ole e ho'ali i ke akua*); the sacred decrees (*kanawai la'a*) of these chiefs were applied to the violators without their being dedicated to the gods (*'a 'ole e 'amama a'e i ke akua*). Anyone who was seen by the *ilamuku,* the executive officers of the chief, or the *iwikuamo'o,* his relatives who had charge of his personal needs, to have defiled the chief's things (*la'a i na nea kapu*) was bound with a rope and was given up to the chief *ilamuku* to be burned in fire, (*puhi i ke ahi*) without offering him to the gods; or to be grasped and held until drowned in the sea or in fresh water without a dedicatory prayer to the gods. If a man was about to die because of a kapu of a god, and chiefs of these ranks were opposed (*ho'ole*), he would not die, but would live. Only these chiefs could release (*wehe*) the kapus of the gods, hence they were called "life here on earth," *he ola ma ka honua nei.* If there were a heiau dedication (*he kapu heiau*), chiefesses of these ranks alone could enter the sacred place (*kahi kapu*) and eat of the bananas, the coconuts, and the pigs; no other chiefesses could enter. Not a single daughter of Kamehameha I could enter this place, lest she die. There were only two *pi'o* chiefesses known in his time, Kalanikauiokikilo and Nalanipipi'o.*

---

* November 3, 1870.

KANAWAI: LAWS AND EDICTS

Life might be spared in the ancient days by means of a ruler's edict, a *kanawai ali'i*. It decreed life or death. A chief who had been taken captive and was about to die, or a man who had been beaten almost to death, was saved if the king (*mo'i*) pronounced his fundamental sacred edict (*kumu kanawai la'a*), the *kanawai Kolowalu*. When two kings were at war against each other, and there was slaughtering on both sides, when the defeated chief and his warriors were taken captive and were to be slaughtered, if the victorious king uttered this fundamental sacred edict, a universally sacred decree (*papa holahola kanawai la'a*), then the defeated side was saved. No one could be killed, no one beaten; not a drop of blood could be shed after the sacred decree had been pronounced. One who violated this decree paid with his own blood for the shedding of the blood of a captive. Even though he were a chief or a favorite of the king he would not be saved. The chiefly decree was sacrosanct (*la'a*).

Sometimes a whole *ahupua'a* or *'okana* land section got into trouble through violating some kapu of the gods, perhaps on a ceremonial day (*la kauila nui*), or perhaps by forgetting when the kapu day came, and treating the kapu ceremonial day as a "free" day. All who lived on that *ahupua'a* or *'okana* became subject to death. The only thing that could save them from being slaughtered by the people who wanted to slay them (*po'e luku make'e*) for violating the kapu of the gods was for the king to place his sacred chiefly decree upon them. This decree of the king was a "refuge of life," *he pu'uhonua ho'ola*. It was a very ancient decree, observed by every king who ruled the land; an edict belonging to every chief who ruled over a kingdom.*

The names of the *kanawai Kolowalu* of some chiefs of the Kauai line were: the Ua'alakawai of La'amaikahiki; the Pu'ua of 'Ahukini-a-La'a; the Maea of Kamahano; the Ka'ikananu'u of Kaumakamano; the Malokea of Ka'oao [Kahakuakane?]; the Pikele'ula of Kuwalupaukamoku; the Haku'alamea of Kahakumakapaweo; and the Loa of Kalanikukuma. Of the Oahu chiefs, there were: the Paliloaali'i of Kuihewa (Kakuhihewa); the 'Anaha of Kanekapu-a-Kuihewa; the Kaiewalu of Kaho'owahaokalani; the Papaholahola of Kauakahi-a-Kaho'owaha; and the Ni'aupi'o Kolowalu of Kuali'i. Of the Maui chiefs, there were: the Kohola of Kekaulike and the 'Ao'ao'ele'ele of Kahekili. These were the fundamental edicts, the *kumu kanawai*, of some chiefs who ruled over kingdoms.**

There were two kinds of *kanawai* observed by the Hawaiian people from the very ancient days: the *kanawai akua*, or gods' laws; and the *kanawai kapu ali'i*, or sacred chiefly laws. Such were the laws in ancient times, as this writer of history has set them forth.*

The first laws made were those which established the ritual periods (*kapu Sabati*; literally, Sabbath kapus) of the year. These days, kapu to the gods, were established in the time of Wakea, and they were very sacred days. At the time of

---

* March 10, 1870.
** March 17, 1870.

Luhaukapawa, the first prophet, and the priestly order of Lihau'ula, and in the time of the later prophets, the laws of the kapu days became very strictly enforced. Men were sacrificed as "burnt offerings" (*mohai kuni*), and fragrant things were burned with offerings and sacrifices. In the period of Wakea, offerings of fragrant things and human sacrifices were unknown. It was 700 or 1,000 years later that men became burnt offerings, and were baked in an imu or broiled over a fire until the body grease (*hinu*) dripped, and then were placed on the *lele* altar. This was often practiced in the time of the Hawaii chief, 'Umi-a-Liloa. Moa'ula, in Waipio valley, Hawaii, was the heiau where most of the offering of human sacrifices was done in his time.

Hakau-a-Liloa, the high chief who ruled over Hawaii, was one of those laid on the altar as a burnt offering for the god by 'Umi. The story is well known, and thousands of persons were eyewitnesses that the god came down from heaven in a billow of floating clouds, with thunder and lightning and dark clouds, and the tongue of the god quivered above the *lele*. The god was not seen; his body was in the heavens, but his tongue quivered downward like lightning, and the burnt offering became a billow of smoke and rose up and was gone. It was not so long ago that 'Umi-a-Liloa ruled—it was six or seven hundred years ago, about fifteen generations from his time to this. But the sacrificing of humans did not originate with 'Umi; it originated after the time of Kapawa, who established the kapus of the chiefs and the kapus of the gods, and who caused a separation between the kapus of the chiefs and of the gods.

The *ilamuku* were the executioners who watched over the sacred kapus of the chief; those who broke the kapus of the chief or of his sacred things were burned in fire. One who broke a kapu of the god became a burnt offering for the god and was offered as a sacrifice. The *ilamuku* who guarded the kapus of the gods were kahunas; they guarded all the kapus of the gods. Both chiefs and people were subject to these kapus. The chiefly mana of a chief could not save one who broke the kapu of the gods. But if a kapu of the chief and that of a god were combined, the man could be absolved through the kapu of the chief, and if the breaking of the god's kapu carried a death penalty, he could be saved.

The god to whom men were offered as burnt sacrifices was Ku, that is, Kunuiakea. The symbols in which he appeared to the eye and accepted (*maliu ana*) the sacrifices and offerings and gifts laid before him were Kuka'ilimoku, Kukeolo'ewa, Kuho'one'enu'u, Kukalani, and Kukalani'ehuiki. These symbols were wooden images below (*po'e akua la'au malalo*), enveloped in layers (*ka'ai kananu'u*) of tapas of the *'oloa, 'ape'ula,* and *ha'ena* varieties. On the head was a very fine feather, which drooped and streamed down to cover the head (*he hulu e kuwelu me ke kiaweawe makali'i e uhi ana i ke po'o*). When the god revealed his approbation (*ho'ike 'ia mai ka 'oia'i'o*), the feather stood straight up, twisting about like a waterspout, as if full of lightning, and flew from its place and rested on the head of a person and fluttered about his head, his arm, or his shoulder. These were signs that the god had said he would help, *kokua,* and would give him his blessing in war, or in the prospering of the kingdom.

So it was that people observed the ceremonial days (*la kauila*) and the ritual periods (*na kapu Sabati*) from ancient times down to the time when the kapus were abolished (*ke au 'ainoa*). Then the kapus of the gods and the chiefs, and the *kauila* kapu days, were done away with, and the people lived a godless and thoughtless (*'aiahulu a 'aia*) life until the American missionaries arrived. They were given over to pleasure-seeking and disbelief; a kingdom of unrestricted common people was ascendant (*lanakila*) [during that period].

SOME KANAWAI OF GODS AND CHIEFS

The edict Kai'okia was the ancient *kanawai* given by the god after the subsiding of the Kai-a-Kahulumanu, or Kai-a-Kahinali'i. The edict pledged that the god would not again destroy the living things on earth and the breathing things that live in space; the sea would be "cut off" (*he kai 'oki 'ia*), and be kept separate from the land, and would not again rise up over it. The sign that set the separation, that the Kai-a-Kahinali'i would not again rise over the land, was the *ala muku* rainbow. The god who set forth this *kanawai* was Kane, that is, Kanenuiakea.

The older generations of Hawaii respected this great edict, and the *kanawai* Kai'okia became an important one for this people. If a parent was angry with a child, or a husband with a wife, or a sibling with a sibling (*hoahanau*), or a father with his father, or a mother with her mother, and they came to dissension and breach, one of them would swear by this edict, which was extremely binding, that he would not see the one sworn against "until death." Only by making an atonement (*uku*) to the god, with offerings for the breaking of the oath, could the person who had sworn by this *kanawai* be free from the anger (*lili*) of the god over the flouting of the oath taken under his *kanawai*. The person who had sworn the oath by this *kanawai* of Kai'okia atoned thus: he took a pig, a whole *'awa* root (*pu'awa*), a complete *'awa* plant (*'awa lau*), a tapa, a red fish, and many other things, and went to the one he had wronged and against whom he had sworn his oath. Then the one who had sworn the oath, and the one against whom it was sworn, made a dedicatory offering (*mohai ho'ali*) of their love offerings (*mohai aloha*) to the god for their wrongdoings, and so they were spared from the repercussions (*ho'ohiki 'ino*) of the *kanawai* of the god. Their offerings could be eaten by relatives and close friends after they two had eaten of the offerings for the forgiveness of their wrongs (*mohai hala*).

The *kanawai* Kai'okia of Kane is often mentioned in the traditions and stories of the people of old, and also in meles; for example:

Wilia i uka, wilia i kai,	Turned to the land, turned to the sea,
Wilia i kaua a ka ho'ole akua,	Turned away are we, and withdrawn from the god,
Ka ho'omalu ka ho'omaloka.	The disbeliever, and the unbeliever.
E Pele, e wakawaka ka'oaka o ka lani,	Oh Pele, jagged flashing one of the heavens,
Ke'apapanu'u, ke 'apapalani,	[You spirits] of the firmament, of the heavens,

O Manokalanipo, o Keakaleihulu,	Oh Manokalanipo, Keakaleihulu,
O Pe'aleihuluomanu, o Manukiu,	Pe'aleihuluomanu, Manukiu,
O Manukiu o Manuaha'i,	Manukiu, Manuaha'i,
A ha'ina ae ana ka mana o ko akua iwaho la, e ha'ina.	Reveal the mana of your god out there, reveal it,
E kukulu ka pahu kapu o ka leo,	Establish the inviolability of the utterance [literally, "set up the sacred drum of the voice"],
E ho'ohiki kanawai he akua, he Kai'okia,	Make binding the *kanawai* of the god, the Kai'okia,
He ala muku no Kane me Kanaloa.	[Show us] the *ala muku* rainbow of Kane and Kanaloa.⁸

The *kanawai* Kai'okia is also mentioned in the meles which begin: *Ua la'a aku la i ke Kai'okia a Kane* ("It has been made sacrosanct by the Kai'okia of Kane"). It is mentioned in many places in the prayers of the kahunas.

Here are some other *kanawai* belonging to gods: Pu'ukoamakai'a and Ka'upukea were the *kanawai* of Kaho'ali'i; Kiki'i was the *kanawai* of Ku, Laulili'i was Kanaloa's; Inaina was the *kanawai* of Kuliliaka, Hawanawana the *kanawai* of Kanehekili, Kupou the *kanawai* of Kukauakahi; 'Aliamoku was Kuka'ilimoku's, a *kanawai* that there must be no widespread fire during his rites; the *kanawai* Papamau was Honuamea's (Pele's), the Paukukaula was Hoku's (Ho'ohokukalani's).⁹

Some *kanawai* were wicked edicts that put men to death and shed blood to please the bloodletting gods (*na akua ho'okahe koko*). Others were laws that benefited the people and the kingdom, and were laws superior to those of any other kingdom on earth.

The *kanawai* Pu'ukoamakai'a was a very revolting edict. It decreed that someone's eye must be scooped out. The *kanawai* Pu'ukoamakai'a might be pronounced (*kau 'ia*) during an assembly, perhaps at a feast where the king would also be present, when the god Kaho'ali'i possessed the man-god of this name (*noho iho la*). He wanted an eye, to be taken as a relish with the cup of 'awa [to be offered to the god in the body of the possessed Kaho'ali'i]. The assembly was dedicated to getting an eye, and they sat and looked at each other until the man was found whose eye was wanted—and his eye would be scooped out. It was a very harsh edict.

The *kanawai* Ni'aupi'o Kolowalu was an excellent one, promulgated during the reign of the Oahu ruler Kuali'i Kunuiakea Kuikealaikauaokalani. It was a fixed decree, constant and unchanging. It provided that old men and old women could go and sleep [in safety] on the highway, and also that farmers and fishermen had to welcome strangers and feed the hungry. If a man said he was hungry, he must be fed. If he invoked this *kanawai,* then the food became dedicated and could not be withheld by the person whose food it was—it was lost to him through the *kanawai,* and he had to give it up. But a person who invoked this law of the king took care that he invoked it rightly, lest the punishment be upon himself. If he invoked the *kanawai* only to rob another of food and provisions, then the burden of the punishment would rebound upon himself. The wrongdoer who had refused him food, and who had been about to die because of that, was released.

Because of the righteousness of his *kanawai,* and the good care Kuali'i took of his government, the gods guarded him and gave him a long life. It was he, the king of Oahu, who is mentioned in the traditions of *ka po'e kahiko* as having lived for four times forty years and fifteen more—until he was bent and feeble, with eyes drooped and bleary, with skin like a dried hala leaf, and was bound up in netting as though he had been made an ancestral god (*pa'a i koko me ka 'aumakua 'ia*). He died at Kailua, Ko'olaupoko, Oahu, in the year 1730, at the age of 175 years.*

Kanela'auli was a chief noted for observing the *kanawai,* and he thought of many others to benefit chiefs and people. But the ruling chiefs did not agree to the *kanawai* he proposed. They were interested only in pleasure, and in laying burdens upon the people and seizing what belonged to them. Because of proposing these good edicts to them, Kanela'auli was put to death [to silence him].

The *kanawai* Mamalahoa was the *kanawai ali'i* of Kamehameha I, which was promulgated during his reign. Its great characteristic (*'ano*) was as an edict that determined life or death. If a chief was about to die, and Kamehameha placed the *kanawai* Mamalahoa on him, he would live. If, on the other hand, the chiefs and the *kuhina nui* (chief counselor) wanted the man to live, but Kamehameha did not agree and pronounced the Mamalahoa, then nothing could release it; it was absolute (*pa'a loa*) and the man died.

The *kanawai* Mamalahoa said, "Let the old men, the old women, and the children sleep [in safety] on the highway." This became the law over the whole Hawaiian group in the time when Kamehameha ruled over the kingdom. He gave the name of Mamalahoa to the law for his escape from death when he was beaten by the fishermen at Papa'i in Kea'au, Puna, Hawaii. He had a wound on his head from being struck with a club (*i ka hoa i ka hahau 'ia i ka la'au*);[10] his body streamed with blood, and he was in great pain. At this time, there was a great war going on between the chiefs of Kona and those of Hilo and Ka-'u. Kamehameha and all his chiefs and war troops were staying at Laupahoehoe, in Hilo Paliku, and Kamehameha had sailed over to Papa'i in Puna to make war there. But he met with this misfortune and was almost killed, and because he escaped from death, he named the *kanawai* Mamalahoa; it was the great life-saving law.

In the year 1792 Kamehameha was at war with Keoua Kuahu'ula, the son of Kalani'opu'u, and the chief of Ka-'u. Both sides were resting from the fatigue of battle. Kamehameha and his chiefs were building the heiau of Pu'ukohola at Kawaihae, and Keoua was staying in Ka-'u with his chiefs and his war troops. Two of Kamehameha's counselors (*kuhina*), Keaweheulu and Kamanawa, sailed over to Ka-'u to flatter Keoua and to persuade him to give up fighting and come to meet Kamehameha and rule with him over the people as Kalani'opu'u had ruled together with his younger brother Keaoua [Keoua, father of Kamehameha]. Keoua was "taken in" (*ua puni*), and he and his company were slaughtered at Kawaihae. Only one man out of the forty on the double canoe with Keoua escaped—that was Kuakahela, the grandfather of Kama'ipu'upa'a. He escaped by crawling among the

---

* March 17, 1870.

thousands of dead, when it would have been impossible to hide a moving form in the open. He is said to have been "saved by the grace of the god" (*he ola na ke akua*).

On the day that Keoua and his followers were killed, a double canoe was lying outside with the chief Ka'oleioku, the younger brother of Keoua and said to be the first-born son of Kamehameha. Many chiefs begged to have him put to death. Keli'imaika'i, Kamehameha's younger brother, insisted upon it, and the counselors clamored for his death. In the confusion of voices, all condemning Ka'oleioku to death, Kamehameha declared, "He shall not be put to death," and commanded Kalaimamahu to proclaim the great law of life, the Mamalahoa law. The proclamation of this law allowed Ka'oleioku to beach the canoe in safety with his chiefs and paddlers, almost forty of them. It saved the life of Kuakahela, who was hiding from capture, and it prevented the slaughter of several thousand of Keoua's chiefs and people, including women and children, who had come in a procession from Ka-'u and who were there on the heights. They heard that Keoua Kuahu'ula and the chiefs on his canoe had been killed. Then Ka'oleioku landed alive; the *kanawai* Mamalahoa had been proclaimed. All the captives were thereby saved, and great was their relief (*'oli'oli*). A thousand and more people were saved on that day through the *kanawai* Mamalahoa.

The followers of Keoua Kuahu'ula who had been saved by the Mamalahoa law had been dancing and rejoicing, singing songs exalting their chief and disparaging Kamehameha, belittling him in songs which they had composed while in Ka-'u. Yet Kamehameha did not harm them. It was his wish to save them by pronouncing the law, which he did against the opposition of his executive officers, his counselors, and powerful chiefs. His power was supreme through the Mamalahoa law.

Ka'oleioku was the younger brother of Keoua Kuahu'ula Kalani'opu'u through the same mother, Kanekapolei. Kalani'opu'u was the father of Keoua Kuahu'ula, who was slain at Kawaihae and offered as a sacrifice at Pu'ukohola, and Kamehameha I was the father of Ka'oleioku. He was a renowned chief, this child of Kamehameha. It was not, however, Kamehameha's chiefly power that saved his son, nor his position as ruler of the kingdom. He had been made ruler of the kingdom by the strong support of his counselors and his chiefs through battle and the shedding of blood. It was not within Kamehameha's power as king to rule absolutely; he had just been given the power of king through the consent of the counselors and the chiefs. How was it, then, that Ka'oleioku was saved? It was through the Mamalahoa law. How was it that this law carried such power? It was because the counselors, the chiefs, the kahunas, and all the powerful persons had agreed that the Mamalahoa law was Kamehameha's birthright, from the time he came from his mother's womb. When Kamehameha escaped death at Papa'i in Kea'au, Puna, it was recalled that the day of his birth at Kokoiki in Kohala had been a propitious day (*la pomaika'i*), auguring that he would not die in battle, but would live to old age, unless he committed some sacrilege (*ho'ohewahewa*), in which case he would die. The *kanawai* Mamalahoa gave him unlimited power while ruler of his kingdom. Anyone so unfortunate as to be taken captive and about to be killed could be saved by Kamehameha pronouncing the Mamalahoa law; it was consecrated to the saving of lives and fortunes (*pomaika'i*). Ka'oleioku and the thousands there lived because of the pronouncing of the Mamalahoa law. It was a righteous thing (*mea kupono*) that Kamehameha did, against the opposition of his friends, because the outcome of the war for the kingdom was still undecided.

The sacred *kanawai* of the kings was a "refuge of life," *he pu'uhonua ho'ola*. When captives taken in war, though they numbered some hundreds or thousands, marched before the king and he placed his sacred decree over them, they were no longer captives, nor could they be seized to be treated as "slaves" (*po'e kauwa pio*). They won not only life, but freedom also, to go where they pleased, or to return to their homes. Kahekili pronounced his *kanawai* in the war on Oahu with Kahahana at the battle of Ka'opuaki'iki'i. So did Kalanikupule in the battle of Kuki'iahu in Kalauao, Oahu; the slaughtering stopped, and the lives of some of the chiefs and warriors were saved, and they were released to return to their lands on Kauai. So also did Kamehameha use the Mamalahoa law to stop the slaughter at the battle of Nu'uanu, and Ulumaheihei Hoapili used such a law to stop the men of Hawaii from killing the men of Kauai at the "pig-eating" battle (*kaua 'ai pua'a*) on Kauai in 1824. The *po'e kahiko* of Hawaii well knew the sacred *kanawai* as a refuge of life. Because the chiefs regretted the slaughter of men and the killing of women and children, they were given *kanawai* with which to stop slaughter. The slaughterers knew that the *kanawai* had a sacred power beyond the mere spoken word of the king; the *kanawai* was an absolute edict (*'olelo pa'a loa*).*

PU'UHONUA

A place to which one could escape and be saved from being taken captive or from being put to death was called a *pu'uhonua*—a place of refuge. The king was called a *pu'uhonua* because a person about to die could run to him and be saved; so also were called his queen (*ka Mo'iwahine*) and his god. They were sacrosanct, and therefore their lands were sacrosanct, and were *'aina pu'uhonua,* lands of refuge. Some fortifications (*pu'u kaua*) were *pu'uhonua,* when they were close to those about to be captured in battle.

In the time of Kamehameha I the old *pu'uhonua* were abolished, and Kamehameha set up new *pu'uhonua* as he wished. The old ones were abolished because they were taken over by the chiefs, war leaders, and warriors who had fought Kamehameha's wars for him, and therefore they ceased to be *pu'uhonua*. Only on Kauai did the old *pu'uhonua* remain, because Kamehameha's wars did not extend to Kauai; hence these lands were not distributed to his war leaders. Kauai did not become a dependency, and the kingdom remained under its hereditary chiefs. The *pu'uhonua* lands on Kauai were, Keonekapu-a-Kahamalu'ihi for Waimea, Kekaha for Mana, and Wailua for Puna, and there were some others besides. There were also *pu'uhonua* refuges on Hawaii, in Kohala, Hamakua, Hilo, Puna, and Ka-'u. But in the battles between the chiefs of Hilo, Ka-'u, and Kona, the Kona chiefs won

---
* March 24, 1870.

and the *pu'uhonua* lands were lost to the war leaders of Kamehameha. Only the *pu'uhonua* at Honaunau, Kona, remained, perhaps because the Kona chiefs won the kingdom, or perhaps because the land on which the *pu'uhonua* was situated was of no value. The *ahupua'a* of Honaunau was separate from the *pu'uhonua*.

The *pu'uhonua* in ancient times was an *ahupua'a* portion of a district (*ahupua'a 'okana*), like Kailua and Waikane for Ko'olaupoko district on Oahu, and also Kualoa, which was a very sacred land and a true *pu'uhonua*, where persons marked for death were saved if they entered it. There were such places all over Oahu. The stronghold (*pu'u kaua*) Kawiwi in Waianae was a *pu'uhonua* in time of war. The *pu'uhonua* of Honaunau was not like these. A real stone wall enclosed it like a fortress (*pa kaua*), and it had the characteristics (*'ano*) of a heiau within. It may have been a *pu'uhonua* for men only to escape to.

The famous *pu'uhonua* of Honaunau in North Kona had the walls of a fortified heiau (*pa kaua heiau*), made of large rocks placed on top of each other. Its two walls made an angle (*huina pa'ewa*) between Honaunau and Keamoali'i. One wall was a furlong (*kesadia*, or *kekakia*) and 19 fathoms (*anana*) long, and the other 67 fathoms long; the height was 2 fathoms, and the breadth, 2½ fathoms. Outside the *makai* wall was a stone called the Keoua Stone, and then a shoal, and the sea. There were two heiaus inside the walled area. One was at the northwest corner, adjoining the wall; this was the Hale-o-Keawe. The other [called 'Alealea] was the large *pu'uhonua* atop the stone platform near the Hale-o-Keawe, and at the curve seaward of Keamoali'i; it faced toward Keokea.

The Hale-o-Keawe was a heiau in which were placed the bones of the chiefs enclosed in sennit caskets (*pa'a i ke ka'ai*). On the North Kona side of it was the lava flat of Akahipapa. Around the kapu enclosure (*paehumu*) which surrounded the Hale-o-Keawe were fixed wooden images (*ki'i la'au ho'olulu*), and on the right (*'akau*) of the entrance to the enclosure was the refuse pit (*luapa'u*).

It is said that Keawe-ku-i-ke-ka'ai built these *pu'uhonua* 300 or 400 years ago, when the chiefs of Kona, Hilo, and Ka-'u were warring all over Hawaii. About him it is said, *Ho'i no Keawe a ku i ke ka'ai* ("Keawe was brought to his lasting resting place and set up in a sennit casket"). Some people say that it was in the time of Keawe-i-kekahi-ali'i-o-ka-moku, the grandfather of Kalani'opu'u, 200 or 300 years ago, and that this Keawe built these *pu'uhonua* at Honaunau. But in the time of this Keawe there was peace; Keawe was the chief who was raised up and made the supreme ruler (*ali'i nui*) by the consent of the rulers of the kingdoms (*na'li'i 'ai aupuni*) of Hawaii island. Keawe-ku-i-ke-ka'ai was the brother of the kapu chiefess Keakamahana, who was the *pi'o* child of Keli'iokalani and Keakealanikane; Keawe was the son of this Keakealanikane by Kalanimakali'i. He was the one who built the *pu'uhonua* at Honaunau, and the house to contain the caskets of the chiefs (*hale ka'ai*). Because Keawe-i-kekahi-ali'i-o-ka-moku became supreme and had been encased in a sennit casket like Keawe-ku-i-ke-ka'ai and placed in the *pu'uhonua* house built by Keawe-ku-i-ka-ka'ai, the house was called Hale-o-Keawe.

The concept (*'ano*) of *pu'uhonua* came down from ancient times, and *pu'uhonua* lands had always been observed. They were sacrosanct and inviolable lands; no blood of wrongdoers could be shed once they entered into these *pu'uhonua* lands. In the time when Kamehameha was ruling chief of the kingdom, all the lands belonging to his favorite wife Ka'ahumanu and to his war god (*akua kaua*) Kuka'ilimoku were made *pu'uhonua* lands. Ka'ahumanu's lands that were set aside as *pu'uhonua* were: Paunau for Lahaina, Waipukua for Waihe'e, and Kaniamoko for Hana, on Maui; and Kalua'aha for Molokai. Kuka'ilimoku's lands on Maui were Kukuipahu [Kukuipuka] for Kahakuloa, Polipoli for Napoko, and Ka'ili at Pu'uhaoa in Hana. There were also other lands belonging to Ka'ahumanu and to the war god of Kamehameha. Thus the ruler converted the lands of his favorite wife and of his god into *pu'uhonua* lands to save persons who had done some wrong [that is, violated some kapu], had shed blood without cause, or who had killed a man unintentionally. Ka'ahumanu herself was at times a *pu'uhonua,* when a lawbreaker who ran to her was saved from death. Kamehameha was also a *pu'uhonua.* A lawbreaker who had killed another unintentionally ran straight to Kamehameha, and his pursuers could not shed his blood; the king released the lawbreaker.*

THE MAKAHIKI FESTIVAL

The Makahiki festival was a time to rest, and a time to make great feasts of commemoration (*'aha'aina ho'omana'o*) for life and health of the body, and for the help received from the god. All manual labor was prohibited and there were several whole days of resting and feasting. Chiefs and people made many joyful Makahiki feasts at the end of each year. The custom (*malama*) of feasting came from very ancient times; and from the time that chiefs became rulers of the kingdoms, yearly feasts (*'aha'aina makahiki*) were held in commemoration. This perhaps was the main reason for the observance of the feasts.

[They gave thanks] to the god for his care, and for his help; from him came life, blessings, peace, and victory.

They made kapu the last three months of the year. The Makahiki began (*e kauwelu ai*) in the month of Hilina, and at this time pork, coconut, and fish were placed under kapu; the eating of flesh foods (*'i'o*) was kapu during these months.[11]

On the kapu day of Kane, the 27th day, in the month of Ikuwa, the ruler of the kingdom who had first prohibited the kapu things would free from kapu (*noa*) the things that had been prohibited, and would also free his *luakini* heiau which had been consecrated to the god of the Makahiki. Then the chiefs and people observed their own kapus; and when they were through, it became *noa,* or free, to eat the flesh of the pig, the coconut, and the *ulua* and other fishes that had been made kapu.

At the beginning of the new year the people rested and feasted joyfully and took part in amusements and in sports that strengthened the body.

The way in which the Makahiki was observed in the time of Kamehameha I was in some ways different in the ancient days. For one thing, the months of the

---
* March 10, 1870.

year of the people of ancient times were not the same as when he ruled; they were changed to be according to the counting of the Hawaii island people perhaps. The months of the Hoʻoilo season were changed to the Makaliʻi, and the months of the Makaliʻi season became those of Hoʻoilo. Also, the Makahiki gods made a circuit of the island to ask for and to seize the wealth of the people. These were new practices and were not observed by *ka poʻe kahiko*. Some of the gods of Kamehameha I who made the Makahiki circuit were new gods who had been created (*hoʻoakua*). Lonoikamakahiki had been a real man of Hawaii, and Kihawahine had been a chiefess of Maui; the man-god (*akua kanaka maoli*) Kahoʻaliʻi of Kamehameha had been made a god, perhaps because the spirit of an ancient god by the name of Kahoʻaliʻi possessed him (*noho pu ana*). These were the Makahiki gods who went about the land.

When the Makahiki kapu was ended, the *akua paʻani*, the god of play, came forth. His work was to promote the strengthening of the body. A place had been made ready before the *akua paʻani* came, and the *maika* sites and level places (*puʻuhonua*) were full of people in readiness for competitive sports (*hakaka leʻaleʻa*). Those on the side of the god were trained for boxing (*mokomoko*), fist-fighting (*kuʻikuʻi*), *lua* fighting (*kuʻialua*), wrestling (*hakoko*), chest-pushing (*kulakulaʻi*), and hand-gripping (*puʻili*); for spear-throwing (*ʻoʻo ihe*), a pushing contest in a squatting position called "playing turtle" (*honuhonu*), wrist-turning (*umauma*), tugging with hooked fingers or arms (*loulou*), *maika* rolling, dart-throwing (*paheʻe*), sliding (*koi*), turning somersaults (*kuwalawala*), noosing (*pahelehele*), and other games that strengthened the body.

The selected players (*moho*) from among the people had also been trained, and they knew how to "size up" a man (*ʻike i na aouli o ka ʻano o na kanaka*) and knew what kind of bruises he could inflict. Their opponents did not escape the knuckles of the people's players, who had studied them well for signs of their weaknesses. Many an opponent would receive a punch in the chin breaking the jaw, and be left "floating on the water" (*hoʻolana i ka wai;* semiconscious). These were the doings of the *akua paʻani* all around the island. The food (*ʻai*) of his followers (*poʻe kanaka*) was whatever they seized and pulled up.

After the *akua paʻani* came the *akua kapala ʻalaea,* a god painted (*pena ʻia*) red with *ʻalaea* earth. On one side he was kapu, and on one side, free. After him came the *akua loa,* who was the Makahiki god, and most of the other gods. The *akua loa* made a right circuit of the island. Afterward the *akua poko* appeared with the female gods, and his procession went to the left, along the beach of Waikiki. The *akua loa* and the *akua poko* met at Kalaeokaʻoʻio, the cape of Kaʻoʻio [the dividing line of Koʻolaupoko and Koʻolauloa districts] at Kualoa and Kaʻaʻawa. This is the reason for the names Koʻolaupoko and Koʻolauloa. At the spot where the companies of the two god-images met, the images were furled up and the *kaʻupu* bird ensigns twisted around (*papio ke akua a ʻowili ka hae kaʻupu*).

Much wealth was acquired by the god during this circuit of the island in the form of tribute (*hoʻokupu*) from the *mokuʻaina, kalana, ʻokana,* and *ahupuaʻa* land sections at certain places and at the boundaries of all the *ahupuaʻa*. There the wealth was presented—pigs, dogs, fowl, poi, tapa cloth, dress tapas (*'a'ahu*), *'oloa* tapa, *pa'u* (skirts), malos, shoulder capes (*'ahu*), mats, *ninikea* tapa, *olona* fishnets, fishlines, feathers of the *mamo* and the *'o'o* birds, finely designed mats (*'ahu pawehe*), pearls, ivory, iron (*meki*), adzes, and whatever other property had been gathered by the *konohiki,* or land agent, of the *ahupua'a*. If the tribute presented by the *konohiki* to the god was too little, the attendant chiefs of the god (*po'e kahu ali'i akua*) would complain, and would not furl up the god nor twist up the emblems and lay him down. The attendants kept the god upright and ordered the *ahupua'a* to be plundered. Only when the keepers were satisfied with the tribute given did they stop this plundering (*ho'opunipuni*) [in the name] of the god. Most of the wealth received in this circuit of the god was given to the crowd—to the people who attended to the god, to those who carried the image, to the people in the procession. Only the most valuable things were saved and displayed before Kamehameha.

When the god returned and went into the heiau and into the house of the god, then he was kapu again. The people would not see him again [until the next Makahiki circuit]. He was very kapu. The attendants who anointed him, the ruler, and the kahunas would be the only ones who would see him, at the time of the *ulu 'ohi'a, haku 'ohi'a, lama,* and the *kapu loulu* heiau ceremonies.

In the kapu period of Kane, the people of Kane [that is, those whose god was Kane] observed the kapus on the day of Kane and also on the day of Lono. When the kapu Kane and the kapu Lono came along no fires were made nor tapa beaters sounded, and all other sounds were silenced. Neither chickens nor owls must make a sound, lest the success of the [king's] ritual be destroyed (*o lilo ke ka'i ana o ka 'aha*). At dawn of Mauli, men, women, and children went *hi'uwai* bathing, then dressed in their best. They feasted joyfully in their fine clothing, with chanting and dancing. The kapus of the Makahiki had ended, and all was free, *noa*.*

NOTES TO PART ONE

[1] For Kamakau's version of the Hulihonua genealogy, see Kamakau (1961, p. 433). For the Wakea-Kapawa generations, see Kamakau (1961, p. 434).

[2] In *Ke Au 'Oko'a,* October 21, 1869, Kamakau relates that the gods Kane, Ku, and Lono made the first man, Kanehulihonua, out of soil, and the first woman, Keakahulilani, from his shadow, at Mokapu peninsula, Oahu. How widespread this account was at the time of his writing is not known, but it is an invention of the times and has no basis in authentic ancient Hawaiian tradition. See Barrère (1961, pp. 422-425).

[3] See Malo (1951), pp. 54-55, Sections 12-14: he applies the term *ni'aupi'o* only in context; to the child (or children) of a high chief with a full or half-sister (brother), or with a niece (nephew), with the additional terms of *pi'o, naha,* or *ho'i* identifying the mating, and applied to the child. Kamakau does not specify a blood relationship between the parents; his generalization applies the term to a child born to two *ni'aupi'o* chiefs who might be only distantly related, or even unrelated. Kamakau does not mention Malo's two-generation, or *ho'i,* union; the term *naha* was in later times applied to such a union. See Fornander (1919, pp. 307-311).

---

* February 17, 1870.

⁴ Kamakau is mistaken in this genealogy. Kamahana (Kumahana) was the first-born son of Peleioholani by Lonowahine (Halaki'i); Lonokahikini was Peleioholani's second wife, by whom he had a son, Ke'eaumoku, and a daughter, Kapueookalani. Ke'eaumoku and Kapueookalani made a *pi'o* union, and the *pi'o* chief Kaneoneo was born to them. The chiefess Nalanipipi'o was the *pi'o* child of Kumahana and his sister Ke'elanihonua'aiakama (Lonomahana); his other sister, Ka'apuwai, became the wife of Kaumeheiwa, king of Kauai.

⁵ See Handy and Pukui (1958, Chapter 4), for Hawaiian kinship terminology.

⁶ The kapu of the *ni'aupi'o* chief was the *kapu moe,* or "prostrating" kapu; of the *naha* chief, the *kapu noho,* or "squatting" kapu; of the *wohi,* the privilege of remaining upright in the presence of a chief with the *kapu moe.*

⁷ Kualono'ehu was sent to get the *kapu puhi kanaka* by Kauakahi-a-Kaho'owaha, ruler of Oahu, and the senior grandson of Kahamalu'ihi through her first-born, Kaho'owahaokalani. The kapu then became the birthright of Kauakahi-a-Kaho'owaha's first-born, Kuali'i.

⁸ This mele has been interpreted as a chant to the goddess Pele, whose *kanawai* Kai'okia is believed by Pukui to be the original one, stemming from Pele's separation by the sea from her homeland. The chief Lonoikamakahiki, son of Keawe-nui-a-'Umi, invoked the Kai'okia law as a means of sparing the lives of the vanquished after a contest (Fornander, 1917, p. 291, Hawaiian text); possibly this was the name of his personal *kanawai* Kolowalu.

⁹ The *kanawai* Ka'upukea was the edict that the *ka'upu* bird must be used during the Makahiki as a symbol of the god Kaho'ali'i. The Hawanawana decreed that while it was thundering, that is, in the presence of the thunder god Kanehekili, there must be no whispering, no sleeping on the back, and no open containers left about. The other *kanawai* of the gods were imposed when conducting a rite in that god's name, or for that god, and when the god to whom the *kanawai* belonged possessed his *haka,* or medium, and applied to those who witnessed the possession as well as to the medium himself. Kamakau explains the Pu'ukoamakai'a and the 'Aliamoku *kanawai*. Others known are: Kiki'i—no one may lean backward; Inaina—no one must show wrath or enmity; Kupou—no one may bend forward; Paukukaula—no one may have with him a piece of rope. For the record, the following are added: the *kanawai* of the sorcery goddess Kuamu was that the medium must wear red, but no one else might use red, and no one might have a foot covering; the hula goddess Laka's *kanawai* were the Mokulehua, requiring that *lehua* be on the *kuahu* altar, and the A'e Kuahu, requiring such an altar to "step into." [From M.K.P.]

¹⁰ The original name of this *kanawai* was Mamalahoe, as recorded by Dibble (1843, p. 59), by Andrews (1865, p. 381), and by Kamakau himself in 1867 (Kamakau, 1961, pp. 125-126). The earlier versions all say that Kamehameha was struck with a paddle, rather than with a club (*hoa*), hence the name *mamala-hoe,* "splintered paddle."

¹¹ Kamakau's calendar differs in sequence from those listed in Malo (1951, pp. 33-35); in *Ke Au 'Oko'a* for February 10, 1870, Kamakau gives the following, beginning with the latter half of March:

MAKALI'I SEASON	HO'OILO SEASON
Welehu—March-April	*Ikiiki*—September-October
Makali'i—April-May	*Ka'aona*—October-November
Ka'elo—May-June	*Hanaia'ele'ele*—November-December
Kaulua—June-July	*Hilina*—December-January
Nana—July-August	*Hilinehu*—January-February
Welo—August-September	*'Ikuwa*—February-March

PART TWO

PART TWO

The Family and the 'Aumakua

MARRIAGE

THE MARRIAGE (*mare*) called *ho'ao pa'a* was an ancient custom by which a man and a woman were bound in a lasting union (*ua pa'a loa ka noho ana*), a man not to desert his wife nor a woman her husband. This form of marriage, in which each took a single mate, originated as a command from the god to Hulihonua and his wife Keakahulilani, and lasted from their time down to that of Kahiko Luamea, 27 generations later. It was Wakea ["son" of Kahiko Luamea] who introduced the "sin" (*hewa*) of mating with many women (*moe lehulehu*). Wakea took three wives, and his wife Papa in revenge took eight new husbands: Lua, Makea, Waia, Hinanalo, Kakahili, Wailoa, and a couple of others.[1] After Wakea's time the unions of succeeding generations divided into two kinds, those in which men took many wives and women many husbands, and those in which there were but one wife or one husband. Formerly, the latter were in the majority. It was the chiefs and wealthy people who took more than one wife or husband.

When the people of old married, this is the way they were betrothed (*ho'opalau*). First, the parents of the boy (*kane*) and the girl (*wahine*) discussed the matter until they came to an agreement; they did not discuss it with those who were to be married. When the marriage was settled upon, the parents of the boy and the parents of the girl consulted them and asked the two if it went along with their wishes. If it did, then the parents united them with a vow (*ho'ohiki aku*), using suitable words. The parents on both sides commanded that the boy take care of the girl, and the girl the boy, and that they learn to work in order to be prepared for their living together. The boy would learn to plant and to fish, and the parents of the girl would teach her woman's work. When the advising was ended, the boy and the girl embraced (*honi*) and they became husband and wife. The marriage of the two was binding.

Another way of arranging a *ho'ao pa'a* marriage, perhaps to a woman of another place, was for the man's parents to send a messenger with gifts to the woman and to her parents. These were valuable gifts—feathers perhaps, or ivory, or pearls, or other precious gifts—from the relatives of the man to those of the woman. Then the woman's side sent a messenger with return gifts to the relatives of the man. These gifts were called *lou,* "hooks," or *lou 'ulu,* "breadfruit hooks," and testified to the betrothal of the two parties to a binding marriage. So binding was this mutual consent that it could not be dissolved (*wehe*), and it led to the fulfillment of a *ho'ao pa'a* marriage. In this kind of betrothal, when the marriage day approached, the relatives of the man and of the woman prepared for a feast. The relatives of the man built a house for the marriage ceremony and the feast.

The house, the feast, and the gifts (*waiwai*) were prepared, and when the marriage day came, the relatives of the woman made a *manele* litter and decorated it for her (*manele hu'a ho'ohiwahiwa*). They carried her (*'auamo*) on it with great display to the house of her husband-to-be. Then the relatives of the man gave them rich gifts, and land, if they had it, and the woman's relatives also gave them gifts and land, if they owned land. The marriage agreement was made, and they became husband and wife in a *ho'ao pa'a* marriage until death separated them. The children born to them sealed the relationship between the two families (*puka a maka*). This was the marriage custom (*ho'ao ana*) of the chiefs and the first-born children of prominent people and family pets of *ka po'e kahiko*.

REARING OF CHILDREN

In olden times parents took great pains with the bringing-up (*hanai ho'ohiwahiwa*) of their children; not only the parents who bore them, but also the grandparents on both the father's and the mother's sides. The claim (*kuleana*) of the grandparents upon their children's children took precedence over that of the parents who bore them; the parents could not keep the child without the consent of the grandparents. Whether a man and woman lived together (*noho ana*) or were formally married (*ho'ao pa'a*), when the first child (*makahiapo*) was born, if it was a male child it was taken by relatives on the husband's side; if a girl, by those on the wife's side. The parents did not rear their own child; its rearing was in the hands of the grandparents or their younger or older brothers and sisters, or other lateral relatives (*hoahanau*), or in the hands of the lateral relatives of the parents. When the woman was in labor, all the relatives assembled, and some of them brought wet nurses. As soon as the child was born it was taken away by someone else and the parents were left without their child. Those who took the child to rear taught him how to do a man's work, if it was a boy, or, if it was a girl, how to do a woman's work skillfully.

Sometimes boys thus taken as foster children (*hanai*) were not allowed to do any work, or to carry anything in the hand, or to plant, or to carry anything on the shoulders, or to fish. This was in accordance with a vow taken by the foster parents never to see the child perform any kind of labor as long as they were alive.* It was the same with some girls; the grandparents or foster parents made great pets of them, and they were not allowed to carry anything in their hands, nor were they taught to beat or to print tapa because that was work that soiled the hands. Such children would be seated on piles of mats or tapa, or on the chest or lap of their attendant (*kahu*), to be fed poi by dropping it into their mouths (*e kau ai ka 'ai*), and fish by mouth (*ka i'a a o ka pu-'a*), lest they choke on lumps in the poi or on fishbones; and they would be given water from the mouth (*mumu i ka wai i ka waha*) lest they choke and the precious ones come to harm.

In the ancient days, when a male child was born he was taken immediately to the *mua* (the men's eating house and family "chapel") [to be consecrated, *ho'ola'a*, to the gods]. If he was a royal child (*keiki ali'i*), he was taken to the heiau to be consecrated, and there his navel cord (*piko*) was cut, and the drums sounded [to announce his birth]. The placenta (*ewe*) was washed well in water and taken care of by the kahunas, and the child was washed. He was then wrapped snugly in tapa and taken by the king to the *kuapala* offering stand and presented to the gods. When the rituals of the kahuna were ended, the child was returned home. At the age of 3 or 4, he was placed in the *mua* and his eating made kapu (*ho'ai kapu 'ia*). Never again would he eat with his mother or with any other woman; he was under kapu and was consecrated to the gods.

If the parents or the grandparents of the boy belonged to a kahuna profession (*'oihana kahuna*), then he was taught that profession. He might be taught the profession of reading omens (*'oihana kilokilo*), or of selecting sites (*'oihana kuhi-kuhi pu'uone*), or a knowledge of the earth's configurations (*papa hulihonua*), or the stars (*kilo hoku*), or the profession of Ku'ula (*'oihana Ku'ula,* that is, deep-sea fishing), or the designing and making of implements for tapa work (*'oihana kapala kua'ula*), or the rituals for *'ana'ana* magic (*'oihana kahuna 'ana'ana*)—whatever profession the parents or grandparents were in.

A boy so consecrated to the gods was placed under restrictions (*ho'okapu 'ia*). His food, his food calabash, his water gourd, his clothing (*mea 'a'ahu*), his loincloth (*mea hume*), his mat, and his house were *la'a,* hallowed. His body was *la'a,* and not to be defiled with women. His hair was *la'a,* and could not be cut or trimmed; it grew tangled and snarled (*a wilika'eka*), and the beard hung down (*a kau i kokiki*). When the youth had gone through the final ceremony of training (*pau i ka 'ailolo*) in whatever branch of learning he was being instructed in, and he had been ceremonially cleansed of all his wrongdoings (*a pau i ka huikala*), the god and the kapus were set aside (*kaupale*) and the youth made free, *noa,* to associate with other men. Here is a strange thing: His teachers always knew if a youth had committed any wrong, whether it was disregarding the kapus (*'aiahulu*), eating scraps of dedicated food, or "free" food (*'ai noa*), defiling himself with women, or stealing—nothing was hidden from them. But if a youth took heed of the laws and the rules that were taught him by his teachers, he would have as much knowledge as they and would see all the hidden things of the gods.**

---

* February 3, 1870.
** February 10, 1870.

THE 'AUMAKUA—ANCESTRAL DEITIES

The *'aumakua*, ancestral deities of the family, were the ancient source gods "from time immemorial," (*akua kumu kahiko mai na kupuna mai*)—the gods from whom the ancestors implicitly believed they had come [personified natural phenomena], or one from whom they had actually descended. If a god had mated among them, and a human had come forth, this god was an *'aumakua* of theirs, and a *kumupa'a*, a "fixed origin."[2]

An ancestral god was called an *'aumakua* or a *kumupa'a*, not an *akua 'unihipili* (a deified spirit), or an *akua kaku'ai* (a corpse transfigured into the form of his source *'aumakua*), or an *akua ho'ola'a* (a spirit made into a god through consecration), or an *akua makemake* (a god created through desire or need), or an *akua ho'oulu* (a god acquired by being inspired by one), or an *akua malihini* (a newcomer god), or an *akua haole* (an introduced god). An *akua 'aumakua* or an *akua kumupa'a* was a god who was deeply venerated; he was the god for the day when a god was needed (*he akua no ka la o ka makemake akua*).

The *akua 'aumakua* spoken of by the ancestors were Kane, Kanaloa, Ku, and Lono. The "hosts of heaven and earth," *na pu'ali o ka lani a me ka honua*, are connected to them through the male *'aumakua* to whom they are related. [The "hosts" here are the departed ancestors whose spirits have joined the *'aumakua* in his particular realm.] A myriad of male *'aumakua* "entered into" [were a part of] Kane (*i komo iloko o Kane*), among them Kanehekili, Kanewawahilani, Nakoloilani, Kauilanuimakehaikalani, Kaho'ali'i, Kamohoali'i, Lonomakua, Nahoali'i, Naho'aiku, Kanemanaiahuea, Kaneholopali, Kanepohaka'a, Kaneulupo, Kaneikokala, Kanekoha, Kaneikokea, Kaneikauila, Kaneki'i, Kanelele, Kanehaka, Kaneikapule, and Kaneikamakaukau. So it was with Ku and Lono—but Kanaloa stood alone.

The female source gods, *kumu 'aumakua wahine*, were Haumea, Kahakauakoko, Walinu'u, Walimanoanoa, and Ho'ohoku. They were worshiped through the "hosts of heaven and earth" who were related to the female *'aumakua*. Pele, Hi'iaka, Kapo, Namakaokaha'i, Kahiliopua, and the "women of heaven" (*lani wahine*), who are related to these female *'aumakua*, are related to Haumea. The woman Uli became a part of Haumea (*i komo iloko o Haumea*), as did Nu'a, Nu'akea, Kapa'uanu'akea, and Niho'aikaulu.

In the ritual praying (*kuili pule*) of the people it is well for them to direct their appeals (*pule kahoahoa*) from the place of the sun's rising to its resting place, from the north to the south, and from the highest heaven to the foundation of the earth below, for these regions are filled with spirits. *Ka po'e kahiko* used to pray this way.*

In the ancient days, the *'aumakua* and the *kumupa'a* ancestral deities were havens of forgiveness (*pu'u kalahala*); they were healers; they counteracted (*wehe*) trouble. Death or suffering sent by another [sorcery] were as nothing to the *'aumakua*, and escape from these influences was called "life from the *'aumakua*," *o ke ola ia a ka 'aumakua*. If there was a shipwreck at sea, and one escaped with his life

---

* September 29, 1870.

and made land, it was "a life from the *'aumakua.*" If, in battle, one from the defeated side escaped being killed and passed safely through the slaughtered, it was "a life from the *'aumakua.*" If a man were sick and his eyes clouded in death, and death had been predicted for him, and none could save him, and then he recovered, it was "a life from the *'aumakua.*" Many lives were known to have been saved by the *'aumakua.* Some were restored from the grave itself, and this too was "a life from the *'aumakua.*" Thus there were many lives saved by the *'aumakua* in the ancient days. The reward of right living was an "*'aumakua* life"; the warding off of death from another—death from *'ana'ana* or from *ho'opi'opi'o, kalo ho'ola'a, ho'ounauna, kalaipahoa,* and all the other deaths sent by another—was "life from the *'aumakua.*"

In this new era, the *'aumakua* have become bitter enemies who punish severely the faults of their descendants when they break a vow they have sworn in their names, or who stupidly eat things consecrated to them, or which are their forms, or who eat defiled things; who break laws, commit adultery, and disregard the laws of God, of the land, of parents, husbands, wives, children, and relatives. Because the *'aumakua* are connected with so many things in these days, it has become very burdensome to offer them the gifts and sacrifices needed for the entangled wrongs and faults of men. Many, many more are the troubles of the men, women, and children of the Hawaiian race in these times as compared to times past.*

The *'aumakua* and *kumupa'a* ancestral deities were the "guardian angels" of men, *anela kia'i kino.* When a man died, his *'aumakua* or *kumupa'a* took charge of him after death. If the man was a descendant, a *pulapula,* of one of the *'aumakua* mentioned before, or was related to the *'aumakua* spirits who were related to the *'aumakua* of the heavens (*ka po'e 'aumakua o ka lani*), the *'aumakua* of the firmament (*ka po'e 'aumakua o ka lewa*) would take him unto themselves (*ki'i mai*) in accordance with the relationship of his ancestors to those of the heavens. He could return again (*a pela no e ho'i hou*) and speak to those of the living world, and so could those of the mountains, the ocean, the earth, and the volcano. Many people have died and have returned to tell about this. So it was in ancient times, and so it is today. There are many who have died and have returned to say that they had no claim to an *'aumakua* [realm] (*kuleana 'ole*). These are those souls, it is said, who only wander upon the plain of Kama'oma'o on Maui or on the plain at Pu'uokapolei on Oahu. Spiders and moths are their food.**

In offering prayers to the *'aumakua* their names were included with the famous names of "holy" people (*po'e hemolele*), or perhaps of chiefly ancestors, or those of kahunas of priesthood lines of succession (*po'e kahuna o ka mo'o*), or other famous people. However, if it was a *kahuna lapa'au,* a medical kahuna, he would put in the names of the *'aumakua* and the ancestors in the priesthood line of the *kahuna lapa'au* who had trained him in medicine. And so with the *kahuna 'ana'ana* and *kahuna kuni*—he would put in his prayers the names in the line of the *'ana'ana* and *kuni* kahuna who had trained him. This was so that the prayers might not be

* September 22, 1870.
** September 29, 1870.

"lost" (*nalowale;* go unheeded), and so that he would be helped in his work by his own '*aumakua* and those of the line of the kahuna who had trained him. Thus did each person who had an '*aumakua* call upon his '*aumakua* and his ancestors—those directly related to him—for help in times of sickness, for the increase of fish and food, for the forgiveness of a specific wrong (*ho'okalahala*), or for the forgiveness of all his "sins of commission and omission" (*huikala*), or for help in the troubles that come to every family that calls upon the '*aumakua* (*ke ho'aumakua*).

HO'AUMAKUA—THE ACQUIRING AND CONTACTING OF 'AUMAKUA

Some families had no '*aumakua,* that is, had no '*aumakua* handed down from the ancestors. In that case, they could acquire an '*aumakua* (*ho'aumakua aku*) through a grandparent or through a father or a mother who had died. These would call out (*kahea aku*) to all the '*aumakua* [and find among them their rightful place as relatives]. For those families who could do this (*makaukau i ka ho'aumakua*), the '*aumakua* would then be united with these immediate ancestors. It was all right for a family to acquire an '*aumakua* in this way—through the relationships (*'ao'ao*) of their ancestors.

There were two distinct sets of prayers for the contacting of an '*aumakua;* one set was to the male '*aumakua,* and the male ancestors of their direct single branch (*lala ho'okahi*), and the other set was to the female '*aumakua* and the female ancestors of their single line (*lalani ho'okahi*).

Here is a prayer for the contacting of the male '*aumakua:*

E kulou mai e na lani	Bend down, O heavens,
E ho'olohe mai e ka honua,	Listen, O earth
E haliu mai ho'i e na kukulu,	Harken, O pillars [of heaven],
Na 'aumakua i ka hikina a ka la a i kaulana,	[O] '*aumakua* at the rising and the resting places of the sun,
A mai kela pe'a kapu a keia pe'a kapu;	From that sacred border to this;
Eia ka alana a me ka mohai,	Here are the offerings and sacrifices,
He mohai pilikia i ke Akua.	A sacrifice to the gods for our trouble [our lack of an '*aumakua*].

(Here are enumerated the sacrifices and most of the gifts that have been offered)

Ia Kanenuiakea,	To Kane-nui-akea,
Ia Kane o Kanaloa,	To Kane and Kanaloa,
Ia Kanehekili,	To Kane-hekili,
Ia Kanewawahilani o Nakoloilani,	To Kane-wawahi-lani and Nakoloilani,
Ia Kauilanuimakehaikalani,	To Kauila-nui-makeha-i-ka-lani,
Ia Kamohoali'i,	To Kamoho-ali'i,
Ia Kanakaokai,	To Kanaka-o-kai,
Ia Kaho'ali'i,	To Ka-ho'ali'i,
Ia Lonomakua,	To Lono-makua,
Ia Kanehunamoku,	To Kane-huna-moku,
Ia Kaneikaulana'ula,	To Kane-i-kaulana-'ula,
Ia Kahuilaokalani.	To Ka-huila-o-ka-lani.

[The above are male 'aumakua gods; the following are male human ancestors]

Ia Kekumakaha,	To Ke-ku-makaha,
Ia Kapoiau'ena,	To Ka-po-i-Au'ena,
Ia Ola,	To Ola,
Ia Kikiaola,	To Kiki-a-Ola,
Ia Ka'ilihonu,	To Ka'ili-honu,
Ia Kaho'owahaakananuha,	To Ka-ho'owaha-a-Kananuha,
Ia Ka'onohi,	To Ka-'onohi,
Ia Kuhemu,	To Ku-hemu,
Ia Kapakanaka,	To Ka-pa-kanaka,
Ia Kauhiahiwa,	To Kauhi-a-Hiwa,
Ia Kapohakahiaku,	To Kapoha-ka-hi-aku,
Ia Kalani'aukai.	To Ka-lani-'au-kai.
I na 'aumakua kane a pau loa,	To all the male 'aumakua,
Ia 'oukou pale ka po, pale ka make, pale ka pilikia.	It is yours [the mana] to brush aside darkness, brush aside death, brush aside trouble.
Owau nei o Kiha ka pua keia i ke ao;	This is I, Kiha, your descendant in this world of the living;
Homai i mana.	Give me mana.

The following is a prayer for the acquiring of a female 'aumakua:

O na 'aumakua wahine me na kupuna wahine ali'i,	O female 'aumakua and ancestral chiefesses,
Na 'aumakua wahine i ka hikina, a i kaulana a ka la,	Female 'aumakua at the rising and setting places of the sun,
Na wahine i ka lewa lani, i ka lewa nu'u,	Female [spirits] in the firmaments of the heavens and of the clouds;
O Walinu'u,	Walinu'u,
O Walimanoanoa,	Walimanoanoa,
O Kaneikawaiaola,	Kane-i-ka-wai-a-ola,
O Kahinaaola,	Kahina-a-ola,
O Haumea wahine,	Haumea,
O Kanikawi, O Kanikawa,	Kanikawi, Kanikawa,
O Kuho'one'enu'u;	Kuho'one'enu'u;
O Pelehonuamea,	Pele-honua-mea,
O Kalamainu'u,	Ka-la-mai-nu'u,
O Kamohailani,	Ka-mohai-lani,
O Nu'a,	Nu'a,
O Nu'akea,	Nu'akea,
O Hulikapa'uianu'akea,	Huli-ka-pa'u-ia-Nu'akea,
O Uliwahine;	Uliwahine;
Ia Kahawali,	To Kahawali,
Ia Kaneluhonua,	To Kane-lu-honua,
Ia Kukalaniho'one'enu'u,	To Ku-ka-lani-ho'one'enu'u,
Ia Niho'aikaulu,	To Niho-'ai-kaulu,
Ia Leihulunuiakamau,	To Lei-hulu-nui-a-Kamau,
Ia Ka'oa'oakaha'iaonuia'umi,	To Ka-'oa'oaka-ha'i-ao-nui-a-'Umi,
Ia Ahukiniokalani,	To Ahukini-o-ka-lani,
Ia Keahiolalo,	To Ke-ahi-olalo,
Ia Kamakaokeahi,	To Ka-maka-o-ke-ahi,

Ia Kapohinaokalani.	To Ka-pohina-o-ka-lani.
I na 'aumakua wahine a pau loa,	To all the female 'aumakua.
Ia 'oukou pale ka po, pale ka make, pale ka pilikia.	It is yours [the mana] to brush aside darkness, brush aside death, brush aside trouble.
Owau nei o Kiha ka pua kela i ke ao,	This is I, Kiha, your descendant in this world of the living.
Homai i mana.	Give me mana.
'Eli'eli kapu, 'eli'eli noa, ia lahonua;	The kapu has been profound, the freeing profound, in this earthly life;
'Amama, 'amama, ua noa.	It is finished; freed.*

POHAKU O KANE

The *Pohaku o Kane,* the Stone of Kane, was a place of refuge, a *pu'uhonua,* for each family from generation to generation. It was not a heiau; it was a single stone monument (*he wahi 'eo'eo pohaku ho'okahi*), and a *kuahu* altar with ti and other greenery planted about. There the family went to obtain relief. All the men and the boys who belonged to the same family went there if the god [that is, the family's *'aumakua* god] had stricken the family with death, with illness, or with misfortune because they had been irreligious (*'aiahulu*), or had been careless about the kapus (*'aia*), or had eaten or had drunk water with persons who were defiled; also, if they had worn the tapas, or slept in the same sleeping place, or girded on the loincloth, or put on (*peu*) the clothing of a person who was defiled with blood. All these things were defiling, and the people had done wrong against the gods who were their *'aumakua* if they did any of them. The Hawaiians are said to be a people consecrated to the gods; the *'aumakua* gods were "born," and from them man was born (*he lahui la'a i ke akua, hanau ke akua hanau mai ke kanaka*).

When trouble came upon a family for doing wrong against an *'aumakua* god, by being irreligious, or doing any of these defiling things, the cause for this trouble was shown to them by dreams, or visions, or through other signs sent by the god. It was pointed out to them what sacrifices to offer, and what gifts to present, to show their repentance for the wrong committed by the family. They were to go to the *Pohaku o Kane,* their *pu'uhonua,* where they were to make offerings to atone for their wrongdoing (*mohai hala*) and to pacify the god (*mohai ho'olu'olu*).

In the evening the fire-making sticks (*'aunaki*) were made ready, and in the morning the family went with a pig, red fish, tapas (*a'ahu*), and some *kohekohe* grass. Very early in the morning the imu was lighted for the pig in front of the Stone of Kane, and the red fish and tapas buried in front of the stone, as a peace offering to the god. The pig and the *'oloa* tapa were the offerings for forgiveness (*mohai kalahala*). The pig was put to bake, then the *'awa* was chewed. This was done in silence; no one went to relieve nature or did any other defiling thing; no one moved about until the *'awa* was chewed and covered with straining fiber (*pau ka 'awa i ka mama, a uhi ka 'awa i ka mau'u*). Then the kapu was lifted (*noa ke kapu*) and they would open the imu; the group would be seated, the pig cut up,

---

* October 20, 1870.

the *'awa* strained. When the pig had been cut up, the *'awa* would be poured into cups and a prayer offered for forgiveness and repentance for the wrong done by the family. Then a prayer of praise (*pule ho'onani*) to the gods was uttered, and at the end of the prayer the [family] kahuna said, "'*Amama.*" The *'awa* was drunk, and the feast eaten, under kapu. When one was satisfied, he must sit still until the kapu upon the eating was lifted. When it was lifted, the ti leaves used as coverings (*kauwewe*) in the imu, and the trash and stones of the imu, were covered over. The remains of the feast were buried in front of the stone. Some part of the offerings might be taken home, but it was not to be shared with those who had remained at home and not "sat in the smoke" for the purifying of the family.

When this purification of the family was ended, no medicine need be given to cure sickness, nor anything done for the misfortune and troubles that had come to the family. The family would be multiplied by the births of descendants, blessed with bodily health and freedom from accident; they would obtain good crops, and an abundance of fish and of all things. There would be no further trouble or misfortune.

The Stone of Kane was called a *pu'uhonua,* and "a gate to heaven," *puka no ka lani.* It was the *kuahu* altar where men talked to the [family] gods; where men were freed from defilement and wrongdoing; a place at which to ask the gods for blessings. One, two, or three persons could go to their stone altar of Kane and make their offerings for freedom from defilement and wrongdoing. The Stone of Kane was a stone pointed out by the god, not one just set up by men. The god indicated the stone, perhaps in a dream, or in a vision, or by leading someone to the spot.

There were very many Stones of Kane in every *ahupua'a* from Hawaii to Kauai. The *Pohaku o Kane* were different from heiaus; different from the *ko'a* shrines set up for the increase of deep sea fishes (*ko'a ku'ula ho'oulu i'a*) and the *ko'a* to the god Kaneko'a set up along the banks of rivers, streams, and shore and inland ponds (*kuapa me na loko*) for the increase of *'o'opu* fishes (*ko'a ho'oulu 'o'opu*); they were different from the heiaus to Kanepua'a and to Lono to increase food crops, the *unuunu ho'oulu 'ai,* and the *ipu-o-Lono* heiaus; and different from the heiaus for Kukeolo'ewa [the Maui chiefs' "state" god, whose services were held in *luakini* heiaus].*

CUSTOMS AT DEATH

When a man died, the *kahuna 'aumakua* of the dead person came and performed his ritual of offering a pig (*pua'a uko*), or if not a pig, a chicken (*moa 'aumakua*), to make acceptable (*ho'omaika'i*) the soul of the dead person to live together with his *'aumakua,* his ancestral gods. This kahuna must belong to the same family and have come from the same line of *'aumakua.* No other would do.

The bodies of those who were especially beloved, if the relatives did not shrink from handling them, were "embalmed," *i'a loa.* [The body was cut open, the inner parts removed, and the cavity filled with salt.] This was the best way to preserve

---
* March 3,.1870.

the dead. Some people stripped off the flesh (*holehole*) and saved the femur and humerus bones (*'aihau*) and the skull (*iwi pu niu*), then took the rest of the body, the *pela manaku,* out to the deep ocean far beyond land and threw it in. This they did without looking back lest it rise again to the surface; or if not that, they appealed (*kahoahoa*) to it to remain in the depths of the ocean.

For other deaths, it would be made known that the death had occurred, then the relatives of the parental generation, their own generation, and all the kinfolk—men, women, and children—would gather and tell of their deep aloha by lamentations (*kanikau kumakena*) with much weeping, grief, and sorrow. Some people fasted, and refused to eat; others cut off their hair on one side of the head (*kikepakepa*); some burned their skin with fire [brands], or knocked out their teeth, or tattooed themselves (*kakau i ka moli*) on the skin. Those who deeply loved the dead mourned bitterly.

If the corpse was that of one who was widely beloved, such as a kapu chief or a chief ruling over the land, several retainers died with him (*he mau kahu moe pu'u me ke ali'i*). This was not by the wish of the chief who had died, but the wish of the other chiefs to put them to death (*moe pu'u aku*) and have them die together with the chief.*

Even though he did not share the chief's wealth or his bounty, when one of his retainers who lived in the back country (*kua'aina*) heard that his lord (*haku*) was dead, he would "kiss" (*honi i ka ihu*) his wife and children, and without telling them why, would go off to be a companion in death, a *moepu'u,* to his chief. Fearlessly he would go before the chiefs and enter the sacred and hallowed place where the corpse of the chief lay, creep between the dead man's legs and lie down. The man could be saved only if the heir to the kingdom, or some one of the kapu chiefs of the same lineage, discovered that the man was a "*kauwa,*" a "humble servant," of his own. He could then be fetched out and his life spared; otherwise the executive officers (*ilamuku*), or the near kinsmen (*iwi kuamo'o*), of the dead chief would strangle him with a cord. One of these officers or kinsmen would himself die if no one came to offer himself as a *moepu'u.* Only the heir of the kingdom could save him.

The *kahu* of the chief who lived here and there in the back country were themselves near kinsmen or executive officers of the chief, and they resented any words of slander against their *haku* which found utterance in the countryside. Here in the back country, where "food and fish," *'ai* and *i'a,*[3] were plentiful, they did not lose their aloha for their *haku.* Some people in country places were destroyed for grumbling (*'ohumu*) against the ruler of the kingdom, without knowing that the "ordinary man," the *kanaka hemahema,* to whom they had spoken was a *kahu* of the ruling chief.

Another way of lamenting a chief's death was by display of anguish (*na'au'auwa*) among the other chiefs and the people at the place where the chiefly corpse was. They mourned with private parts exposed. The men tied a malo around their loins and just let it hang down (*kuwelu*) in front, and so did the women; they would

---

* September 29, 1870.

hang a piece of kapa in front leaving their bodies bare from top to bottom. They did many indescribably shameless things when they mourned their beloved deceased ruler. The heir of the kingdom, his wives and "sisters" (*kaikuahine*), and the chiefs of his household (*kona mau ali'i 'aialo*) did not take part in this kind of mourning. This was because the heir to the kingdom was separated from the chiefly corpse, for the place where he had died was defiled (*haumia*). It was 15 days before the heir was allowed to return. By this time the bones had been preserved (*i'a loa 'ia iwi*), the remains (*pela manaku*) had been taken to the ocean, and the *kahuna huikala* had performed the ceremony of purification and had cleansed of defilement the land and the place where the body had been.

The corpses of the people in general (*maka'ainana*) were also defiling. All clothing and mats that had come in contact with them were defiled, as were also their water gourds and food calabashes. When the body was taken away to be disposed of (*kanu*), these things were taken and burned in fire, together with all the other things connected with the death. Those who had disposed of the dead were also defiled. After the body was disposed of, they bathed, and then were purified by the sprinkling (*pi kai*) of salted water, or sea water with *'olena* in it, to end the defilement. They kept themselves separated for a few days until the defilement was gone, then they rejoined their families at home.

In carrying the corpse out for disposal, it was not well to take it out through the door that was commonly used for fear the house would become badly defiled. It was better to make a new opening through the gable end (*hakala*) of the house and pass the body out through there, lest the house become contaminated and another death follow. If the house was new and it seemed a pity to break it anywhere, it was better to build a new door outside of the old door. After the body was carried out, the new door was broken and the house thus freed of all contamination of the corpse.

Something to be observed when a person died was whether or not his eyes remained closed and after several hours opened again. Those who watched the body knew that in this case the dead was looking for one of the living. If one of his relatives died soon afterward, the living then recalled that it was because the eyes of the corpse had opened. Other signs were observed in the bodies of the dead. Should tears flow after the corpse was laid out, then everyone recognized them as tears of affection. If it vomited food, or water, or blood flecks, it was a sign that the dead had a great deal of aloha for the living, and they preserved these things. They kept a strand or twist of hair, or fingernails, teeth, or some other part of the body of a loved one, because they were overwhelmed with a grief which stabbed to the vital parts like the thrust of a needle and caused excruciating pain. These things were keepsakes, *kia ho'omana'o*, for the living to remember their dead by.

Sometimes, because of their light weight, the vomit or other things of the body were used in offering the dead for transfiguration into gods unrelated to him (*e kaku'ai 'ia iloko o kekahi po'e akua e aku i pili 'ole i ka mea make*). At other times they were the "bait" used for the *kuni* rituals.*

---

* October 6, 1870.

KUNI RITUALS

The services of the *kahuna 'ana'ana kuni,* or *kuni ola,* or *'o,* were important [in order to divine, and avenge by counter-magic, the death (or illness) of a person who had been the victim of *'ana'ana,* "praying to death," magic]. They were sought because of grief for the loss of a loved one. Their rituals were burdensome tasks requiring an exorbitant price and many gifts for the kahuna. *Kuni 'ana'ana* was not for the poor, nor for those with but few possessions. To relatives and close friends of the kahuna the price was less, and the charge for the *kuni* ceremony was reasonable.

Kuni ola was resorted to when the sick person was yet alive but showed characteristic symptoms (*'ano*) of being prayed to death by someone (*ka 'ana'ana 'ia mai e ha'i*). Perhaps several kahunas had observed the signs that made it evident to them that the sick man was being prayed to death and could not be cured with medicines, or with prayers to absolve his faults (*pule kala*). Then there was only one thing to do: strike back with greater harm (*'ino'ino loa*). This was *kuni ola,* and it had one great value (*ho'okahi waiwai nui*): it caused the death of the person who had first practiced *'ana'ana* and saved the intended victim from death. It was indeed of great worth, for it saved life.

Kuni make, the magic *'ana'ana* prayers used to avenge death with death, was called *kuni pilau,* "vile magic." It was useless; the beloved one was gone. It was a profitable practice for the *kahuna kuni,* however; his gain was greater after a man's death than that of the medical kahuna, the *kahuna lapa'au,* when the man was alive. Perhaps the reason it was resorted to was because intense grief brought the desire to retaliate and to punish the evil-hearted one who had in secret taken away the life of the loved one.

Before Christianity came to Hawaii there was no death-dealing (*pepehi kanaka*) equal in mana to the mana of praying to death in broad daylight (*kuni i ka la 'okoa*). Solid rocks were melted away by the mana of the prayers, and thunder and lightning vibrated like a rattling piece of tapa at the fireplace of the *kahuna kuni.* Any large tree that stood close by was withered as though it had been scorched by fire. That was through the mana of the prayer. Those who lighted the wood in the fireplace and those who threw in the "bait" from the body of the dead person fell down beside the fireplace, and the kahuna would fall down also. Then he and those who served in the *kuni* work saw the *kahoaka,* the spirits of the living persons who had caused the death. The kahuna could name those who had used the *'ana'ana* prayers, the number of persons who had taken his "bait," and the number of kahunas who had prayed the person to death. He prophesied the number of days before they would die, and the kind of fate (*ma'i*) that would cause their deaths—whether a shark would eat them, leaving the entrails tangled on the shore to be devoured by pigs and dogs, or be dragged along the road, or whether, while going out to sea to fish, they would be drowned and cast ashore to be eaten by pigs and dogs. Whatever the kahuna foresaw (*wanana*) would come to pass. But there was not much to be gained by this except that the wish for revenge through the death of the enemies was fulfilled.

The *kahuna 'o,* who, like the *kahuna kuni ola,* counteracted *'ana'ana* prayers for death while the victim was still living, did not have as elaborate a ceremony as the *kahuna kuni.* His work was done either at night or during the day, but not in broad daylight, and it was done in private. The *kahuna 'o* received signs and omens of the death which would befall the enemy, and according to these signs, death did fall on all the bitter-hearted ones. Perhaps it was thunder and lightning that dealt the punishment, or lava that turned them to stone; it was fulfilled according to the mana of the prayer.

There were two principal sins (*hewa nui*) for which punishment was applied while a person lived, and after he died. One was for stealing, *'aihue,* and the other was for taking "bait," *maunu,* for the purpose of *'ana'ana,* praying of someone to death. The punishment of a thief when he was caught stealing by the owner of the property was a stern one—his flesh was stripped off his bones (*holehole*) until he died. This is a saying of the people of old, "A thief denies his guilt until his bones are stripped of flesh," *I ka ho'ole no ka 'aihue a pau na iwi i ka holehole.* A person who took "bait" and practiced praying to death was punished by having his head cut off with an adz (*ko'i*). This is why murderous *'ana'ana* kahunas (*po'e kahuna 'aihamu*) were called *kahuna 'ana'ana po'oko'i,* "adz-head kahunas." For these sins there was bitter punishment and cruelty before death, and the bones of their perpetrators could not be hidden away. In ancient times other sins could be absolved by the gods, and perhaps it was thought that the sin of [outright] murder was less important than these because it was so rarely committed. However, at times the fate of one who killed in secret was a very cruel one.

He whose hands were soiled by accepting "bait" or by stealing from others died a terrible death, with the grease, *hinu,* of his body flowing onto the road, and with a broken and foul-smelling back. Dreadful and horrible were the things that happened to such evildoers (*po'e hana 'ino*), for dogs dug them up. The bones of unprincipled (*kolohe*) people could not be hidden. That is the way it was in the ancient times, and these are the abiding words of the *po'e kahiko,* that the bones of the unprincipled could not be hidden in the ocean, nor in secret caves, nor in the depths of the earth, nor in any other secret place, but that the bones of the wicked would be exposed, and they would be abused and dragged about on the road and become a sight to strike fear, and other cruel things would happen to them. Perhaps this is not so now, for the bones of the wicked and the bones of the righteous are all together in one burial ground. Not so in ancient times; the bodies of the wicked were devoured by dogs, and dragged about on the roads. Even if they were thrown into the ocean after being weighted down with big stones and with sandbags or iron bars tied all around the entire body, they were cast ashore and devoured by dogs. The words of prophecy concerning the wicked were fulfilled—that the bones of the wicked could not be hidden. Today the bones of the wicked are safe; no difference is seen between the bones of the wicked and those of the righteous. Perhaps the reason why this bitter fate has been taken away from the wicked is because of the introduction of law. By law, the whip (*la'au hahau*) is applied to the wicked, and they are imprisoned while living. This may be the reason, and it may not be.*

DISPOSAL OF CORPSES

There were many ways of disposing (*kanu ana*) of corpses. In the very ancient times corpses were buried in graveyards (*kanu ma na ho'oilina*), and these graveyards were well known throughout the islands. The corpses were laid out straight in wooden troughs (*holowa'a*) and buried. That was in the time of peace and tranquility in the land; that was when corpses were actually buried. During the time of wicked, traitorous, and desecrating chiefs, the bones of the dead were dug up out of the burial grounds to be used for arrows for rat shooting and for fishhooks, and the bones and bodies of the newly buried were dug up for food and bait for sharks. For this reason, consternation arose in every family, and they sought places of concealment for the bones of their grandparents, parents, children, chiefs, and relatives. They searched for deep pits (*lua meki*) in the mountains, and for hiding pits (*lua huna*) and hiding caves (*ana huna*) along the deep ravines and sheer cliffs frequented by *koa'e* birds. There they deposited the precious bones of their loved ones, without a thought for their own weariness, the heavy load they carried, or their own possible death; with no other thought except that they were carrying out the "last will," the *kauoha,* of their loved one. For instance, someone who was dying on Hawaii might before his end make his *kauoha* known by saying, "When I die take me to the high-ridged hills of Nakoaka'alahina on Kauai," or "to Kapalikalahale on Niihau." A death might take place on Oahu and the *kauoha* point to Hawaii, or perhaps to Maui. The right thing to do was to fulfill these commands. The places mentioned in the *kauoha* are the burial pits and caves of the ancestors. They are well hidden from the eyes of men, and unknown to the "wizards of the night," *kupua o ka po,* who might reveal them. These caves hold treasures and other hidden things.

There is only one famous hiding cave, *ana huna,* on Oahu. It is Pohukaina. The opening on Kalaeoka'o'io that faces toward Ka'a'awa is believed to be in the pali of Kanehoalani, between Kualoa and Ka'a'awa, and the second opening is at the spring Ka'ahu'ula-punawai. This is a burial cave for chiefs, and much wealth was hidden away there with the chiefs of old. On the Kona side of the island the cave had three openings, one at Hailikulamanu—near the lower side of the cave of Koleana in Moanalua—another in Kalihi, and another in Pu'iwa. There was an opening at Waipahu, in Ewa, and another at Kahuku in Ko'olauloa. The mountain peak of Konahuanui was the highest point of the ridgepole of this burial cave "house," which sloped down toward Kahuku. Many stories tell of people going into it with kukui-nut torches in Kona and coming out at Kahuku. Within this cave are pools of water, streams, creeks, and decorations by the hand of man (*hana kinohinohi'ia*), and in some places there is level land.

According to the traditions of some people, Oahu was said to have once been

---
* September 29, 1870.

a floating land, *he 'aina lewa o Oahu*. The Kahuku side was a wide open gap (*puka hamama*) and this was called *Ka puka o Kahipa a me Nawaiuolewa*, "The opening of Kahipa and Nawaiuolewa." The piece of land that closed it up was called Kahuku, and the hooks that made fast the piece of land and joined it to the island were called Kilou and Polou.

'Iao is the famous burial cave of Maui. It is in Olopio, close to the side of the Pali-o-Kaka'e at Kalakahi. One entrance is said to be under water; the second entrance is on a sheer cliff on the south (or left, *hema*) side. This was a famous burial cave in ancient times. In it were laid all the famous ruling chiefs, the people who had mana and strength, the *kupua* (people possessed of supernatural powers), and all those attached to the ruling chiefs who were famous for their marvelous achievements (*na hana kupua*). The first of the several hundred famous rulers to be enclosed (*papani*) there was Kapawa, the celebrated chief of Waialua, Oahu, and the last was Kalaniku'ihonoikamoku (Kekaulike), who died in A.D. 1736. There is no one remaining of the people who knew the entrances to 'Iao.

Waiuli, on Maui, is a deep pit where the corpses of the common people were thrown (*he lua meki ho'olei kupapa'u ia no na maka'ainana*). It is directly mauka of Honokohau, Honolua, and Honokahua, and for those from Lahaina to Kahakuloa, it was the common burial place (*ho'oilina kupapa'u*). The body of anyone from those places who had died on Molokai was brought back (*ho'iho'i*) to that place. Waiuli is a large disposal pit, possibly miles deep, with fresh water at the bottom. Its location is marked by a small hill called Waiuli. It has a wide open mouth that faces upward (*ua akea no kona waha iluna e hamama ana*), and those from any place can throw in their corpses from their own side. Early in the morning the dead would be brought on a *manele* litter, and all the kinsmen and friends—men, women, and children—would come in a funeral procession (*ka'i a huaka'i ho'olewa*). A *kahuna 'aumakua* of the pit would make the appeal for the corpse (*ka pule kahoahoa kupapa'u*) [to be welcomed by his ancestral spirits in the pit], and would appeal to the *'aumakua* (*ka pule kahoahoa 'aumakua*) there to watch over their ancestors in that pit.

A story is told of Waiuli that at one time, when the body of a certain man was about to be thrown into the pit and everyone had gathered to mourn for him, his daughter wandered off to gather *maile, lehua,* and other forest plants. The people who gathered said that she was a daughter who had no love for her father. But when the body was thrown into the pit, the girl ran to the edge and leaped into the depths below.

The disposal pit of Ka'a'awa is a deep disposal pit inside the crater of Haleakala. It is on top of a lava mound in a pit (*lua*) on the north side, close to Wai'ale'ale [a swamp just outside the crater wall] and the rock that divides the lands [Pohaku Palaha, or Pohaku'oki'aina] on the eastern edge of the Ke'anae gap that opens at Ko'olau. It is a chasm, a *nupa,* or perhaps a deep pit, a *lua meki,* opened up from the foundations of the island by the forces of heaping lava, and may be several miles deep, with fresh or sea water at the bottom. Because of the insipid taste (*'ono 'ole*) of the waters, some people have supposed that the waters of Waiu and Waipu at Kaupo have their source at this pit of Ka'a'awa, or from some disposal pits mauka of Pu'umane'one'o. This pit of Ka'a'awa was like Waiuli; it was the disposal pit for the people of Makawao, Kula, and Kaupo. These pits could be visited in broad daylight because no evilly disposed people could get at the bones and take them away to work mischief. This is the character of *nupa* and *lua meki*—they are pits that mischievous people cannot get at.

Burial caves, disposal pits, and caverns (*ana huna, lua huna, nupa*) were important from Hawaii to Kauai. Very often cherished women were hidden in them, and objects with supernatural force (*mana kupua*) were placed in them, with watchmen of *kupua* powers to take care of them.

When a person requested that his corpse be laid away (*ho'iho'i*) in one of these caves or caverns, it was dangerous for an outsider (*kanaka e*) to take the body there, lest he be killed. Only a "blood" relative, *'i'o pono'i*, a *makuakane* or a *kaikaina*, could safely carry out the request; a brother-in-law would not escape death, even though he might be the parent of a child of the family. If it was the corpse of a chief that was to be taken and hidden, and his *kauoha* had been, "You are to conceal (*nalo*) my bones," and the answer had been, "Yes, I will conceal them," these words might be the cause of the man's death. Only persons of the same flesh (*'i'o ho'okahi*) should conceal them, and only one or two of them.

Some people would be taken away secretly, while they were still alive, and laid in an *ana huna*, a *lua huna*, or a *nupa*. "Food and fish," mats, and their personal things made the spot where they were laid comfortable. Sometimes a sick person close to death was taken and laid in an *ana huna*.

The bodies of the dead were not borne to burial caves with lamentation lest they be spied on in the night, the cave discovered, and the bones therein desecrated. They were taken secretly by canoe to a distant spot and brought back by a devious route. For instance, if Honolulu was the place where a person had died, and the burial pit, *lua huna*, was in Honolulu, the corpse would be taken to Waikiki, then taken up to the plains, and then returned to Oloku in Honolulu and put into the burial pit. When people saw the canoe at Kahala they would think, ah, there is the body! *Eia no ka!* By morning the body was back again. Lamentations would fill the air (*olo ka pihe*), but by then the body was hidden away (*nalo malu*). Thus did they hide away (*ho'onalonalo*) their dead.

Sometimes, when the guards and those who watched over the body were asleep, those who had been commanded while the man was alive and well to dispose of his corpse would remove it through the bottom thatching of the house, and the corpse would be theirs; the bones would then belong to these "outsiders" (*po'e e*). If it was the body of a chief, a man who looked like him would be killed and his body substituted and the chief's corpse taken away secretly. In the morning, lo and behold! there would be a stranger's body (*kanaka e*) in its place.

This is what was proper to do: for the head watchmen, they who were to hide the body (*kekahi po'e kia'i po'o oia kekahi mea a nalo ai*), to go secretively, and for the other watchers over the body (*po'e kia'i*) not to follow those who were carrying away the corpse, lest they be killed.

There were very good places (*wahi maika'i loa*) in the *ana huna, lua huna*, and *nupa* where the corpses were laid, like men asleep, on piles of mats, with pillows, and covered nicely with kapa, not wrapped up like a corpse. "Food," "fish," and all the favorite articles (*kana mau puni*) of the living person were laid there, the place screened off (*paku 'ia a pa'a*), and thus the corpses left within the *ana huna, lua huna,* or *nupa*. Some of the *ana huna* and the *lua huna* were blocked up (*pani*) with hewn rocks fitted together to close up the opening. To go into them, some of them miles long inside, kukui-nut torches (*ihoiho kukui*) were needed.

At Papaluana, near the village of Kipahulu, is the burial cave in which the bones of the famous ancient chief Wahieloa were deposited, and the canoe which Laka used to fetch the bones of his father Wahieloa from Punalu'u in Ka-'u on Hawaii. [In it are also] the bodies of the famous chiefs who helped him with their wonderful deeds (*mau hana kupanaha*), and the body of a small person, a *ma'ihi* (*a me ke kino o kanaka li'ili'i he ma'ihi*). The cave has never been found, from that ancient time to this day.

In the burial cave of Pu'uwepa in Kohala, Hawaii are deposited the bones of Pa'ao, the famous kahuna who built the heiau of Mo'okini at Kohala, and who lived a span of 15 generations before he died. Its entrance is said to be beneath the sea. It extends a long way up into the mountains, and through it people went to get *pala, 'ie'ie,* and *palai*.

Ka'iliki'i is another very famous burial pit. It is in the pali of Molilele, in Ka-'u, Hawaii, and is famous from ancient times.

Kaloko [pond] is another famous burial pit; it is at Kaloko, in Kekaha, Hawaii. [In a cave that opens into the side of the pond] were laid Kahekili, the ruler of Maui, his sister Kalola, and her daughter, Keku'iapoiwa Liliha, the grandmother of Kamehameha III. This is the burial cave, *ana huna,* where Kame'eiamoku and Hoapili hid the bones of Kamehameha I so that they would never be found.

As I have said, there were so many burial caves and pits that I cannot name them all. The skilled people, even if they have a thousand spyglasses, will not discover them; they cannot be found; they are in the care of the gods (*ua molia i ke akua*).

Some chasms (*nupa*) are *lua huna,* burial pits. They are very deep pits (*lua hohonu*), 60 or 70 feet deep, with sides that are sheer cliffs. To get down into the main pit (*lua nui*) kukui-nut torches were burned. Then one could go into the *ana huna,* the burial caves that branched off. In order to get down into the chasm, the *nupa,* the corpse bearers and the wife would let themselves down on ropes. Outside of Waimea, on Hawaii, are such large pits, some for chiefs and others for the people.

A *haole*, Dr. John Pelham, called Dr. Pili by the Hawaiians, saw one of these chiefs' burial pits at Waimea and told me how he discovered it. A certain Waimea chief, then a feeble old man, had been pierced by a *pololu* spear, probably in one of the battles of Kalani'opu'u or Kamehameha I, and the spear had gone through at his waistline (*'api o ka 'opu*), through the ribs on the right side, and had penetrated the ribs on the left side. The point of the spear was barbed and could not be removed; it had remained in his body all those years, from the time when the man was young and healthy until he had become aged. Dr. Pili examined the man and found this to be truly so. He made a request of the man, saying, "When you die, let me have your body. I will make a fine coffin (*pahu maika'i*) for you, and leave you in it until the flesh has fallen away from the bones and I can see just how the piece of wood lies." The man agreed. Some years later he died. Dr. Pili went to those to whom the body belonged, but the daughter refused to give it to him; although he offered to pay for it, he was unable to get it. Thus disappointed, he kept on the alert and watched every night from a secret spot. Late one night when everyone was asleep, the people to whom the body belonged carried it out secretly. Dr. Pili spied on them until they reached the plains beyond Waimea, and located the chasm where they ended their procession and let down the body with ropes. He marked the place well; and the next day, armed with a gun and accompanied by his servant, he went there with a rope and lamps (*ipukukui*). The two let themselves down with the rope, lighted their lamps, and entered. There they saw innumerable helmets (*mahiole*), long feather capes (*'ahu'ula*), short capes (*'ahu*), implements of war (*mea kaua*), and valuables of every description in profusion—and they also saw the remains of ancient chiefs, together with innumerable kahilis, kapas, and mats.

They searched for and found the man, the doctor noticing the place carefully lest his body become mixed up with the others, and about six months later Dr. Pili returned to the place. He located the spear point, but the body was not really clean yet, so he waited until a year had passed and then had a *koa* coffin made for the body. In the meantime, some doctors in Honolulu had directed Dr. Andrews at Kailua [Dr. Seth Andrews, who arrived in Kailua in 1837] to get a skeleton (*kanaka iwi*), and Dr. Andrews had sent the order on to Dr. Pili at Waimea. When he was ready to get "his" body from the cavern he had discovered, Dr. Pili got a skeleton for them; not his chosen one (*kana milimili*), but the skeleton of a man who had not consented [to give his body] to him (*ke kanaka i 'ae 'ole iaia*).

The men who took the skeleton from Waimea to Kailua on Hawaii were told that the contents of their bundles (*pu'olo*) were very valuable and that they must take good care lest they be stolen. The Waimea men who carried them used the bundles for pillows at night. When they arrived at Kailua, Dr. Andrews said, "These are bundles of human bones," and when they were opened, there were the bones. The men were terrified, Dr. Pili told me. Well might they be afraid of the deception. If a man deceives and sends someone a corpse, he is put in jail (*pa'a maoli i Kawa*).

Lahainaluna people will perhaps remember about a skeleton there in 1835 or 1836. This was Dr. Pili's skeleton, whose coffin he had labeled falsely: "Glass case, handle with care, lest the wheels fall apart inside." H. Kuihelani and Amala were the two who carried it at night from Lahainalalo up to Lahainaluna.

If Kuihelani and his companion had heard that the box they carried was a coffin, it is doubtful that they would have stayed in Lahainalalo until late at night; probably they would not have carried the bones of another and, at night, put them in their carpenter shop. When they got to Andrews' place [Lorrin Andrews, at Lahainaluna], they said, "We have handled the glass case very carefully. We thought there might be a clock in it and were afraid that we might dislodge the wheels." "Oh, it is something different," Andrews answered. He set the box upright, inserted the key, opened the lid—and there was the skeleton, complete from head to toes, with the ligaments still attached, and the bones that had fallen away wired back in place, and the teeth grinning. *"Auwe! Auwe! He akua e ke kane!*⁴ We had thought that 'Umiamaka *ma* were gone, but they are still here!" (*Ka inoa ua hala o 'Umiamaka ma, eia no ka!*)⁵

Dr. Pili, however, met with disappointment. Not many days had gone by, not a week perhaps, when a great and dreadful fire broke out from the chasm burial pit (*lua huna nupa*), and for several days or perhaps a week, black, smelly smoke poured out and fire blazed. The bones and treasures within were all destroyed. Well do the people of Waimea and the missionary household remember the day, the month, and the year, when the cavern at Waimea was destroyed. The precious treasures which Dr. Pili had coveted to take as exhibits to his native land of England were all lost to him. The ancient treasured possessions of the chiefs, the famous *pololu* spears of Makakuikalani and Kanaloakua'ana Puapuakea that they used in the battle of Pu'oa'oaka, and the *la'au* clubs of Kamalalawalu and Lonoikamakahiki were all gone. There was no cause for the fire starting, nor reason for its going out. It came from the inside of the pit. Perhaps it was felt that the things would be taken and belittled; or perhaps it was because a *malihini* had seen these things. This is just a guess. And what of the skeleton at Lahainaluna? It was probably consumed when the school building took fire and burned down [on July 18, 1862]. Fire reached out and destroyed everything.

We see what trouble can come from abusing the bodies of the dead. Therefore, they were rounded up (*ho'opoepoe*) like packages of hard poi (*pu'olo pa'i'ai*), or wrapped bunches of banana (*'oma'o mai'a*), and bound around with netting (*koko*). Since the main thing was to hide the bones, they were buried (*kanu me ke pao*) under new houses, in roadways, in banks of taro patches, or any place where they would be concealed. During the time of Kamehameha II and Kamehameha III they were properly buried (*kanu pono,* that is, with funeral ceremony, and in a grave). Then numerous resentments arose among the chiefs, one against the other [as to their relative rights and privileges in the funeral arrangements and rites].*

DEATH

A mounting sickness (*he kulana mai'i*) was often the cause of a man's death. If the sickness reached a vital part, then death resulted. All medical treatment was in vain; one might search for healing and find nothing. Treatment could relieve the sickness but could not put off death. General weakness (*make 'ohemo wale*), accidents (*make ulia*), capture of the spirit of a living person (*make kaka ola*), high blood pressure (*make koko lana*), apoplexy (*make ka'iliponi*), madness (*make ulu nui*), consumption (*make hoki'i*), emaciation (*make mailo*), influences of *kuni 'ana'ana* magic (*make ka'ameha'i*) or sorcery (*ka ha'i make mai ho'i*),

---

* October 6, 1870.

pestilential diseases (*ma'i lele*), epidemics (*ma'i ahulau*), malignant diseases (*ma'i 'a'ai*), sickness from bitter emotions within a person (*make 'awahua iho a ke kanaka*), battle injuries and battle wounds (*make i ke kaua a me ka pahi kaua*), all these were causes of death—including the introduced diseases brought by *haoles* (foreigners). Innumerable were the causes of death.

A person who is dying moves his hands as though making string figures (*hei*), gasps, struggles for breath, and has a ringing in the ears before he is released to the spirit world (*aupuni 'uhane*). For some people there is no way of telling their time. Some people go while sleeping; others struggle; and still others cry out with great fear. As some draw near to the spirit world they become delirious; others are conscious when their time comes to go. In the midst of a pleasant conversation one who was about to die would say, "I am ready to go; this is my time. I have been sent for. Aloha to you all." Then his breath would be taken away and he would be gone into the spirit world. Thus did the righteous die in olden times; their passing was like the closing of the eyes in sleep, and they were gone.

Those who were related to those of the heavens (*o ka po'e lani*) would speak of them, saying, "Heaven is opening for me. Here are those of the heavens, Kanehekili, Kanewawahilani, Kauilanuimakehaikalani, Nakoloikalani. The wings of birds are ready to bear me hence." Then the first-born child (*keiki makahiapo*) would draw near to the mouth of the dying man with wide-open mouth, and the father would expel his breath (*ha*) into his child's mouth as he blessed (*me ka ho'omaika'i*) him and passed on the blessings received from the gods, so that they would continue to help the family of the dying man.

NOTES TO PART TWO

[1] These were the mates of Haumea in succeeding "reincarnations" (*hanau wawa*), one of them as Papa. See Beckwith (1951, pp. 110-116).

[2] For a discussion of '*aumakua* see Handy and Pukui (1958), Chapter III.

[3] "Food," '*ai:* "Food or food plant, especially vegetable food as distinguished from *i'a*, meat or fleshy food; often '*ai* refers specifically to poi" (Pukui and Elbert, 1957, p. 8). "Fish," *i'a:* "1. Fish or any marine animal, as eel, oyster, crab, whale. . . . 2. Meat or any flesh food. 3. Any food eaten as relish with the staple (*poi*, taro, sweet potato, breadfruit), including meat, fish, vegetable, or even salt" (Pukui and Elbert, 1957, p. 87). The idiom "*ka 'ai me ka i'a*" has given rise to the modern expression, "fish and poi."

[4] "*Auwe! Auwe! He akua e ke kane!*" This is a saying that originated on Molokai. A man brought home as a gift to his wife a bundle he had found along the roadside, thinking it contained a calabash and tapa beaters. When she opened the bundle, she found it contained human bones—the skull and long bones—and she cried out, "Alas! Alas! It is a corpse, O husband!" Her words are still used as an exclamation of dismay when an object turns out to be quite different from what was expected. (The Molokai story ran in the newspaper *Ku'oko'a* from October 7 to December 23, 1921.)

[5] '*Umiamaka* was a lesser chief who was remembered for his deceitful actions. He once brought a lobster as a gift to the father of a girl he wished to have. The father gave his consent, and the couple departed. On opening the lobster, the father found it full of sand. '*Umiamaka*'s name has come down as meaning a deceiver, and the quotation is still used in referring to a deceitful action.

PART THREE

PART THREE

The Spirit World

THE THREE SPIRIT REALMS

THERE WERE THREE realms (*ao*) for the spirits of the dead, according to the most learned people in the ancient times of Hawaii, such as the prophets, *po'e kaula;* those who knew the configurations of the earth, *po'e papa hulihonua;* the readers of omens in the heavens, *po'e kilokilo lani;* and the persons who knew sites, *po'e kuhikuhi pu'uone*. There were, first, the realm of the homeless souls, the *ao kuewa;* second, the realm of the ancestral spirits, the *ao 'aumakua;* and third, the realm of Milu, *ke ao o Milu,* that is, of Owa, Kapokuakini, Kapokuamano, and the many other names by which the ancients called this realm.

AO KUEWA, OR AO 'AUWANA

The *ao kuewa,* the realm of homeless souls, was also called the *ao 'auwana,* the realm of wandering souls. When a man who had no rightful place in the *'aumakua* realm (*kanaka kuleana 'ole*) died, his soul would wander about and stray amongst the underbrush on the plain of Kama'oma'o on Maui, or in the *wiliwili* grove of Kaupe'a on Oahu. If his soul came to Leilono, there it would find the breadfruit tree of Leiwalo, *ka 'ulu o Leiwalo*. If it was not found by an *'aumakua* soul who knew it (*i ma'a mau iaia*), or one who would help it, the soul would leap upon the decayed branch of the breadfruit tree and fall down into endless night, the *po pau 'ole o Milu*. Or, a soul that had no rightful place in the *'aumakua* realm, or who had no relative or friend (*makamaka*) there who would watch out for it and welcome it, would slip over the flat lands like a wind, until it came to a leaping place of souls, a *leina a ka 'uhane*. There spirits would be bathing in the sea in an area (*kahi 'oko'a*) where there was a valley in the sea floor (*awawa kai*) below a jutting rock (*pohaku 'oi'oi*). If it found no *'aumakua* soul to warn it (*'uhane 'aumakua kokua*), and it leaped from this soul-catching leaping place (*ua kawa kai po'i 'uhane,* that is, the rock), it would leap into the *po pau 'ole o Milu.* That was the purpose (*kuleana*) of these places that were spoken of frequently by the ancients. Many people who had died and come to life again had pointed them out; and even some people of this age, who have swooned or perhaps lain dead for a few hours or half a day, have related their experiences in these places. There are many stories from the ancients concerning them, and they have been pointed out by prophets inspired by spirits (*po'e kaula i uluhia i na 'uhane*). It became the custom to offer prayers for the dead (*kanaenae*) and bunches of *pili* grass at such places. The reason they were believed in was because so many had died and come to life again and had told innumerable stories about these places.

The *leina a ka 'uhane* on Oahu was close to the cape of Ka'ena, on its right (or north, *'akau*) side, as it turns toward Waialua, and near the cutoff (*alanui 'oki*) that goes down to Keaoku'uku'u. The boundaries of this *leina a ka 'uhane,* it is said, were Kaho'iho'ina-Wakea, a little below Kakahe'e, and the leaping place (*kawa-kai*) of Kilauea at Keawa'ula. At these places would be found helpful *'aumakua* souls who might bring back the spirit and restore life to the body, or if not, might welcome it to the realm of the *'aumakua.* Places within the boundaries mentioned were where souls went to death in the *po pau 'ole,* endless night.

Leilono at Moanalua, Oahu, was close to the rock Kapukaki and easterly of it (*a ma ka na'e aku*), directly in line with the burial mound of Aliamanu and facing toward the right side of the North Star (*a huli i ka 'ao'ao 'akau o ka Hokupa'a*). On the bank above the old trail there was a flat bed of pahoehoe lava, and on it there was a circular place about two feet in circumference. This was the entrance to go down; this was the topmost height (*nu'u*) of Kapapaialaka, a place in the *'aumakua* realm. Here at the entrance, *ka puka o Leilono,* was a breadfruit tree of Leiwalo, *he 'ulu o Leiwalo.* It had two branches, one on the east side and one on the west. These branches were deceiving. From one of them, the soul leaped into the *po pau 'ole;* if he climbed the other, it would bring aid from helpful *'aumakua* (*'aumakua kokua*). From that branch the soul would see the *'aumakua* realm and the ancestors spoken of, Wakea and all the rest, and those of the entire world who had traveled on this same journey.

The boundaries of Leilono were, Kapapakolea on the east, [with] a huge caterpillar (*pe'elua nui*) called Koleana as its eastern watchman, and the pool Napeha on the west, with a *mo'o* the watchman there. If the soul was afraid of these watchmen and retreated, it was urged on by the *'aumakua* spirits, then it would go forward again and be guided to the *'aumakua* realm. If a soul coming from the Alia (Aliapa'akai) side was afraid of the caterpillar, whose head peered over the hill Kapapakolea, and who blocked the way, it would wander about close to the stream by the harness shop. This was not the government road (*alanui aupuni*) of former times, but was a trail customarily used by "those of Kauhila'ele" [figuratively, the common people; the *la'ele,* old taro leaves, as contrasted with the *liko,* the new and choicer leaves—that is, the chiefs]. It was said that if a wandering soul entered within these boundaries it would die by leaping into the *po pau 'ole;* but if they were found by helpful *'aumakua* souls, some wandering souls were saved. Those who had no such help perished in the *po pau 'ole* of Milu.

On the plain of Kaupe'a beside Pu'uloa, wandering souls could go to catch moths (*pulelehua*) and spiders (*nanana*). However, wandering souls would not go far in the places mentioned earlier before they would be found catching spiders by *'aumakua* souls, and be helped to escape. Those souls who had no such help were indeed friendless (*he po'e 'uhane hauka'e lakou*), and there were many who were called by this name, *po'e 'uhane hauka'e.*

There were *Leina-a-ka-'uhane* and *'Ulu-o-Leiwalo* on Hawaii, Maui, Molokai, Lanai, Kauai, and Niihau as well as on Oahu. The traditions about these places were the same. They were where spirits were divided (*mahele ana*) to go into the realm of wandering spirits, the *ao kuewa* or *ao 'auwana;* or to the ancestral spirit realm, the *ao 'aumakua;* or to the realm of endless night, the *po pau 'ole.*

The places said to be for wandering spirits were: Kama'oma'o for Maui; Uhana for Lanai; Ma'ohelaia for Molokai; Mana for Kauai; Halali'i for Niihau; in addition to Kaupe'a for Oahu. In these places the friendless souls (*'uhane makamaka 'ole*) wandered.

Ao 'Aumakua

The *'aumakua* realm, *ao 'aumakua,* was a wide, level realm, containing within it many dwelling places—"In my Father's house are many mansions"—but the realm itself was one, with one overlord (*haku*), one god (*akua*), one chief (*ali'i*), one living (*ola ana*), one kingdom (*aupuni*). There were many places to live in, and many overseers, *luna,* to keep things in order, under one great overlord, *Haku nui.* "Narrow is the entrance, many are the dwelling places" (*Ua pilikia ka puka, a ua nui kahi e noho ai*).

In the *ao 'aumakua* were a *lani kuaka'a* (the highest heaven), a *lani kuakini* [a heaven of myriads], a *lani kuamanomano* [a heaven of multitudes], the *lewa lani* [the heavenly firmament], the *lewa nu'u* [the cloud firmament], *na paia ku a Kane* (the standing walls of Kane), *na kukulu o ka lani* (the supporting pillars of heaven), those [spirits] of the spread-out earth (*ko ka honua palahalaha*), the ever-beautiful sun (*ko ka la mau nani*), the bright-shining moon (*ko ka mahina koha'iha'i*), the ever-adorning stars (*ko na hoku mau ho'ohiwahiwa*), and all the other places, too numerous to mention, that were called realms of the *'aumakua.* What god created them? It was Kanenuiakea, the god who created man. He was called the *'aumakua* who created heaven and earth and mankind, and the ancients of Hawaii called him an *'aumakua.* A god-spirit, *akua,* who had been born as a human being was an *'unihipili* [that is, a god created by deification, as contrasted with the cosmogonic gods].

There were many doors by which to enter the *'aumakua* realm. If a man and his descendants were related to beings in the heavens (*ina ma ka lani ka pili ana*), they were not strangers to their relationship to their rightful place—their *kuleana*—

in the heavens. They knew very well that they had a *kuleana* in the heavens. If the *lewa lani* [heavenly firmament] was the *kuleana* of a man and his family, he was prepared to go to the *lewa lani*. If the deep ocean was the *kuleana* of a man and his family, it was known that his *kuleana* was there; and if the pit of Pele at Kilauea was the *kuleana* of a man and his family, it was known that theirs was an irrevocable *kuleana* (*kuleana hemo 'ole*) to go there. If it was at Uluka'a, or at *na paia ku a Kane,* it was known that he would be taken there.*

Each person knew his own *kuleana;* and at the time when a man's last illness came upon him, even before he became feeble he might say to his family, "Kanehekili *ma* have come to take me away." The family might say, "Do not consent to their taking you away; stay with us; no one knows what comforts (*pono*) there will be in that world, and if you go we shall be helpless." "I cannot be held back when it is the god who sends for me. When I die, observe (*malama*) the god." After a few days had passed, he would be just taken away, at times without anyone's knowledge. Some people would be taken bodily, and some while still breathing; but the soul had already been taken away by the *'aumakua* and it belonged to them. It was said that those who were taken to the *lewa lani,* the *lani kuakini,* and so forth, had wings and had rainbows at their feet. They were not in the *ao kuewa,* the realm of homeless spirits; they were the beloved of the heavens. If the sick person belonged to an unknown place in Uluka'a (*kahi 'ike 'ole i Uluka'a;* an unknown ancestral land in Kahiki), Ha'enakulaina, or Kauaniani, then he would say, "Kanehunamoku has sent for me to be taken to Uluka'a." The family might say, "Do not consent to their taking you." Sometimes the sick man would be taken alive into the sea without ever becoming a corpse. And so it was that Pele-Honuamea, Kaho'ali'i, Kanakaokai, Kamohoali'i, or the "guardian angel" (*anela kia'i;* personal *'aumakua*) of every man helped him to go to the *ao 'aumakua.* If it was the dead grandparents or parents that the sick man said had come to get him, this was a "fetching by deified spirits," *he ki'i 'uhinipili 'ia.* He would be united with the "guardian angels" and be led to the *'aumakua* realm. The faces of these people would be revealed and would be visible to him. This was a common thing with sick persons while laid low with an illness. Sometimes the sick person might be mistaken, but usually he spoke the truth.

Persons with this right, *kuleana,* in the *'aumakua* realm did not fear death or have any misgivings about dying, for what was death to them, or what was the body but a useless thing to those who had seen before their eyes the glory of the place prepared for them? I have seen such a man smiling and his cheeks dimpling with laughter, and if you asked him the reason for his happiness he would tell how the door of heaven had opened and a wondrous beauty not seen in this world had been revealed, and that he heard many voices calling him to go there. For such a person, the *ao 'aumakua* was ready to welcome him, in the heavens, perhaps, or on the earth—at whatever place was prepared for him in his *'aumakua* realm (*ao 'aumakua nona*) by the "guardian angels" and the *luna 'aumakua* (overseeing guardian spirit).

---

* October 6, 1870.

In the *'aumakua* realm there are many beloved—friends, relatives, and acquaintances—all united in thought and all joined together in the *'aumakua* realm, from the heavens, *lani,* to the firmaments (*lewa lani, lewa nu'u*), to the supporting pillars (*kukulu*), and to the standing walls of Kane (*na paia ku a Kane*). Those of the heavens are known to have wings like the wind (*me na 'eheu makani*), and their bounds are above the firmaments of the earth; those of the ocean are gathered together in the deep purple sea of Kane, the *kai popolo huamea a Kane.* So are gathered together those of the whole earth who belong to the *'aumakua* realm; all are united in harmony.

AO O MILU

There are many names in Hawaiian traditions for the realm of Milu: *po pau 'ole,* endless darkness; *po ia Milu,* the dark world of Milu; *po kinikini,* deep darkness; *po manomano,* intense darkness; *ka papa ia 'owa,* the stratum of the cleft [figuratively, of the forsaken]; *ka papa ia ka haoa,* the scorching stratum; *ka papa ia ka halelo,* the rocky stratum; *ka papa ia ka ha'aka* [*'a'aka*], the arid stratum.

It is said of this realm that it is a realm of evil, a friendless realm, one without family; a terrifying, fearful realm, a realm to be patiently endured, a realm of trouble, a realm in which to bear cruel treatment. It is said in the traditions and legends of Hawaii that there is fire there, and that it is not very dark, but rather light. There is a chief, an *ali'i,* there, to whom belong the fire and the darkness and the dreadful cruelty. Manu'a is the chief below of the *po pau 'ole*[1]— Milu is another person. Because of Milu's evil and foul deeds, he was cast into the *po pau 'ole.* He was a chief of Waipi'o, Hawaii, and he has become well known through the expression *ilalo ia Milu,* "down to Milu."

In the legend and tradition of Mokulehua, he went to get his wife Pueo from this realm. She had strangled (*ka'awae*) herself and died, and her soul had gone down and come under the rule of Manu'a (*a hiki i lalo lilo i Manu'a*) in the *po pau 'ole.* Pueo was imprisoned there, and Mokulehua went with his god Kanikani-a'ula to search for her. He found her through the mana of the god and they escaped from the fire and from many cruel deaths.

In the Hawaiian tradition of Malua'e, it is told how the man Malua'e sought for and found the spirit of his son Ka'ali'i in the *po pau 'ole.* Malua'e was a planter in the uplands of Manoa, Oahu. Kanaloaho'okau was his land. He raised a lot of bananas as food for the gods, and he planted other food, *'ai,* for himself, his wife, and his son. Malua'e's son choked while eating of the bananas of the gods without regard to the kapu on them (*i ka 'aia i ka mai'a*), and the gods Kane and Kanaloa cast his soul into the *po pau 'ole.* When Malua'e returned home from his farming, there was Ka'ali'i, dead, with a banana still in his mouth.

Malua'e grieved for love of his son. The gods revealed to him that the soul of Ka'ali'i had been cast away (*kiola*), and that it was there under Manu'a in the *po pau 'ole* (*aia ilalo o Manu'a i ka po pau 'ole*). One would think that when Malua'e heard of the death of his son because of the gods' anger that he would seek pity through penitence and appeals. But instead, Malua'e swore (*ho'ohiki*) that he would eat no food and would die together with his son. He carried his son into the house, closed the door, laid him down, and lay down beside him. Kane and Kanaloa no longer heard his voice in prayer each morning and evening, making offerings of food to them. Ten days and ten nights passed and the door did not open; 20 days and 20 nights, and the door did not open; 30 days and 30 nights passed. Kanaloa said, "Perhaps Malua'e is dead. We were too hasty in punishing this man who grows 'awa and gathers bananas and offers us food morning and evening. This is the server who has cared for us and cultivated 'awa, bananas, and sugar cane for us. How shall we repay him?" Kane replied, "Let us go and heal Malua'e and let him go and get the soul of his son who has gone down to Manu'a."

After 40 or so days, Malua'e grew feeble and darkness settled like cobwebs across his eyes. When Kane and Kanaloa saw this, they were filled with regret. They went and revived him, and Malua'e recovered from the destruction of his starving and fasting for the love of his son. He became strong and well, and his body recovered its vigor, and all the functions of his body were restored. The gods asked, "Do you love your son Ka'ali'i?" "Yes, with an endless love." "Can you get the soul of Ka'ali'i from Manu'a?" Malua'e denied that he could, saying, "I cannot do it, but you two have the mana that would make it possible for me to get the soul of Ka'ali'i." "We can grant your wish, and this will be our reward to you. You will also see the mana of the god who helps you; I will go down with you, and I will protect you in the fire and in the darkness." Kane considered how Malua'e could fetch the soul of Ka'ali'i from the *po pau 'ole,* and realized that he could not go in human form, so he changed him into a spirit form (*'ano kino lani*). It was this spirit form of Malua'e that fetched the soul of his child and made it possible for him to undergo all the dangers of the *po pau 'ole* of Manu'a.

At the time when Malua'e went to get the soul of Ka'ali'i, the god gave him a marvelous cane (*ko'oko'o mana*) called Maku'uko'o. Within this cane were all sorts of food and all the sweet things of the earth; in it were weapons for battle; in it were life and death; in it were fire and lava; in it were the sea and fresh water. There at the entrance, at Leilono in Moanalua at the breadfruit tree of Leiwalo, *ka 'ulu o Leiwalo,* Malua'e went down into the *po pau 'ole* beneath Manu'a. It is said that Malua'e encountered many dangers on the way, but was victorious over his enemies and slew them, until he got down under the foundations of the earth to the stratum of the forsaken, the *papa ia 'owa,* and the scorching stratum, *papa ia ka haoa,* of the *po pau 'ole.* That was where Ka'ali'i was imprisoned, still expiating the fault of eating the banana that had choked him to death, and for which he was being punished.

It is said of the *po pau 'ole* that there are two separate places in it: one for the people who are being punished for the "venial sins," *hewa li'ili'i,* of man; and one for the "mortal sins," *hewa make,* of man. There are two heinous sins, *hewa 'ino loa,* for which men are cruelly punished in Kapokuakini [the latter division]. But Ka'ali'i was not imprisoned in Kapokuakini, nor was Pueo, the wife of Mokulehua. Her obtaining had been extremely difficult, but not so that of Ka'ali'i; he was quickly obtained, and was given treatment (*lapa'au*) after Malua'e had brought his soul up from the *po pau 'ole.*

Kawelu is another famous woman in Hawaiian traditions and legends. Hiku went down to get the soul of Kawelu, and found her soul under the rule of Manu'a (*ilalo o Manu'a*). It was brought back and she was warmed and revived with *'awapuhi, maile, pala* fern, and many other fragrant things to induce the soul to remain in the body, and thus she was restored to life.

There are a great many Hawaiian traditions and legends about spirits and about those whose bodies have died and whose souls have gone down to the *po pau 'ole*. All these stories which are told about people who have gone to get souls and have restored them to life are false and lying tales. They are persistent tales, and the right thing to do is to call them falsehoods and lies. But this is the truth and is to be believed: It is not an unfamiliar thing for Hawaiians to hear of a place of intense darkness, of endless night, a pit of everlasting fire, and a place where people who have done wrong are held fast. This is clearly to be seen from the tradition of Milu. Because Milu was a bad and cruel chief, his soul was thrown down into the *po pau 'ole*, and he fell under the rule of Manu'a (*ua ha'ule ilalo lilo i Manu'a*), to the darkness of Manu'a (*ka po ia Manu'a*) and the darkness that was Manu'a's (*ka po lilo ia Manu'a*). Because of Milu's evilness, souls were cast down to him and came under the rule of Milu (*a i lalo lilo i o Milu la*). The *po pau 'ole* was not Milu's; he was only an evil chief who had been cast down into it. The *po pau 'ole* had been well known to the whole Hawaiian race from ancient times; and also in this time, when writing and the Word of God has been brought—these are the new things.

The ancients of Hawaii recognized four realms: this world that we live in; the realm of homeless and wandering souls, the *ao kuewa*, or *'auwana;* the *'aumakua* realm, the *ao 'aumakua;* and the realm of endless darkness, the *po pau 'ole*.*

NOHA ANA—MEDIUM POSSESSION

Spirits often return and speak through (*maluna*) a person who is inspired because he has become possessed (*ma ka uluhia ana mai a noho iluna*). Some possessed persons speak crazily. Some speak as inspired prophets (*uluhia kaula*) or prophesiers (*uluhia wanana*), some just talk, and some give inspired help. There are many kinds of spirits that help for good and many that aid in evil. Some lie and deceive, and some are truthful; it would not be possible for a man to do these things without the aid of his possessing spirit.

> . . . believe not every spirit, but try the spirits whether they are of God: because many false prophets are gone out into the world. Hereby know ye the Spirit of God: Every spirit that confesseth that Jesus Christ is come in the flesh is of God: And every spirit that confesseth not that Jesus Christ is come in the flesh is not of God. . . . (I John 4:1–3)

According to these words of the Holy Scriptures, the people of Hawaii have not been in error; not only here in Hawaii was there this possession of spirits (*uluhia a 'uhane*). But the workings and possessions of the spirits were a little

---
* October 13, 1870.

different in ancient times, and people were possessed to foretell the coming of misfortunes or blessings.

There was Kekio Pilakalo, a *kaula* in the time of Peleioholani, who prophesied the coming of a race of people with bright shiny eyes, and other similar peoples, and "children of Kamapua'a" [figuratively, "beastly people"]; animals that people would ride on, and large animals with horns on their heads. So also in the time of Kuali'i, Peleioholani's father, prophets had foretold the coming of the *haole*, or foreigner; and in the time of Kahahana, the king of Oahu, the *kahuna nui*, Ka'opulupulu, prophesied the coming of the *haole* and of people who would dwell in houses of rocks, and in large hollow logs. Shortly after the time of Kahahana and the *kahuna nui* Ka'opulupulu, Captain Cook, called Lono, arrived. Kapihe was the *kaula* in the time of Kamehameha I; Ka'onohiokala and Keaweawe'ulaokalani were his gods. The prophecy of Kapihe was: "The ancient kapus will be overthrown, the heiaus and *lele* altars will be overthrown, and the images will fall down. God will be in the heavens; the islands will unite, and those of the heavens [the chiefs] will fall, and those of the earth [the lesser people] will rise," *E hiolo ana na kapu kahiko, a e hiolo ana na haiau a me na lele, a e hina ana na ki'i; Aia ke Akua i ka lani, e hui ana na moku, e iho mai ana ko ka lani, e pi'i aku ana ko ka honua nei.* This prophecy was spoken about three years before the coming of the first missionaries who brought the Holy Scriptures.

It is a wonderful thing how the spirits (*'uhane*) of the dead and the "angels" (*anela*) of the *'aumakua* can possess living persons. Nothing is impossible to god-spirits, *akua*. Persons are possessed, first, when the gods desire to reveal hidden things and to foretell important events that will come to pass (persons so possessed are called *kaula*, or prophets); second, when persons are chosen by the *'aumakua* and directed to take care of their physical forms (*kino*) and the things pertaining to these forms; third, when *'uhinipili* (*'unihipili*) spirits directed by the *'aumakua* possess; fourth, when spirits that have been consecrated (*'uhane ho'ola'a*) possess, at the desire of these spirits; fifth, when *'unihipili* spirits, combined with spirits of the *po pau 'ole* [that is, evil spirits], possess.

In the old days in Hawaii, prophetic utterances and hidden sayings (*'olelo huna*) were relied on and the words of the *kaula* fully believed in. The words of the *kaula* were always fulfilled; no chief or ruler of a kingdom would disregard the words of the prophets and of those possessed by an *'aumakua* or by the ancestors. Their direction was always right. Kamehameha I is thought (*i mana'o ai*) to have placed his entire confidence in one of his gods, Kaho'ali'i—he who was the man-god of Kamehameha I—but that is not so. Kamehameha relied upon the god Kaho'ali'i who would possess (*noho mai*) this human *kahu* of the god Kaho'ali'i. So also with Kihawahine. She was a female image with hair bleached with lime (*pukai 'ia*); and sometimes the image of Kihawahine was decorated with *olena* and *puaniu* and *pokohukohu* tapas. This image was only a symbol. The spirit of Kihawahine would possess a man (*noho 'uhane*), or if not, she showed herself in some awesome and terrifying god form (*kino akua*). So it was with others of Kamehameha's gods. These gods were called the *'aumakua* gods of Kamehameha, and they were *'aumakua* for the chiefs. So it was with this and that god kept (*malama*) by Kamehameha.*

There were many *kahu* of *'aumakua* gods, who were the personal gods, *akua pili kino*, of the chiefs and people [that is, the ancestral gods or cosmic forces to whom they were related—sharks, thunder, lava, and so on]. The *'uhinipili* gods, *akua 'uhinipili*, were family gods, *akua 'ohana* [that is, deified spirits of deceased members of the family]. They were included (*huipu 'ia*) with the *'aumakua*, and the *'aumakua* were grouped with (*huipu me*) the angels of heaven (*na anela o ka lani*).

When such spirits would inspire [persons] to prophecy and to "speak in strange tongues" (*'olelo e*), this was called "predicting by prophets," *wanana a na kaula*. Spirits that possess a person when he is ill are murderous spirits (*'uhane pepehi kanaka*) aiding thieves and those who would rob from others. In this age most of these spirits escape. Some are virtuous spirits (*'uhane 'oia'i'o*) who lead their *kahu* and their medium (*haka*) to do good and to safeguard the welfare of the family, and they may be angels of light. But most of the spirits of this age are lying spirits who lead their mediums into trouble and bring them to punishment according to the laws of the land. This is a result of the joining together of the *'uhinipili* spirits with the spirits from the *po pau 'ole*.

VISIONS AND DREAMS

Dreams are of two kinds: dreams at the moment of falling asleep (*hihi'o*); and dreams in deep sleep (*moe 'uhane*). A vision, *akaku*, is unlike either of these. It is what one sees when one is really awake, and it is raised up by the mana of the *'aumakua* and by the mana of the supreme *'aumakua* in the *lani kuaka'a*. *Akaku* and *kuaka* visions are the same—they have unlimited scope (*palena 'ole*) of revelation. Their revelations come from the supreme *'aumakua* of the *lani kuaka'a*. Some people have great gifts (*ha'awina*) of vision, and some have small. As the Holy Scriptures say: "And the devil, taking him up into a high mountain, shewed unto him all the kingdom of the world in a moment of time" (Luke 4:5), so he who has a revelation (*'ike kuaka*) might see in a single moment all the kingdoms of the earth, and every kingdom of this world, and every race of people—red, white, or black. All things might be revealed to him; nothing would be hidden from his sight. If he desires to see the kingdoms of Europe and America, then these things are before his eyes, if he at first has said he wants to see them, and if it is his gift (*kana ha'awina*) to see whatever he desires. If he wishes to see heaven and earth unite, the heavens will lower to meet the earth, through the mana of the *'aumakua* of the *lani kuaka'a*. This kind of revelation (*'ike*) is a *kuaka*, or an *akaku*. There might be revealed before his eyes the pillars of the earth, and the ocean and all its hidden things, and he will recognize them as though his eyes had always seen them. If it is his god whom he desires to see, or perhaps all the *'aumakua*, then he will see them and talk with them; they will shortly be revealed to him. Or, if it is the spirits of all those who have preceded him into the

---
* October 13, 1870.

'*aumakua* realm that he wishes to see, he will see them all just as he has wished—all will appear like living persons and talk with him in ordinary speech. Such a vision is called an *akaku* or a *kuaka*. Some who have such visions see the angels of heaven flying in space, and the heavens opened, and the depths of the ocean exposed, and villages there in the deep ocean, and people walking on the surface of the sea. These are *akaku* and *kuaka*. Many people in the old days saw visions of this kind. The reason is that they were so frequently possessed by spirits and so frequently inspired by them to prophesy (*uluhia mau na 'uhane i 'ano kaula*), that even when they were not actually being possessed (*noho hou*) they were inspired by *akaku* and *kuaka* revelations and would then tell what they had seen.

A *hihi'o* is a dream (*moe 'uhane*) while dozing (*i ka lau o ka lihilihi*), while the mind is yet awake and one can still hear conversation. Then one is wafted away into the spirit world (*ao 'uhane*) and meets spirits talking about important or perhaps strange things. Some of these waking dreams are worth while, but most of them are worthless things that concern only the spirit kingdom.

True dreams, *moe 'uhane,* are very important to man. Most of them are idle dreams, but occasionally a dream of great significance is had by a man. To dream the same thing repeatedly brings good luck (*pomaika'i*) to a man if it has brought him good luck in the first place, and bad luck (*po'ino*) if it has before brought misfortune. To dream of riches at night is useless—it will not bring riches by day. If one dreams at night of dying, he will not die when day comes.

Most dreams are in the form of parables (*nane*) and are difficult of interpretation; but dreams of a canoe, a foreign ship, exposed genital organs, a person blind in one eye, a drying rack, a corpse, of hands crossed behind the back, and things of that nature are easy of interpretation. If a man has a dream such as one of these, and he is planning to get his food the next day by fishing or trading or by any other means of gain, he may as well spend the day idly and put off the work until another day. If he insists on going fishing, he will be unsuccessful and return with nothing. Or if he means to work with his hands or to engage in trading, he had better give up the idea—it will be futile. If he insists on going fishing he will not get enough to eat, or if he wants to get bait to make into chum, it will take him a long time to get it. He has had a meaningful dream (*moe kahua*) in the night. So with some other bad dreams (*moe 'ino*) of the night. If he dreams of drawing out his own intestines, or a tooth, or something of this nature, the dreamer can guess (*koho*) that this does not pertain to any outsider (*ha'i*), but to one of his own "flesh and blood" [literally, of his own navel, *piko*] who will die. If he dreams of taking out his tooth and holding it before him (*ma ke alo*), it means he will be struck by a stone [a "stone" of grief] in front of him [misfortune to someone very close to him]. Bitter dreams (*moe 'awahua*) about a man's own body do not pertain to the dreamer himself.

There are many kinds of dreams, some of them terrifying and striking the soul with awe and causing the body to tremble. As the soul is awestruck, so is the body set atremble by some wondrous dreams; there are many dreams of this kind. Dreams of being chased by a bullock or by a wild animal signify the enemies of the day, although they are not the same kind as those of the dream. Dreams that are bitter to some people are mild to others, and they are revelations of the gods (*ha'awina a ke akua*).*

AKUA 'AUMAKUA—THE 'AUMAKUA GODS

There is one great *'aumakua* god, and he made the highest heavens—the *lani kuaka'a*—and the earth, and the things that fill them both. He is Kanenuiakea, a single god and many gods in one god. Kunuiakea and Lononuiakea are included within (*huipu oloko*) the mana of this god; they are one god. The *'aumakua* gods (*na akua 'aumakua*) and the multitudinous hosts of chiefly spirits (*na pu'ali ali'i 'uhane*) under them are worshiped by men; and the names of the *'aumakua* gods previously mentioned, Kane, Ku, and Lono, are attached (*ho'opili*) to them. Those three names are split up (*hahae*) into the multitudinous hosts in the heavens above and in the earth below, and they are worshiped under such names as:

Kanehekili (Kane-the-thunderer)
Kane-wawahi-lani (Kane-breaker-of-heaven)
Kane-i-ka-pualena (Kane-in-the-golden-dawn)
Kane-i-ka-malamalama (Kane-in-the-light)
Kane-i-koli-hana-a-ka-la (Kane-who-works-in-the-heat-of-the-sun)
Kane-i-ka-molehulehu (Kane-in-the-dusk)
Kane-i-ka-wana'ao (Kane-in-the-early-morning)
Kane-i-ka-pule (Kane-in-the-prayer)
Kane-i-ka-makaukau (Kane-in-readiness)
Kane-ki'i (Kane-the-fetcher)
Kane-haka (Kane-the-gazer)
Kane-maka-hi'o-lele (Kane-of-the-darting-eyes)
Kane-lele (Kane-the-flyer)
Kane-i-koha (Kane-in-explosive-sound)
Kane-pa-'ina (Kane-in-crackling-sound)
Kane-kaka'a (Kane-the-roller)
Kane-koa (Kane-the-warrior)
Kane-i-ko-kea (Kane-of-the-white-sugar-cane)
Kane-i-kokala (Kane-in-the-*kokala*-fish) [called a shark god by Kamakau]
Kane-huli-honua (Kane-overturning-the-earth)
Kane-i-kaulana-'ula (Kane-resting-in-the-rosy-clouds)
Kane-mana-ia-pai'ea (Kane-who-gives-power-to-Pai'ea)
Kane-makua (Kane-the-parent)
Kane-huna-moku (Kane-of-the-hidden-island)
Kane-i-ka-papa-honua (Kane-in-the-foundation-of-earth)
Kane-ki'ei (Kane-the-peeper)
Kane-halo (Kane-the-peerer)

---
* October 20, 1870.

    Kane-'ohi'ohi (Kane-the-talkative)
    Kane-milo-hai (Kane-accepter-of-sacrifice)
    Kane-pua'a (Kane-the-pig)
    Kane-pua-hiohio (Kane-of-the-whirlwind)
    Kane-ne'ene'e (Kane-the-creeper)
    Kane-mana-ia-huea (Kane-who-gives-power-to-Huea)
    Kane-pohakuka'a (Kane-of-the-rolling-stone)
    Kane-holo-pali (Kane-running-on-the-cliff)
    Kane-i-ka-'onohi-o-ka-la (Kane-in-the-eyeball-of-the-sun)

There are thousands and thousands of names that are separated (*mahae 'ia*) into names of the same form. There is only one form (*'ano*), and the names only fit the work done. There is one *kuahu* altar, and one place to make offerings—the *Pohaku-o-Kane*—and among all who are inspired by a Kane god (*a o ke Kane ulupo a pau*), one *kahu* should not despise another. They should all eat together of the sacrifices and the offerings. It is in edicts (*kanawai*) and consecrated things (*mea la'a*) that each is different.

In the dividing (*mahae ana*) of Kunuiakea, the names became those of the hosts of chiefly "angels of heaven," *na pua'li ali'i anela o ka lani*, and they were worshiped by the names into which they had been divided, such as:

    Ku-kaua-kahi (Ku-the-warrior)
    Ku-waha-ilo (Ku-maggot-mouthed)
    Ku-ho'one'enu'u (Ku-moving-the-heights)
    Ku-ka-lani (Ku-the-chief)
    Ku-ka'ili-moku (Ku-snatcher-of-land)
    Ku-ke-olo'ewa (Ku-the-supporter)
    Ku-ke-ao-loa (Ku-of-the-long-cloud)
    Ku-ke-ao-poko (Ku-of-the-short-cloud)
    Ku-ke-ao-ho'omihamiha-i-ka-lani (Ku-in-the-clouds-that-dot-the-sky)
    Ku-moku-hali'i (Ku-spreading-[forests]-on-the-land)
    Ku-pulupulu (Ku-[giver-of]-verdure)
    Ku-pa'aike'e (Ku-smoother-of-rough-places)
    Ku-pepeiao-poko (Ku-the-short-eared)
    Ku-ho'oholo-pali (Ku-who-slides-[the-canoe]-down-the-cliff)
    Ku-alono-wao (Ku-of-the-mountain-heights)
    Ku-ka-'ohi'a-laka (Ku-of-the-*'ohi'a lehua*-tree)
    Ku-mauna (Ku-of-the-mountain)
    Ku-lili-aka (Ku-of-the-patchy-shadows)
    Ku-lili-'ai-(ke)-kaua (Ku-who-is-furious-in-battle)
    Ku-hai-moana (Ku-traversing-the-ocean)
    Ku-kaha'ula (Ku-of-the-sensual-dream)
    Ku-i-ke-alai (Ku-[who-stands]-in-the-way)
    Ku-i-ka-uweke (Ku-the-releaser)
    Ku-i-ke-kala (Ku-the-liberator)

Ku-i-ke-pa'a (Ku-the-binder)
Ku-i-ka-ha'awi (Ku-the-giver)
Ku-i-ka-loa'a (Ku-the-prosperous)
Ku-i-ke-pi (Ku-the-stingy)
Ku-i-ka-pono (Ku-the-righteous)

The thousands of hosts of *'aumakua* (*tausani pu'ali 'aumakua*) into which this branch of the "godhead" (*lala o ke akua*) had been divided pertained to death and life, and the freeing (*wehe*) and forgiving (*huikala*) [of men's faults].

The second branch under the single "godhead" included:

Lono-i-ka-ou-ali'i (Lono-in-the-chiefly-signs-in-the-heavens)
Lono-maka-hi'olele (Lono-of-the-darting eyes)
Lono-'opua-kau (Lono-of-the-omens-in-the-clouds)
Lono-kina'u (Lono-who-notices-defects)
Lono-i-ki'eke (Lono-of-provisions)
Lono-iki-aweawe-aloha (Lono-in-the-yearning-of-love)

It is said that for all the thousands divided up into these names of Lono, there was only one important thing to do—to pay heed to them and observe their kapus (*o ka ho'olohe a malama*).

Regarding the *'aumakua* previously said to be Kanenuiakea, and the divisions made by this or that man or family, it is only the names that are different. It was a single god, a single mana, a single god-spirit; the mana was a single mana within a single god and within a single spirit. So it was with Kunuiakea and Lononuiakea; they were combined within (*huipu ai iloko*) the one god and thus were regarded as sacred by the *po'e kahiko*. In the kapus [the ritual ceremonial observances] of the heiaus—the *kapu loulu, kapu luakini, kapu unu*, and also the ceremonies of the *waihau* heiaus—the three gods were joined together within a single kapu. And so it was in the acquiring of *'aumakua* (*ho'aumakua ana*) by some people—three or four might be joined together.

Because of the confusions (*pohihihi*) caused by people of later times, and people of this time, some people today are utterly "mixed up" (*ua lauwili*). They acquire or contact the *'aumakua*, in accordance with what they have been told by their parents—or under the direction of certain kahunas or other persons who know—who say: "So-and-so is your *'aumakua*" (*He mea ko 'aumakua*).* But they do not understand how to contact the *'aumakua* and are told, or are directed by a kahuna: "Thus must you do to please the *'aumakua*." If the *'aumakua* is a *mo'o*, they get a reddish-brown dog, or a brown one, or a mottled one, or a dog with a spot on each jowl, or one striped like a caterpillar, or a brindled dog, and whatever the persons directing them say in the way of tapas—a saffron yellow tapa (*'olena*), or a light yellow one (*he mahuna*), or one the color of ripening *hala* fruit (*he halakea*), or one the color of the blossom of the coconut (*he kapa pua niu*)—and other things, including a whole *'awa*, and wrap all the sacrifices

---

* October 20, 1870.

in a striped tapa (*kapa moelua*). Then, when all is quiet (*noho a hano ka leo*), they take the bundle to a pond fed by springs and hide it in the water. Or they might take it to the ocean, or to the mountains, or to the pit of Pele—wherever the kahuna or the one who knew had pointed out or had taught them was where the *'aumakua* was. Because they did not have the names of the *'aumakua* to call on (*e ho'aumakua aku ai*), the names of a man's parents, or of the woman's parents, or that of a child of theirs who had died were used; and these became *'aumakua* (*lilo aku la no ia i mau 'aumakua*). These ways of contacting the *'aumakua* (*mau hana 'aumakua*) were not the correct or true way. It was just a good way to seek a lessening of troubles, and, in the seeking, they found some relief—even in this false way of seeking it.

Very different was the calling upon of the *'aumakua* (*ho'aumakua ana*) by *ka po'e kahiko* in the setting to rights of the punishments and troubles sent by the *'aumakua* to this or that family. Each offering to be sacrificed was a light one. It was just a "wave" offering (*o ka ho'ali wale*) that the god desired in his name. The sacrifices and offerings were eaten by the people (*kanaka*), with repentance for their wrongdoing, and that would cause the god to look upon them with favor (*ho'omaliu 'ia mai*). The god would not be pleased with sacrifices just offered carelessly without proper procedure (*ho'olei wale 'ia aku me ka pono 'ole*). The god was not in the water, nor in the deep ocean, nor in the sea, nor in the pit of Pele, nor in the high heavens; the god was in the place where the offerings (*ho'ali*) were made with repentance and humbleness of heart. Then heaven would bend low. But no matter how many the offerings and sacrifices, if they were not properly offered in accordance with the desire of the god, the heavens would remain high, the ocean deep, and the pillars of heaven remote.*

NOTE TO PART THREE

[1] Manu'a as chief of the underworld appears elsewhere only three times: among the gods listed in the introduction to *The Legends and Myths of Hawaii* (Kalakaua, 1888, p. 48); in a paraphrasing of this 1870 account of Kamakau by Fornander (1919, p. 337); and as a brother of Uli in a legend by Rice (1923; p. 43). He appears to be an "invention" of Kamakau, as does the description of the *po pau 'ole* itself, with its "strata" so identifiable with the Christian hell. It is in this passage that Kamakau most clearly displays the influence of his Christian training in his attempt to reconcile the ancient beliefs with the new. Compare the attempt of Kepelino (Beckwith, 1932, pp. 48-54). For the earliest recorded Hawaiian concept of the underworld and of Milu (Miru) see Ellis (1917, pp. 274-276). For Milu, see also Andrews (1865, p. 391).

* October 27, 1870.

PART FOUR

PART FOUR

Kaku'ai — Transfiguration

HOSTS OF HEAVEN AND EARTH

IT IS CLEAR from the ancient accounts of the remote forebears of this group of islands that the ancestors believed in the true god. This true god they worshiped was Kanenuiakea. He was the source who made heaven and earth. He made all things in heaven and in space; he made the sun, the dots of light in the heavens, and all things that were made in space; he was the god who made the highest heaven. His was the mana that made the earth and the things that fill it, and the waters under the earth. The tradition says that Kanehulihonua was the very first man that the god made out of earth, and that Keakahulilani was the first woman. They were the earliest ancestors of Hawaii; because of them, it is said, the god became the friend of mankind. In the time of their child Kapapaialaka[1] the earth was separated from heaven, and the god looked toward mankind with love, and men became the children of god. In his time men made sacrifices and offerings to the god of the first things they obtained—the first-born of their animals, the first fruits of the earth, and the first fishes caught. Men gave these things as sacrifices and offerings to the god, and the god was pleased with the offerings of men.

So it went on for a long time through the generations, until the time of Kahiko Luamea. He is said to have been a devout chief and his kingdom a pious one. The god blessed his rule and the people prospered. Kahiko Luamea had two sons; Lihau'ula was the elder, and Wakea was the younger. Lihau'ula entered the priesthood ('oihana kahuna) and performed the sacred offices for the god. In his time the kapus and the things consecrated to the god multiplied until they became burdensome. Wakea was set apart to be the progenitor of chiefs (*kuamo'o kupuna ali'i*), and Lihau'ula to be the progenitor of the kahuna line of Milipomea. Thus through Kahiko Luamea came the high priests of the god. When Lihau'ula carried on his priestly work, certain foods were made kapu to women—pig, shark, *ulua* fish, red fishes, most bananas, yellow coconuts, and certain dark and pink pois. It was made kapu for men and women to eat together. This was to separate from the worship of the god those who were unclean and defiled by blood; and so all those who were polluted were kept separated because the god desired only those who were clean and pure.

Long after these kapus had begun to be observed (*malama*), bones of the dead began to be placed on the *kuahu* altars together with sacrifices and offerings. Then the kahunas saw that the spirits (*'uhane*) of those who had been offered with sacrifices to the god were being revived (*ho'ala*) through the worship paid the god; they grew strong and had great mana. They were seen to come in bodily form (*hele kino ana mai*) to eat of "food and fish," or to do some deed of mana like killing an "enemy," or really attacking in a battle. When it was seen that real life (*ola maoli*) could be brought back into the corpses by treating the souls (*ma ka lapa'au ana o na 'uhane*) so that they came back into the bodies, that caused the deserting of the true god. People began to worship the "hosts of heaven," *pu'ali o ka lani,* and the race fell to worshiping this thing and that, according to each man's inclination (*makemake*). Chiefs gave (*ha'awi*) their children to the gods and made offerings at the *kuahu* altars of the heiaus in order that they might have mana, retain the kingdom, and be brave and famous. If they died first, they were themselves made into gods. If the father and mother died first, then the children made the offerings in order that their spirits would become strong (*kahukahu a lilo na 'uhane i mea ikaika*), and they became the gods to be worshiped.

In place of the true god whom they had forsaken, the people worshiped the "hosts of heaven and earth." They transfigured, *kaku'ai,* the souls of their forefathers so that they would be kept joined to their descendants; and they bowed their heads and worshiped them. Transfiguring, *kaku'ai ana,* was a common practice among the Hawaiians, and it is still practiced today.[2]

VOLCANIC MANIFESTATIONS—PELE

For a dead beloved one whom they wished to become a volcanic manifestation (*e lilo i pele*) of the crater (*luapele*) of Kilauea on Hawaii, the Hawaiians would act in this way: They would take to the volcano the bones, hair, fingernails, or some other part of the dead body, sacrifices and offerings for the gods (*akua*), gifts for the priests and prophets and guardians of the volcano, a pig, *'awa,* and a tapa garment of whatever color the relatives to whom the body belonged chose to be a visible sign to them—whether striped, red and white, or red and black—and they would ascend to the pit of Pele, *ka lua o Pele.* There they ritually killed the dedicatory pig (*ho'omoe kapu ka pu'a me ka ho'ohiki ana, he pua'a hana*) for the dead newcomer, the *malihini,* to become a native, a *kama'aina,* of Kilauea. If the ritual went well (*ina he maika'i ka ho'omoe ana*), a pouring rain would pelt the uplands and the sounds of thunder would reverberate to the sea, as a sign of consent to the admission (*ho'ohui*) of the *malihini.* In the morning, the pig was roasted, the *'awa* was chewed, and all would feast. Then the prophet of Pele, the *kaula Pele*, and the relatives of the dead, from 10 to 40 as eyewitnesses, would take the corpse and the offerings—a live pig (*pua'a mohai ola*) and some *'awa*—to the very center (*'onohi*) of the fire, where the fires were quiet and where fiery lava (*ahi pele*) welled up (*hua'i*) instead of tossing about or rolling in great waves.

The prophet stood and pleaded (*kahoahoa*) for the acceptance of the *malihini* and for his being united with the *kama'aina* of the pit, and he recited the ancestry of the dead one so that his ancestors in the crater of Kilauea would know him as one of them. It was useless to make offerings to them, for they were just the *kama'aina* of the place, not the gods. When the *'awa* and the pig were thrown in, they were immediately consumed. When the body of the *malihini* was thrown in, it was as though it were being fondly lifted by a procession of people and borne tenderly upon fingertips into Halema'uma'u, the home of the *kama'aina* chiefess of this place. She, Pele, had built this place to warm the strangers who came to the mountain through icy mists. The body was borne along for the distance of a chain or two without the tapa that covered it being scorched; then, like a swelling wave, a flame swept over it and the *malihini* vanished. Some minutes later a flame appeared and billowed, and a column of fire appeared, streaked with whatever color the relatives had chosen to wrap the body in. They would hear the sound of many voices making a din, chanting *hula* and *oli* and *mele*, and the colored column which was the *malihini* they had brought would move about joyfully. Then the people to whom the *malihini* belonged would wail and call out the name by which he had been known in life and say, "You live! You live!" The "sign," *ho'ailona*, which the relatives saw was their beloved one; this was the body of their beloved.

Should Hawaii be overrun by lava, if they saw the *ho'ailona* of their own volcanic spirit (*pele*) in the fountains of fire the people had no fear of death—it was their own *kama'aina* who surrounded them with fire. If they were within the blazing fires, they would come to no harm; they had their guide, and they could go forward victoriously (*hele i ka lanakila*) and without harm. Such was the belief of some people about volcanic spirits in the old days.

If the corpse was that of a chief, some people divided the body into 40 or more pieces and distributed the little pieces among the districts (*moku'aina*) of Hawaii. Those of each district could take their pieces to be made into a *pele*. There might be 40 or 100 pieces, and so each person might become a "multitude" (*lehulehu*) of volcanic spirits. The danger in making the body of a high chief, or perhaps a ruler, into so many spirits was that they might burst forth and devastate the land. The *kaula Pele*, therefore, did not like to do this. Those who did yield to the pleading of certain people and consent to do so were called "destroyers of the land" (*ho'ino 'aina*) and "troublemakers to the kingdom" (*ho'opilikia i ke aupuni*). That is the reason why chiefs killed prophets of Pele in the old days, and why the prophets acted in great secrecy. If there was a great eruption that devastated the land, the people became greatly excited and believed that a high chief had been taken into the pit of Pele. The mistaken idea (*mana'o kuhihewa*) that many spirits are banded together in the pit of Pele has persisted from ancient times to this. It is a place free from all defilement, according to the belief of these people.*

Many people wished to become volcanic spirits, and their relatives would make the appeal for them—perhaps because they believed that they would continue to live in the volcanic fires. There were many signs to be seen if one could not become a spirit of the volcano. A person did not become such merely by the making of a great many gifts and offerings; many are the eyewitnesses and prophets who can testify to this. When the prophet and the relatives of the dead one took his bones, hair, fingernails, or his spittle, perhaps, and the prophet made the appeal and threw the bundle into the glowing fire, if the bundle fell into the fire and was thrown back again to the place from which it was thrown without the tapa wrappings being burned, then the prophet would retrieve the bundle and ask what the obstructions (*na kumu hihia*) were that had caused it to be thrown back. If, when it was thrown a second time into the fire, it vanished into flame, then it had first been returned because of the obstruction that had now been cleared up. But if the bundle broke open and the bones or fingernails or whatever it was scattered, why was this? It was because the person had been spurned. He had no right—no *kuleana*—there, and had no relatives in that place. He became a wandering spirit at Kamaʻomaʻo, a catcher of dragonflies, a shredder of spiders in the *wiliwili* grove of Kaupeʻa.

The persons who have a *kuleana* in *Ka lua o Pele* are the direct descendants (*pulapula ponoʻi*) of Haumea, Kanehekili, Kahoʻaliʻi, Kanewawahilani, Kauilanuimakehaikalani, Nakoloilani, Kamohoaliʻi, Pele, Hiʻiaka, and Namakaokahaʻi. If one of these *ʻaumakua* is in the family of a person, they are all in his family [as they are related to each other]. Through giving birth in human form, one of them joins a person's blood to theirs and becomes a *kumupaʻa,* a "fixed origin"; they are all *ʻaumakua*. The *kuleana* does not come by consecrating a spirit to be one's god (*hoʻolaʻa*), or by pretending to be possessed by a god (*hoʻonohonoho akua*) and feigning insanity (*hoʻopupule*) and speaking in whispers, or by bowing down and worshiping them, as some do, or by calling upon them to come and inspire him as he wishes. Only through the blood lineage (*koko i eweewe mai*) of the ancestors does the *kuleana* come. The god recognizes that blood kinship and clings forever to his descendants in the living world. Persons who can claim such birth, even those who live on Oahu or Kauai, or those who have sailed away to foreign lands, have a *kuleana* in *Ka lua o Pele*.

When persons become volcanic spirits (*pele, a i ahi;* literally, lava or fire), their *hoʻailona* are flames, earthquakes, or tidal waves within these volcanic manifestations (*ahi pele*). They become the "worker slaves" (*kauwa lawelawe*) of the earth-devouring spirits (*ahi ʻai honua*) of the volcano who direct these "fires" to wherever they want them to go. The "fires" heed their desires, and from that place to this they are directed by these spirits. When the spirits are angry, they appease their anger and chagrin (*lili*) by ruining the land and causing death to man. The only way to make them stop is for the ruler himself to take a pig and offer it as a "burnt sacrifice" (*mohai kuni*) to the gods with his own hand.

* March 24, 1870.

The fishpond of Kiholo in North Kona, Hawaii, was constantly being threatened by lava flows while Kamehameha was ruler of the kingdom of Hawaii. A flow came down close to the pond of Kiholo; Kamehameha brought a pig and cast it in; the "fires" stopped. The flow had gone down as far as Ka'upulehu and Mahai'ula and had almost plunged into the sea. Kamehameha's bringing of a pig and offering it made the flow stop. There were eyes in the lava to see Kamehameha, and ears to hear his appeals and his words of prayer, and the great blazing lava flow died down.[3]

That is how the good lands of Hawaii often escaped when the lava flows came down from Kilauea or Mokuaweoweo, or from whatever place the earth-devouring fires came forth. It was a time, perhaps, when the fires had ears and would listen to the words of men. Today Wainanali'i fishpond, and lands of Kiholo and Kapalaoa in North Kona, and Kalahuipua'a in South Kohala are covered with lava. In Puna and in Ka-'u, and on lands that had never known the desolation of lava flows, there are places where lava has overrun the land.

In the old days men feared the volcano; they did not descend into Kilauea as they pleased. Neither did most of the *kahu Pele,* the attendants of the volcano. Not more than ten of them made the dedications and took care of *Ka lua o Pele.* But today anyone can go there and descend with the bones or hair of the dead and the gifts that accompany the dedication (*mau makana i ho'ohiki ai no ka pele*). From Kauai to Hawaii come visitors with their bones and their gifts and their offerings vowed to Pele (*na 'alana no ka ho'ohiki no Pele*).

The principal god among those there is the goddess Pele (*o ke kumu o keia akua, he akua wahine o Pele*). She has many lesser bodies, each with its own name. So do those called the "younger sisters" (*kaikaina*) of Pele—the Hi'iaka sisters—and so do their brothers. Haumea was Pele's mother, and Kapaliku her father; Namakaokaha'i was her older sister (*kaikua'ana*). These gods came from Kahiki. Some had human forms and some had spirit (*akua*) forms. Pele and Hi'iaka, and also Namakaokaha'i, had both forms, but most of them had only spirit forms and did not take human forms. Pele, Hi'iaka, Namakaokaha'i, Kapo, another sister of Pele, and the *mo'o* goddesses, Kalamainu'u, Walinu'u, and Walimanoanoa, were among the group of gods (*pae akua*) and the line of goddesses (*lalani akua wahine*) that reached thousands upon thousands in number.

It is said that these gods were not of Wakea's time; nor were they Kanenuiakea in visible form (*kino maoli*), that is, Kanenuiakea who made the heaven and the earth. But they had been made into "hosts of heaven," and had come down in their spirit forms. In this form, it is said, Kane, Kanaloa, and Haumea came from Kahiki and from the firmament (*mai ka lewa mai*). They were first seen by a couple of fishermen outside of Ke'ei, in South Kona. Kuheleimoana and Kuheleipo were the two fishermen who first saw these spirits (*po'e akua*) coming over the surface of the sea. When the two men saw these wonderful beings they knelt in profound respect, and they gave them white fish and pointed out the *'awa* plants mauka of 'Alanapo in Ke'ei. Those of us who study and understand clearly the prophetic chants (*mele wanana*) know that the name of Haumea was given to the woman who came with Kane and his companion because she was a woman of mysterious and recurrent births (*no ka mea o Haumea ka wahine hanau kupanaha a hanau wawa*). Here is a *mele* of the *po'e kahiko* that makes this clear:

Holo mai Kane mai Kahiki,	Here comes Kane from Kahiki,
Holo a i'a iloko o ke kai,	Coming like a fish in the sea,
Ke kekele 'au i ka moana;	Gliding through the currents of the ocean;
O Haumea ke kaikuahine	Haumea the sister
O Kanaloa ia me Kane.	And Kanaloa are with Kane.
E ki'i e ka i'a kea i kai,	We get the white fish from the sea,
La'a i ku'emake o Kane,	That is sacred to the eyebrows of Kane,
La'ahia i ke kanawai,	Consecrated to him by his edict,
He mau lawai'a i ka moana,	We two fishermen on the ocean,
O Kuheleimoana O Kuheleipo,	Kuheleimoana and Kuheleipo,
E kaka ana i ka malie,	Who are deep-sea fishing in the calm,
I ka la'i ku pohu malino,	In the windless calm,
I na kai malino a 'Ehu.	In the calm seas of 'Ehu.
Hukia i ka 'upena luelue.	The bag net is drawn up.
E ho'i kakou i ka uka,	We return to shore,
E 'alana i ka pu 'awa hiwa;	And offer the choice 'awa;
Ha'awi i ke kaikuahine.	It is given to the sister.
Elua 'olua ko Haumea i ke keiki.	There are two of you, and Haumea conceives a child.
I hanau i kana hiapo,	She gives birth to her first-born,
O Ka'ulawena Konohiki Wawanakalana.	Ka'ulawena Konohiki Wawanakalana.

The woman called Mapunaia'a'ala was Ka'ulawena; she was the daughter of Kuheleipo and Haumea, it is said. She was a little while before Maui-a-Wakalana.[4]

It is frequently told that, in the traveling about of Kane and Kanaloa, they made water gush from hills and cliffs and from lands parched by the sun. These waters are called "the waters of Kane," *na wai a Kane,* from Hawaii to Kauai, and the rocks from which the waters came are called "the rocks of Kane," *na pohaku o Kane.*

The coming of Pele and her companions, and her becoming an *akua* and an *'aumakua* and a *kumupa'a* for the Hawaiian people happened between the time of Paumakua and that of La'a, or La'amaikahiki.[5] That was also the time when Kalananu'uikuamamao, Humu, and Kamaunuaniho came from Kahiki as humans do— that is, by canoe. These became ancestors for the people of Oahu. They intermarried (*huipu*) with others who had also come from Kahiki—the Olopana and Kahiki'ula families. Olopana and Kahiki'ula married Hina, the daughter of Kamaunuaniho. Their children were Kahikihonuakele and Kekeleiaiku, and also Haunu'u, Haulani, Ha'alokuloku, and Kamapua'a. The first-mentioned children, Kahikihonuakele and Kekeleiaiku, became ancestors for the people of Oahu and Kauai; when Kamapua'a lived with (*noho ana*) Pele, he became an ancestor for those of Hawaii. Because their child brought forth (*hanau*) real ancestors (*kupuna maoli*), Pele and Kamapua'a are called *kumupa'a.* Their child was 'Opelunuikauha'alilo; this was the child born from Pele who became an ancestor of chiefs and people, and his descendants therefore call Pele their *kumupa'a* because he was born from her body. She became an *'aumakua* and a *kumupa'a* for the descendants born from her body. She was consecrated and made a god (*ho'ola'a*) by persons not related by blood descent; and that is how Pele became an *akua* for this race. There were no formal prayer rituals (*kuili*) for her, nor were heiaus erected for her where people bowed down; nor were people taught to worship her—such things were unheard of. Only her actual relatives (*po'e pili kino*) commemorated her and observed the kapus of their ancestress. Persons who were inspired by her to prophesy, and others who wanted her as a god, became the *kahu*, the "administrators," of Pele. But to people who talk boisterously and deny the mana of the goddess, to them will the goddess show her mana through her "angels," those who have become volcanic spirits.

THUNDER AND LIGHTNING FORMS

Kanehekili, Kanewawahilani, Kaho'ali'i, Kauilanuimakehaikalani, and the many other gods who belong to the upper and lower strata of the firmament (*ka lewalani, ka lewanu'u*), are called "gods of the heavens," *na akua o ka lani*. Kanenuiakea's place was elsewhere. The first *kahu* who observed the kapus of these gods was named Hekili (Thunder). He lived at Papa'aea in Hamakualoa, Maui. The land of Papa'aea where this man was born is a place where thunder claps very loudly, with double claps, and there come flashes of lightning that smash to pieces the forest of 'O'opuloa.

Everyone knew Hekili as a man who had mana, so that everything he said was fulfilled. He had but to speak to the thunder and lightning, and they avenged him instantly upon his enemies; those persons who cursed him and abused him were all killed suddenly by thunder and lightning. His enemies therefore plotted in their hearts to kill him and whispered about it in secret. While they whispered, thunder struck. His enemies ceased to plot and to think evil thoughts.

People feared Hekili as a man of great mana, and they all called him Kanehekili. They believed him to be a man with the mana of a god, and they relied on him as a man of mana and as a *kahu* for the "gods of the heavens." His heiau for the gods of the heavens stood above Ke'anae in the Ko'olau district. There Hekili died, beneath the *kuapala* offering stand. When the brother-in-law of this man of the thunder spirit (*kanaka akua hekili*) entered the heiau and found him dead, he cut off his head and took it to Lanai, and thus it came into the possession of Lanai. The men of Hamakualoa missed him, and searched, and found his body in the heiau above Ke'anae. When they found that this *kahu* of great mana was dead, they took the body and divided it into small pieces and distributed the pieces to various places around Maui. These became their *kuleana* to worship thunder. Those persons who had the head worshiped through the head and eyes of Kanehekili. They were called "the eyeball of the god" (*ka 'onohi o ke akua*), and "the mouth of the god" (*ka waha o ke akua*). [They were the seers and prophets of the god in thunder.] Those who worshiped through the buttocks "fostered with filth" (*hanai lakou i ka lepo*).[6]

Ka po'e kahiko were familiar with the god in the thunder. Sometimes he appeared in human form (*kino kanaka maoli*), but without changing his character as an "angel," to associate with men and to speak to them in visions and trances (*akaku, hihi'o, kuaka*). At other times he showed his supernatural form (*kino akua*), which was like that of a man, with his feet on the earth and his head in space among the rolling clouds. The right side of his body, the god side, was a very deep black from head to foot, and the left side, white from head to foot. At other times he took the form of a real man and spoke with men. But the dark marking of his skin never changed—it was always there so that his descendants in this world could not mistake him. That was Kanehekili's "angel" body in a man; his body as a god (*kino 'ano akua*), which no man has ever seen, is the thunder. There are many angelic spirit bodies (*kino akua anela*) in the thunder, and Kanehekili is their high chief, their *ali'i nui*. There are Kaho'ali'i and Kanewawahilani, and many other chiefs in (*iloko*) Kanehekili.*

From the very beginning Kanehekili appeared with one side a deep black. This is the reason why Kahekili, the ruler of Maui, was tattooed a solid black (*kakau pa'ele*) from head to foot on the right side. His whole company of warrior chiefs (*po'e pu'ali ali'i*) and household companions (*na 'aialo*) were tattooed in the same way as Kahekili. He himself had an ancestor who had been born from thunder (*mailoko mai o ka hekili*). This was Kahekilinui'ahumanu, the son of Kaka'alaneo and Kapohauola. As a child Kahekilinui'ahumanu was taken to the thunder (*lawe 'ia na ka hekili*) and so became (*ho'olilo*) a child of the thunder. The royal child was consecrated to the thunder at Papa'aea in Hamakualoa, a land of thunder. His mother was of the thunder (*he makuahine hekili*), and so the descendants of thunder have come down to this day.

Among the offspring of the descendants of thunder, if a child is born from his mother's womb daubed with black (*pala hiwa 'ele'ele*) on one side, it is a sign that he has been chosen by the god Kanehekili, who has placed the mark on the child he desires to be his. The mark appears to this day, but only among the god's own descendants. Ulumaheihei Hoapilikane was an offspring of thunder. His face was marked with deep black, visible to all; and everybody said he was a child of thunder. His mother, Keli'iokahekili, came from thunder.

I saw a man at Ka'anapali named Mahi whom I took to be an offspring of thunder from the black marking of his face. If questioned, he will admit that he is descended from thunder. This sign holds true from Hawaii to Kauai. A man or woman marked with black on one side of the face from the eye down the cheek, while the other side remains unmarked, has the sign of Kanehekili. If both sides are marked with black, that person is not from Kanehekili; that mark shows he belongs to Kukauakahi or Luaipo. If the right hand is streaked with black, he is recognized as belonging to Kaho'ali'i. If a child born to some descendant of Kaho'ali'i has the hand streaked with black and a black ring around one eye, he will be a man who "scoops out eyeballs," a *pu'ukoamakai'a*. A child that is born with a rough marking, as from a sharp stone, below the loins and is dark from the line of the malo straight

---

* March 31, 1870.

across the loins and downward is marked with the sign of Kauilanuimakehaikalani. His descendants are known by this sign.

When a family wished to give one of their beloved dead to the thunder and lightning, this is how they did it. They took the corpse, or some part of it, wrapped it in a dark tapa head covering, blue-black or blue-gray, and took it to the *kahu* of Kanehekili, together with whatever offerings they chose.

The kahuna also wore dark tapas—one for a malo, and another wound around his head (*me ke ka'ei 'ele'ele ma ke po'o*). If the *kahu* was a woman, she wore a dark *pa'u* and a dark tapa wrapped around her head. My grandmother and grandfather have told me that they were both kahunas and descendants of Kanehekili and of those others of the heavens, and that in the old days they had real mana and they heard and saw the *akua*. When they called for thunder and lightning, immediately thunder and lightning came. At the time when a person was being transfigured, *kaku'ai nei,* into thunder and lightning, thunder and lightning would come with such force as to stop the breath; the house would be destroyed; stones and trees smashed to pieces. Then people would say that someone was being transfigured into thunder and lightning; and when a great thunderbolt came that stopped the breath, then, they said, another one (*he mea hou*) had been transfigured, *kaku'ai 'ia*.

On the night when a body was to be transfigured, strict regulations were imposed (*ho'omoe kapu*), and all things were provided in accordance with the *kanawai* pertaining to Kanehekili, Kanewawahilani, Kaho'ali'i, Nakoloilani, Keololani, Ka-'oaka, Kauilanuimakehaikalani, and all the heavenly beings. All things *la'a* to them were supplied, and prescribed ritual prayers were offered continuously until day. Then there came black threatening storm clouds, and shining black storm clouds, and lightning like the tongue of an ox licking at the bushes. The earth trembled, and, like the rattling to and fro of a sheet of tapa, came the persistent rolling of thunder until one great bolt sounded that seemed to crush the earth with its force. A billow of smoke arose, and the sacrifices that had been offered mounted into the air upon the smoke, and the corpse that had been transfigured was carried into the firmament and vanished.

While the kahuna or the *kahu* of Kanehekili stood outside appealing to the heavens, lightning flashed and darted and tumbled about their dark tapa head coverings. When the thunder struck with a burst that made the earth tremble, the family of hunchbacks, *'ohana kuapu'u,* were seen darting about on the earth. Who were they? They were Nakoloilani *ma*. Everyone in the household, even if a hundred or more, would see this family of hunchbacks. Sometimes the gods would appear also, but at other times only the hunchbacks. Then those to whom the body of the dead belonged would see with their own eyes the "angel" form of their beloved one walking about in the thunder. That is how a person became thunder and lightning in the old days.

Some persons are still living who have seen these "angelic" beings. When a man named Kana was killed by thunder (*ua make 'oia i ka hekili*) in the year 1834 in Hamakualoa, Maui, persons in their houses saw the hunchbacks and the multitude of "angels." Also when a certain man, who served the chief Ka'u'ukuali'i, was killed by thunder in the year 1835 in Nu'uanu, Oahu, many persons inside the house saw wondrous things, and all the angels, and the family of hunchbacks.

At Kipahulu in the year 1847 a girl was killed by lightning and thunder. Her mother and father and the rest of the family are all living, and the man who was with her when she was struck, Kaumaea, is now a mature man. The house was struck first, and the main post to which the ridgepole was fastened was split in two and blazed as if on fire. The family inside were all stunned, and those who were near where the lightning struck were almost killed. The girl and her companion were at the back of the house where there was a wet taro patch with a bank around it. The thunderbolt struck with such force as to crush and char the girl as black as a black satin dress. The man Kaumaea turned black from thigh to foot, and he fell into the taro patch and lay in the water. The leaves of the taro were shriveled, but the man's life was saved. The girl was killed. Persons are still living who saw the angel hosts at this time.

At Pu'uiki in Hana just a few years ago, a house was cut in half by lightning and thunder. One side of the house, where most of the people were gathered, was separated from the other side, where there was but one woman. The house spun around with the people inside, and the angelic host and the hunchback family of Mai'akuapu'u were seen. They were darting about the foundation of the house and coming to gouge out the eyeball of the woman. She did not feel her eyeball being taken, but it was taken according to the *kanawai pu'ukoamakai'a*. Her shining eyeball was taken because she had defiled [Kaho'ali'i's] *kanawai* with her mouth, and her god was angry with her for talking too much. If she had been an "outsider" the punishment would have been death; as it was, her life was spared, but her eye was taken.

Thunder and lightning were very strong in the old days when they were worshiped by their descendants. They killed people who were their enemies and turned them into stones or dark charcoal. If someone were being offered to become thunder and lightning and was rejected, the bones fell to pieces and were scattered; then the persons to whom the body belonged would have to gather up the pieces. The direct descendants (*pulapula pono'i*) of Kanehekili, and those related to the heavenly beings, did not need to be transfigured, however; nor were their bodies deified. They had a fixed right, a *kuleana pa'a*, to become "angels" in the thunder and lightning. The death of one of these was called *he make kumupa'a*, the death of one with a "fixed origin." If Kanehekili was their *kumupa'a* (actual god-ancestor) he always stayed close to his descendants; so did all the *kumupa'a* of the ancestors.

In the old times when there was a violent thunderstorm and the house was destroyed by lightning and the leaves of trees were being shriveled, and taro was ruined by the breaking down of the stone walls of the ponds, and chiefs and people were breathless in the storm, a *kahu* of Kanehekili—a descendant, or perhaps a prophet, of his—would come out wearing a black tapa covering on his head and carrying a coal-black pig. While the thunder crashed and lightning flashed, the pig squealed and was licked up and became smoke. The anger of the thunder and lightning was appeased.

SHARK FORMS

There were many reasons for transfiguration. One was so that the "lions of the ocean" would become loving friends of man. The shark is a ravaging lion of the ocean whom none can tame. It is able to swallow a man down whole. If a man arouses its anger, it will show its rows of shining teeth with the sea washing between—and nothing can equal the terror which seizes a man when a shark chops to pieces the *ama* of his canoe and tosses him up and down in the sea. Holding the man securely between its upper and shorter lower jaw, it jerks him about on the surface of the sea.[7]

There are people still living who have seen such things, and there are some who have been bitten by those two wild "lions," Pehu and Moanaliha, two man-eating sharks of Maui and Hawaii. Pehu and Moanaliha had been transfigured and were worshiped; they were not ancestral sharks, not *kumupa'a* or *'aumakua,* but "itchy-mouthed *'uhinipili"* (deified spirits), and "made gods," *akua ho'ola'a.* These two devoured men regardless of the presence of chiefs or their households—even in the presence of Kamehameha. At one time the shark-worshiping altars (*ko'a ho'omana o na mano*) for these two at Kailua, Kona, Hawaii, were set on fire. While their *kahu* were living on Maui, at Honokohau, Lahaina, and Wailuku, innumerable people all about Maui were devoured by these two. But they were afraid of Oahu, where there was a *kanawai* that no *malihini* shark who thought to bite people would escape with his life.

Oahu was made a kapu land by this *kanawai* placed by [the shark gods] Kanehunamoku and Kamohoali'i. But their sister Ka'ahupahau broke the law and devoured the chiefess Papio. She was taken and "tried" (*ho'okolokolo*) at Uluka'a [the realm of these gods], but she escaped the punishment of death. It was her woman *kahu* who paid the penalty of the law because it was her fault—she reviled Papio. The trouble arose over a *papahi* lei of *'ilima* flowers which belonged to Ka'ahupahau that her *kahu* was wearing. [The *kahu* refused to give it to Papio, and] Papio said, "I am going bathing, but when I come back you shall be burned with fire." But Ka'ahupahau devoured Papio before she could carry out her threat, and she was punished for this. That is how Pu'uloa became a [safe] thoroughfare (*alahula*). After her confinement ended several years later, Ka'ahupahau was very weak. She went on a sightseeing trip, got into trouble, and was almost killed. But she received great help from Kupiapia and Laukahi'u, sons of Kuhaimoana, and when their enemies were all slain, the *kanawai* was firmly established. This law—that no shark must bite or attempt to eat a person in Oahu waters—is well known from Pu'uloa to the Ewas. Anyone who doubts my words must be a *malihini* there. Only in recent times have sharks been known to bite people in Oahu waters or to have devoured them; it was not so in old times.

There was, however, a shark who did bite in the old days—a shark with one tooth, who nipped like a crab. He was known to all the *po'e kahiko.* He frequented the waters of Kahaloa at Waikiki, and Mokoli'i, at Hakipu'u and Kualoa, in Ko'olaupoko. *Malihini* may be skeptical that he had only one tooth, but this was known to everybody.* We all know that sharks have rows and rows of teeth, but this shark, called 'Unihokahi (One-toothed), had but one tooth. He was known to Peleioholani, Kahekili, and Kamehameha I. When the chiefs went surfing at Kapua in Waikiki, if a man was bitten by this particular shark that left a single toothmark, it was a warning that an enemy of the sea was approaching. Chiefs and people went hurriedly to shore; it would not do to hesitate, for soon the dorsal fin and side fins of an approaching shark would be visible.

In 1834, during the time of Kaomi, a *malihini* shark came to Waikiki in search of food. When he reached Ka'alawai and Kaluaahole, he was refused by the guardian sharks of that place (*ka po'e kama'aina kia'i o ia wahi*) and then he came to Kapua, where the guardians of Waikiki were, and argued with them. They decided to kill him and to leave visible proof of it, so they forced his head into a cleft in the rocks at Kuka'iunahi, makai of Kupalaha. It could not get free, and there it was with its tail—two or more *anana* in length—flapping in the air, and a little companion shark swimming around it. If this had been done by men it would have been impossible to hold it fast without tying it with ropes, but as it was done by those whom men had made into supernatural beings, the shark was made fast without ropes. When this wondrous sight was seen, men ran with ropes and tied them to the tail and dragged the shark ashore, still alive, with its eyes blinking and its body turning from side to side. It died from being dragged here and there, and by the time they reached Honolulu it was all flabby.

Most of the sharks who had become supernatural beings (*ho'olilo 'ia i akua*) were people who had been changed into forms of their shark ancestors (*kaku'ai 'ia iloko o na mano kumupa'a*). These ancestral sharks, *mano kumupa'a*, were not beings deified by man (*ho'omana 'ia e kanaka*); they got their shark forms from the god. Nor did their angel forms remain permanently in sharks—but when they showed themselves, it was in the form of sharks. They did not show themselves in all sharks, but only in those which had been given distinguishing marks (*ho'ailona pa'a*) known to their *kahu* and offspring, and known to their descendants in the world of light. If a *kahu* were in trouble and in danger of death on the ocean he would call upon his own shark, and that shark would come and get him, and so he would escape death. Hawaiians are familiar with sharks coming to the rescue of their *kahu* or their descendants. Not only one person, but many—ten to forty—have been saved at one time by such a shark.

I will tell now about our ancestors who sailed the ocean, Kaneakaho'owaha *ma*, Kaiahua *ma*, Kuakapua'a *ma*, and Luia *ma*, and of the hundreds they led across the ocean, unafraid of storms, the south wind, the north wind, and all the winds of the ocean. They did not come to harm, nor did they fear death, for they were guided over the desolate wastes like beloved children by a single great guide: the shark named Kalahiki. When it was stormy and the ocean was rough, he swam in front of the canoe fleet, and when land was out of sight, he led them back to land. If they lay becalmed at sea with land out of sight, he lay with his head in the direction of land. A fire would be lighted on the lead canoe and *'awa* and *aumiki,* the after-drink,

---

* April 7, 1870.

would be prepared. The shark that was guiding the canoes would come up close and open its mouth and the *'awa* would be poured into it. After it had partaken of the drink-offerings it had been fed, it would turn its head and in whatever direction the head turned, the canoe fleet would go. If there were forty canoes, they must all turn alike. If they had been becalmed, a good wind would instantly spring up; one that would bear them along until they sighted land.

The man who chewed the *'awa* and offered the drink-offering to this shark died in 1849. He had sailed with Luia *ma* from Kauai to Hawaii without any of them getting even the least glimpse of land because of the fog and mist that covered the ocean. These people were famous for sailing the ocean, but the basis of their skill and knowledge was the shark. From Luia has come down to us today the knowledge of the arts of fishing for flying fish and of steering canoes in the deep ocean. Many can testify to the deeds of Luia *ma,* and to their being guided by the shark.

Kanehunamoku, Kamohoali'i, Kuhaimoana, Ka'uhuhu, Kaneikokala, Kanakaokai, and some others were *mano kumupa'a.* Most of them came from Kahiki. They were not beings deified by man; they came as angels of many forms (*kino lau*). Each had a shark and bird or some other form, and also a human form. In their human forms these divine beings met and conversed with men and talked to those who served the gods. Thus some people were inspired to become prophets, *kaula,* others to become god keepers, *kahu akua,* and others to become kahunas for these gods. They showed themselves in trances and visions in the forms they assumed as sharks, owls, *hilu* fish, *mo'o,* and so forth. There were many forms that these ancestral gods, the *'aumakua kumupa'a,* such as Kamohoali'i and Kanehunamoku *ma* and other ancestral beings from the *po* (spirit world), assumed.

It was not the *'aumakua kumupa'a* who laid kapus upon their descendants of these times, but those who were deified, *ho'ola'a,* and transfigured, *kaku'ai,* to be with their *kumupa'a;* these are the ones who punish their *kahu* and their mediums (*haka*) and the heads of the households (*pa'a mua*) and those who protect wrongdoers. Such persons are smitten with afflictions if they do wrong, but the people who observe their *kanawai* are blessed. This is the cause of much illness among the Hawaiian people. When an introduced disease (*ma'i malihini*) is combined with a native disease caused by flouting the *kanawai* of a *kumupa'a* (*ma'i kama'aina kumupa'a*), the skill and knowledge of a medical kahuna cannot cure it; but if the introduced disease is not combined with a native one, health is quickly restored by medicines and doctors (*po'e kauka lapa'au*). The *kanawai* of the deified are very harsh ones over this race.

In the country districts of Maui I have often seen persons who had been maimed by a shark—a foot cut off, a hand cut short, one side, or both, of the buttocks gone, the back badly scarred, the face marred, the eye and cheek torn away, and so forth. I saw one woman whom I pitied especially. She lived at Ma'onakala in Kanahena, Honua'ula, when Mahoe was the schoolteacher, in this era of writing (*ke au palapala*). She was nearly engulfed by a shark, and I saw the horrible scars made by the teeth of the shark on the back and front of her body. The woman had dived to set a fish trap, and after making it fast in the current, she returned to the coral head where her companion was chewing bait, took the bait, and dived again to put it into the trap. When she turned to go back to the coral head she saw a small shark pass in front of her; then she felt the sea warm about her feet and herself being gulped down. Her whole body was inside the mouth of a shark, and its top jaw was just closing over the lower jaw when the small shark crossed and held up the top jaw and pressed the lower jaw down on a rock. Her companion saw her and called out, "So-and-so is being eaten by a shark! *Pau o Mea i ka mano!*" Here was the woman inside the shark, and the little shark circling above the large one. She saw an opening between the rows of sharp teeth and struggled out, with the help of that little shark who splashed and drove the other away. She was badly torn, and lay on the rock and fainted dead away; but she was still living. I first saw this woman at Lahaina in 1845 at the home of Mahoe and his wife Kealoha. Ho'oikaika was her daughter, and they belonged to the household of the Reverend Mr. Baldwin. I actually saw the marks of the shark's teeth on her body; it was cut and ridged back and front from her head to her feet.

I have heard of other persons who had been swallowed by sharks and escaped with their lives. In the story of Puniaiki it tells how he went into a shark and escaped with his life.[8] It is told that in the time of the rule of Kaka'alaneo on Maui, when 'Ele'io was the chief of Hana and all east Maui, probably at the time when Kahoukapu was the ruling chief of Hawaii, a chief of Hawaii named Kukuipahu was swallowed by a shark and lived a great many days inside the shark. The shark came ashore at Hana on Maui, with the chief inside; and the Hana chief gave his daughter Ahukiokalani to the chief from Hawaii. The story is well known about his being swallowed by the shark and staying inside it. His hair all fell out, but he came out alive after living inside the shark.

Because sharks save men in times of peril, protect them when other sharks try to devour them, and are useful in other ways in saving lives at sea and on the deep ocean, some people were made into shark *'aumakua,* or guardian gods; they became forms of Kamohoali'i, Kanehunamoku, Ka'uhuhu, Kaneikokala, Kanakaokai, Ka'ahupahau, Kuhaimoana, or other ancestral shark gods. Thus many sharks appeared who had been deified by man. Some were evil, some were man-eaters, some were as fierce and untameable as lions, who even devoured their own *kahu* who had transfigured and deified them. Such were Kapehu (Pehu), Moanaliha, Mikololou, and other evil sharks. Others who were worshiped (*ho'omana 'ia*) became beloved friends if their *kanawai* were properly obeyed; they became defenders and guides in times of trouble and danger on the ocean, quieting the stormy ocean and bringing their people back to land. If their canoes came to grief and were smashed to pieces, their shark would carry them safely to shore. But those who had no such friend were like castaways without a guide; when land was out of sight, they would drift about until they died. If the canoe broke to pieces, their dead bodies would be cast up on Lanai or at Hanauma. They were people who had no claim upon anyone in the sea (*po'e kuleana 'ole iloko o ke kai*).

Such people would take a loved one who had died—a father, mother, child, or some other beloved relative—to the keeper of a shark, a *kahu mano,* or to one who had shark *'aumakua,* to be transfigured into whichever shark *'aumakua* they wanted, and it was done according to their wishes. The gifts and offerings to the *kahu mano* were a sow, a bundle of tapa, and a clump of *'awa.* If the *kahu* was satisfied with the gifts, he would command the persons who owned the body to prepare the ritual offerings for the god, as well as the gift offerings, for the body to become a shark. All was made ready on the sacred day of Kane, the most important day of the kapu periods (*na la kapu Sabati*). At dawn of this day, a fire was lighted at the *kuahu* altar of the *ko'a* shrine or heiau of the ancestral shark, Kamohoali'i, Kanehunamoku, Ka'uhuhu, Kaneikokala, or whichever one it was. Then the owners of the body and the *kahu* of the shark god brought the sacrifices and offerings, the pig and the *'awa* being the most important, and also the whole body of the dead person, or a bundle of his bones or some other part of the body, wrapped in a distinctive tapa. The shark would take on the character of the wrapping. If the tapa was a *pa'i'ula,* a red-and-white tapa, the shark would be reddish; if it was a *puakai* tapa, it would be all red; if it was a *moelua* tapa, it would be striped. The persons who owned the body would thus be able to recognize their own after it became a shark.*

The fire was lighted at the *ko'a* shrine and the food and the offerings were made ready; the "wave" offering of pig (*pua'a ho'ali*), and the sacrifice offering of pig (*mohai kaumaha*), and the "wave" and sacrifice offerings of *'awa.* The "wave" offerings of pig and *'awa* were not offerings to be eaten (*mohai 'ai*), but were given to the god, and bowls were filled with them as gift offerings to the god for changing the body into a shark. Then the persons to whom the body belonged and the *kahu mano* went with the bundled corpse and all the offerings to be given to the shark, while the *kahu mano* murmured prayers. Then the shark appeared, of a size immeasurable. Beside the cliff was a place two or three *anana* deep with a sandy floor, where the shark lay. When the *'awa* and pig were taken there, the shark rose to the surface of the sea and opened its mouth and the *'awa* and pig were poured into it. If the shark was very large it drank down the *'awa* and the pig and bananas and other offerings besides. Then the body was given to it, being placed close to the "belly fin," the *halo,* of the shark. The *kahu mano* and the owners of the body returned to the *ko'a* and made ready their *mohai* offerings and their *'awa* and took the pig out of the imu. They offered [the essence] to the god (*kaumaha i ke akua*), and when they had finished eating of these *mohai 'ai* offerings they threw the remainder into the sea. This ended, they went home.

The *kahu mano,* however, took *'awa* at dawn and at dusk for two or three days, until he saw clearly that the body had definitely assumed the form of a shark and had changed into a little shark, with recognizable marks on the cheeks or sides like a tattoo or an earring mark. After two or three days more, when the *kahu mano* saw the strengthening of this new shark that had been transfigured, he sent for the relatives who had brought the body to go with him when he took the *'awa.* If he had gone constantly, morning and evening, it strengthened quickly, and when the relatives came they would see with their own eyes that it had really

---

* April 14, 1870.

become a shark, with all the signs by which they could not fail to recognize their loved one in the deep ocean. If the relatives should go bathing or fishing in the sea, it would come around and they would all recognize the markings of their own shark. It became their defender (*pu'u pale*) in the sea.

This is the main reason why the people of Maui worshiped sharks—in order to be saved from being eaten by a shark when they went fishing. At Kaupo, Kipahulu, Hana, Ko'olau, Hamakuapoko, Ka'anapali, Lahaina, and Honua'ula a fisherman was in danger of being devoured by a shark when he was out fishing with a dip net (*'upena 'aki'iki'i*), or fishing for octopus with a lure (*lawai'a lu'uhe'e*), or setting traps for *hinalea* fish (*ho'olu'ulu'u hinalea*), or diving with a scoop net (*lawai'a uluulu*), or setting out fishnets (*lawai'a 'upena ho'auau*), or whichever kind of fishing a man would be doing alone. It would be better to stay ashore, but the fisherman craves fish to eat, and so might be devoured by a shark. Hence the people of that island worshiped sharks. Most of the people of that land do not eat shark even to this day; those who do are *malihini*— the *kama'aina* are afraid to eat shark.

Few people have been eaten by sharks in late years, but a number of people were devoured at the time when the Reverend Mr. Conde was pastor in Hana. A man named Kehopu, who was an assistant tax collector for Hana and a deacon of the church, was fortunate enough to escape from a shark. One day in 1848 he went to the home of Kihuluhulu at Kalua, adjoining Pa'ako in Honua'ula. On the morning of the day following, Kihuluhulu and his companions set out to sea to catch *'opelu*. As the sun grew warm Kehopu paddled out to look for Kihuluhulu at the *'opelu* fishing ground (*ko'a 'opelu*). He was in a canoe by himself. There were a number of canoes floating about with *'a'ei* nets for surrounding *'opelu*. Kehopu drew close, and when he was perhaps four or five chains away he heard a smacking sound behind him. When he turned, he was terrified to see behind him a mouth opened as if to swallow both man and canoe. The shark's body, as it lay lengthwise of the canoe, was twice as long as the canoe. Then a little shark blocked the way of the big one to divert its rage, but the big shark swam right across the front of the canoe, turned back with its head toward the back of the canoe, flipped the canoe upside down and made short work of the *ama* and the *'iako*. Kehopu climbed up on the keel and began to beg forgiveness for his "sins" and for the wrongs he had committed by eating without observing the kapus. The little shark got in the way of the big one's mouth, and that is how Kehopu escaped a terrible death. The men who were fishing for *'opelu* were too frightened to paddle one stroke. Kehopu kept on appealing and praying to the god to forgive his misdeeds. The little shark interfered and obstructed the way of the big shark, and the shark's wide-open mouth was downward as he brushed his rough skin against the length of the overturned canoe. Because of how Kehopu escaped with his life, and because so many had witnessed it, they said to him: "That little shark was your *'aumakua*— it was he who saved your life." Not only Kehopu was saved by a "guardian angel," *anela kia'i,* but many others whose "guardian angels" have come to their rescue.

Close to the door of my house where I lived at Kaupipa in Kipahulu, perhaps a chain and a half away, a man named Kalima was eaten by a shark. He was fishing for octopus (*luhe'e*) when a great number of people were heard shouting: "Kalima is being eaten by a shark!" Everyone saw two sharks—one a large shark called Kapehu (Pehu) who was pursuing him to eat him, and a little shark that had gotten in the way and was warding off the enemy. The little shark was fighting the big shark, somersaulting this way and that, and its tail was flipping upward and dashing up the spray. The people thought that the man was carried away by the little shark to a place close to the pali where there is a narrow cleft and the sea is deep. Here the sea is dark below and the pali too smooth and steep, perhaps, for the little shark to have put him ashore. The crowd on the pali above could not see him and they believed that he had been eaten by the big shark, but they were puzzled by the absence of blood. One man, Ka'ai'ohi'a, insisted that the big shark was lying quietly at the sandy area down at Mokupapa, and that the little shark had disappeared and perhaps had the man. The man might have been saved if he could have been brought ashore. Down at Mokupapa the big shark rose to the surface and swam toward the cleft, where people pelted it with stones. As the sea receded, the shark went out and sank, then reappeared when a wave rose and, dodging the stones with which it was being pelted, entered the cleft and edged along in the shelter of a rock. The people were on the two headlands on either side of the cleft, which were not more than three *anana* apart. The shark entered and went along close to the edge of the pali where the man was with the little shark, as they knew when the sea turned red with blood and the shark reappeared with the man in its mouth. The big shark took the man far outside and jerked him up and down and set him head up, then thighs up, then doubled up with head and body erect, and then it bore him away to the sea of Mokuahole and disappeared into its hole. That is the way men were handled by sharks—they were jerked about on the surface of the sea. Sometimes the body was bitten in two, and the head and trunk alone mauled about. It was because of such terrifying occurrences that people transfigured their beloved into sharks.

If they had source *'aumakua* (*kumu 'aumakua*) of many forms—such as shark, volcanic fires, thunder, lightning, and so forth—into which they could change the bodies of their beloved, the bodies might be apportioned (*mahele ai*) for transfiguration accordingly. But they had to be accepted by the *'aumakua,* and this acceptance was given only to their true descendants, those related to them by blood.

People knew that the spirit of the person transfigured lived again and went into a shark when the shark had all the markings of that person's body. His body assumed that form, and the remembrance of him was on the shark, without his spirit living permanently in the shark. It was the same with other forms—a volcanic fire, a bird, or whatever the body had been changed into to live again. The spirit would become strong and would return and possess (*noho*) his parents, relatives of his own generation, or other relatives perhaps. Then it would say: "My bodies are such-and-such and such-and-such. When you are in trouble, in sickness, and near death, and you see such-and-such, it is I. You can ignore the trouble; there is no trouble. If you hear that a relative is in danger of death elsewhere and you see this thing, it is I; you can ignore the danger; there is no danger. If you go to war and those on your side are being slaughtered and you are taken prisoner, and you see this thing, it is I; there is no danger; do not fear, but follow after it; it is I made visible. If you are seized and are to be put to death and your hands are tied behind you with a rope and you are led to the place where you are to die, if you see this thing, it is I. Wherever it goes, you must follow. When you are sailing on the ocean and are in danger of death and your boat or canoe breaks up and you see this thing, it is I. You will not die."

In this way his relatives knew what his bodies were. At the same time he would decree those things which were kapu for them to eat and would say: "Such-and-such things are my bodies; do not eat them. Do not allow yourselves to inhale smoke from their cooking, or eat from a dish or from a calabash or drink water from a water gourd that has been in contact with these consecrated things, and do not eat in the houses of others (*i kauhale*)." That is the reason why there were so many kapus, some of which remain to this day. These kapus concerning the consecrated things (*kapu ho'ola'a*) were binding only upon those connected to the bones, flesh, and blood—the relatives. How can this defilement and pollution be removed? This requires deep thought.

The Jews are called the "Children of Abraham," and because Jehovah first called Abraham to him, Jehovah is their *'aumakua* and *kumupa'a*. Jesus Christ was a "consecrated one," *he ho'ola'a 'ia*, because he was born a god-man (*akua kanaka*) in human form. He was called a *ho'ola'a* and an *'unihipili* (deified one) in human form. In the same way those of Hawaii *nei* believed that the real offspring (*pula-pula maoli*) of real *'aumakua* (*'aumakua maoli*) did not need to be [ritually] transfigured; they were not deified (*ho'omanamana*) by pig and *'awa*. Their *'aumakua* came and took away their corpses, leaving not a scrap of bone, nothing but the tapa covering and trough-shaped container (*holowa'a*) that had held the body. I have personally seen two instances of this kind, when only the tapa and the trough were left. This was something often seen, and there may be people who have seen the god-spirits of this group of islands.

In 1827, at the time when Kamehameha III was staying at Wao'ala, and Ka'ahumanu and some other chiefs were at Maeaea in Waialua, Oahu, the *ko'a* altars and burial places on the curve of the beach there were being closely watched. Something kept sparkling (*lapalapa*) on the beach, and some of the chiefs thought it must be diamonds, since torches and lights were forbidden at night. But this was a usual thing on this beach; it was phosphorescent light (*ahi makaihuwa'a*)—the innumerable fires of the *'aumakua o ka po,* the divine ancestors of the night.

There died at that time an old woman named Manoheli'i who was a grandparental relative (*hanauna kupunawahine*) of my family. Her place was near her brother's house and the houses of my relatives, and in the morning she was buried close to the back of her house and perhaps a chain away from the back of my family's, in a hollow deep enough for a man to stand upright in. The coffin was an old-fashioned trough, and the body was wrapped in two *pa'iula* tapas. Not the first night after her burial, but the second, the shark came and took her. It was extraordinary how the body could have been gotten out whole—the grave was seven feet deep. A hole about 16 inches in circumference wound downward to the coffin, and there was a hole made through the lid of the trough at the head. The body must have come out through this hole. The spot was about 20 feet above sea level, and tapa was scattered on the beach, and the "belly fins," *halo,* and "side fins," *'eheu,* of the shark had made a ridge in the sand from the edge of the sea to the grave. When the coffin was opened no trace of a human body could be found—not even a scrap. The body had been taken whole into the sea. The woman's brother, Kuaila, died in 1828. He was buried inside the house and covered over with dirt and with the mats on which the wife and family slept. An opening was made at the side of the house and the body was taken away by the shark. I had often heard that Kamohoali'i used to possess him. I made inquiries and learned that it was customary from ancient times in this family for a body buried in the upland to be taken away whole into the sea. Not a bone would be left on land. The sea, it was said, was the place for the bones to be laid.

Another well known tradition (*mo'olelo*) of this family is that if any one of them "sinned" against the sacred things of the god, perhaps by eating a forbidden food, he was punished by being laid beside the shark in the sea for from two to four days, close to the *halo* of the shark. On the third day he would be brought to shore alive. I have indeed wondered how a man could live thus, but the family were all dead before I grew up. It was, however, confirmed by persons who witnessed this, and I have myself seen the "hole," *lua,* of Kamohoali'i where the bodies were laid for two or three days and nights without dying. A person would hardly believe so extraordinary a thing unless he had seen it. One who has seen everything on earth would say that no one could live in the sea for an hour—or even for 30 minutes—but relatives of my parents' and grandparents' generations say that hundreds (*mau haneri*) of people saw them alive, and saw them lying in the sea and returning to shore in a weakened condition after they had lain as long as five days with the shark in the sea. This is no mere tale (*ka'ao*) or dream, but a thing actually seen. Their descendants from Waialua to Ka'ena have heard their grandparents tell about it. They were familiar with this living long in the sea.

I heard in Hana about a man named Po'okapu, and I saw him with my own eyes. He lived with us, and his wife is still living in Kipahulu with the children. His relatives, including his own sister, say that they, with others, saw him taken by the shark from Maka'alae in Hana and carried to the pali on the coast of Hawaii and returned again and landed at Waiohonu in Hana. This was in 1844, when the Reverend Mr. Conde was the pastor for this district. The shark that took him was Moanaliha.

These are things that I am familiar with concerning the people who "keep" sharks, *ka po'e kahu mano,* from knowledge obtained from the grandparental generation in these people's present families. They themselves do not impose kapus, or pretend to receive kapus from these gods; they do not decree that certain things shall be kapu to you or kapu to themselves; I have not seen them bow down and use the sacred containers, *ipu kua'ahu.* Perhaps this is due to the kapus having been abolished (*no ka 'ainoa ana paha*). But I know about these many little kapus of the people who were transfigured and deified. These are kapus that can destroy (*kapu 'aihamu*), and they persist unto this day.

MO'O FORMS

Kalamainu'u, Laniwahine, Hauwahine, Kanekua'ana, and Kihawahine, and the myriads (*kini a me ka lehu*) of interchangeable body forms (*kino lau*) of the *mo'o* (water spirits) used to be worshiped constantly. Persons would be transfigured to become such strange beings (*kino 'e'epa*), but it was not done by merely being buried along a stream or river or beside a spring or by having their bones thrown into the water. If they were not related to the *mo'o*, or a bird form, or a shark, they had no rightful place, *kuleana*, in the *kino lau* of the *mo'o*, or the shark, or the other forms. It is a mistake to suppose that by dying in the ocean or in fresh water that one is changed into a shark or a *mo'o*, or any other creature living in the sea or in fresh water. Those who had no *kuleana* had not the least right to any of these forms, said the *po'e kahiko*. Their souls just drifted about in the currents. But those who had a true *kuleana* were brought to shore alive; or, if one had come to the end of his years, his body was taken and his bones were never found. That was one reason why *ka po'e kahiko* worshiped their god until they were old and feeble. Then when the god decided to take them, their bones would not be seen on land or sea. When these people came near to the end of life, they said to their sons, daughters, grandchildren, and relatives: "The god is coming to take me." Then they would all watch carefully, day and night, thinking to hold him fast. When the old person became too weak to creep about, they would go to sleep, and when they awoke, he was gone. When they searched, he could not be found. The next day they would search for the corpse and never find it at all. He had been taken by the god. With some persons, the god came right in and contended for the man. That was often seen to happen, even after the abolition of the kapus (*au 'ainoa*), and in the time of learning, during the rule of Kamehameha III. This writer of Hawaiian history has seen it with his own eyes, and so have many other people now living. Perhaps these things no longer happen since the gods have been abandoned for so long.

This is why some of the old folks are so emphatic that their gods have mana, can talk with them, and can protect the lives of their *kahu* up to the time when one "walks with a cane, has eyes blurred like a rat's, is yellow as a *hala* leaf, and reaches extreme old age," *a kani ko'o, a haumaka'iole, a pala lau hala, a kau i ka puaneane*. The reasons why people "kept" sharks (*malama i ka mano*) were personal ones—for health and blessings to themselves, and for fish. When the men went fishing at their *ko'a* fishing grounds, to fish with *'upena lu'u*, or *wahanui*, or *lau apo*, or *laulele*, or *aumaiea* nets, or other kinds of fishing, the *akua mano* would lead fishes right to them—the *kule, kala, kawakawa, kawele'a, 'o'io, 'aweoweo, 'ahi, uhu, opule, a'ua'u*, and all kinds of fishes. The fisherman would be urged to go fishing in a dream in the night by the words of the *akua: He malihini o ke kai* ["There are fish in the sea"]. That is why *ka po'e kahiko* cared for them.

Akua mo'o were kept for the same reasons—for the health and welfare of the people, and to bring them fish. Some people put all their trust in the *akua mo'o*. On Oahu, and similiar lands, where there are walled ponds (*loko kuapa*) and large fresh-water ponds (*loko wai nui*) like Uko'a, Ka'elepulu, Kawainui, and Maunalua, some people depended entirely upon the *akua moʻo*. They were the guardians, the *kiaʻi*, of the ponds all around Oahu.

The *moʻo* that were chosen to be worshiped were not the house or rock lizards (*moʻo kaula, moʻo kaʻala*) or any of those little creatures with which we are familiar. No indeed! One can imagine their shape from these little creatures, but these were not their bodies. The *moʻo* had extremely long and terrifying bodies, and they were often seen in the ancient days at such places as Maunalua, Kawainui, and Ihukoko at Ukoʻa. They were not seen just at any time, but when the fires were lighted on the *koʻa* altars beside their homes. There was no doubting them when they were seen. They lay in the water, from two to five *anana* in length, and as black in color as the blackest Negro. When given a drink of *ʻawa*, they would turn from side to side like the hull of a canoe in the water.

The *moʻo* Mokuhinia has been seen on Maui at Kapunakea, in Lahaina, and at Paukukalo and Kanaha in Wailuku; and she showed herself at Kalepolepo at the time that Kamehameha Kapuaiwa died. She has appeared before hundreds and thousands of people. At the close of the year 1838 she almost capsized Kekauluohi, who was going by canoe across the pond of Mokuhinia from Mokuʻula on her way to church at Waineʻe. Many people from Hawaii to Kauai have seen the terrible form of the *moʻo*. They have places where they lay aside these wondrous *ʻeʻepa* bodies, but their nests where they lay them aside are not known. Has the *moʻo* none but that terrible body? That body is only one of the spirits in this form—they had many "angel" forms (*kino anela*). Laniwahine of Ukoʻa has often appeared in human form, even in this time of writing and knowledge. Such an appearance foretells that some terrible event is to happen at that place. It is the usual form these wondrous beings show themselves in to reveal hidden things.

Kanekuaʻana was the *kiaʻi* of ʻEwa, and the *kamaʻaina* from Halawa to Honouliuli relied upon her. Not all of the people of ʻEwa were her descendants, but the blessings that came to her descendants were shared by all. When *pilikia* came to the *iʻa* at ʻEwa, and their children were in distress because of the scarcity of *iʻa*, the descendants of Kanekuaʻana erected *waihau* heiaus for Kanekuaʻana, and lighted the fires [for the cooking of offerings] to bring blessings upon the whole people. What blessings did they obtain? *Iʻa*. What kinds of *iʻa*? The *pipi* (pearl oyster)—strung along from Namakaohalawa to the cliffs of Honouliuli, from the *kuapa* fishponds of inland ʻEwa clear out to Kapakule. That was the oyster that came in from deep water to the mussel beds near shore, from the channel entrance of Puʻuloa to the rocks along the edges of the fishponds. They grew right on the *nahawele* mussels, and thus was this *iʻa* obtained. Not six months after the *hau* branches [that placed a kapu on these waters until the *pipi* should come in] were set up, the *pipi* were found in abundance—enough for all ʻEwa—and fat with flesh. Within the oyster was a jewel (*daimana*) called a pearl (*momi*), beautiful as the eyeball of a fish, white and shining; white as the cuttlefish, and shining with the colors of the rainbow—reds and yellows and blues, and some pinkish white, ranging in size from small to large. They were of great bargaining value (*he waiwai kumukuʻai nui*) in the ancient days, but were just "rubbish" (*ʻopala*) in ʻEwa.

What other *i'a*? The transparent shrimp, *'opae huna,* and the spiked shrimp, *'opae kakala,* such as came from the sea into the *kuapa* and *pu'uone* fishponds. *Nehu pala* and *nehu maoli* fishes filled the lochs (*nuku awalau*) from the entrance of Pu'uloa to the inland 'Ewas. Hence the saying of the *kama'aina* of this land: *He kai puhi nehu, puhi lala ke kai o 'Ewa e, e noho i ka la'i o 'Ewa nui a La'akona* ("A sea that blows up *nehu,* blows them up in rows, is 'Ewa, until they rest in the calm of great 'Ewa-a-La'akona").

Other famous *i'a* of 'Ewa, celebrated land of the ancestors, were the *mahamoe* and *'okupe* bivalves and many others that have now disappeared. When all these things supplied them by their *kia'i* Kanekua'ana appeared, then her descendants believed that the old woman had returned from the "pillars of Kahiki," *kukulu o Kahiki,* out of aloha for her descendants, perhaps. These are the people who told me about the "pillars of Kahiki" and other unknown lands.

Laniwahine was the *kia'i* of Uko'a, in Waialua, and Uko'a was the "long house" (*hale halau*) in which she lived. She was the *kama'aina* woman of Uko'a, and all her deeds centered about that fishpond. The "native sons," *keiki kama'aina,* never failed to recognize her deeds, but few of her descendants are left now—perhaps none. Uko'a was a very strange fishpond—extraordinary fishes lived there. A fish might be a *kumu* fish on one side and an *'anae* mullet, on the other; or one side might be a *weke pueo,* and the other an *'anae;* or a fish might be silver white like a white cock and when scaled the flesh might be striped and variegated inside. It was understood by all Laniwahine's descendants that these strange fish belonged to her, and that it was not right to eat them. The mullet of Uko'a were usually full of fat, but sometimes they were not—and sometimes the fish did not come at all. Sometimes they were thin, with woody heads, and sometimes they disappeared altogether. That was a customary thing in all fishponds, and then the thing to do was to do honor to (*ho'omana'o*) the *kama'aina* guardians of the ponds. Then the ponds would fill with fish, and the fish would be fat. Thus it was with Hauwahine, at her ponds of Kawainui and Ka'elepulu, and with Laukupu at her pond of Maunalua. They were the guardians who brought the blessing of abundance of fish, and of health to the body, and who warded off illness and preserved the welfare of the family and their friends. This honoring was a fixed rule (*kanawai pa'a*) on these lands and brought the young fish to the sea and to the ponds.

Sometimes, when the land was blessed with an abundance of young fish in the sea, the overlord (*haku*) of that land, or the land agent (*konohiki*), would become haughty and indifferent to the welfare of the poor and the fatherless; and when they saw the boys and girls with their gourds for storing "fish," *ipu wai kahakai,* they would become overbearing, seize the gourds and break them without pity for the fatherless, and smash the gourds of the women without giving them a chance to speak. An *ipu wai kahakai* could do no harm—it could not take away all the oysters and shrimps, but for no cause at all (*"mai ka lani mai ka honua"*) the overbearing "shark" would come and break the gourd in pieces. Then the guardian *mo'o,* who loved the poor and the fatherless, would take away all the "fish" she had given for high and low alike, for the rich and the poor. When she saw the rights of the many abused, she took away the blessing altogether, leaving nothing but the rocks which endure and the earth which crumbles. Her chagrin (*lili*) could not be appeased by supplication (*kalokalo*) but by penitence and restitution; that was the only way to bring prosperity back to the land.

Walinu'u, Walimanoanoa, Kalamainu'u, and Kihawahine were ancestral *mo'o* and *mo'o* rulers (*he po'e kuamo'o, a he po'e mo'o ali'i 'ai aupuni*), and the kingdom that "kept" them prospered. They were represented by post images (*po'e kia ho'omana'o*) in the heiaus, where they were in the line of goddesses (*lalani akua wahine*). The rule of the chief who had faith in these *mo'o* to watch over his kingdom would not be shaken.

Walinu'u, Walimanoanoa, and Kalamainu'u were '*aumakua* with many bodies. A certain chiefess of the island of Maui named Kihawahine was transfigured into (*kaku'ai 'ia iloko o*) Kalamainu'u, and she became a goddess with the body of a *mo'o*. Kihawahine was a famous *mo'o*, perhaps because she had been a chiefess and an ancestor of chiefs, and had been born a real human being. But when she was transfigured she turned into an *'e'epa*, a *mo'o*. She was deified by the chiefs of Maui and Hawaii with kapus, with the setting up of kapu sticks (*pulo'ulo'u*), and with the kapus of the chiefess Kihawahine. She was a sacred goddess and people had to prostrate themselves because of her kapu; people in canoes crouched down in their canoes in the presence of her kapu. A person who broke her kapu died.

Kihawahine had been transfigured on Maui into an *akua mo'o*; and when Oahu and Maui became Kamehameha's, Keku'iapoiwa Liliha, her daughter Keopuolani, and their goddess Kihawahine were taken captive and they became his. Kihawahine was an ancestress of theirs, and her *kahu* were all chiefly people. Ulumaheihei Hoapili *ma* were her *kahu*. Kihawahine was frequently seen at Mokuhinia, at Kapunakea, at Paukukalo, and at Kanaha; and when Kamehameha added her to his gods, she was one of his gods that united the kingdom from Hawaii to Kauai. He said: "If you take (*'ai*) Oahu, I will build a house for your *akua* in the calm of Waikiki—a *puaniu* house for Kalamainu'u, the *akua* of Kihawahine."

Kalamainu'u was an '*aumakua* and a *kumupa'a;* so were Walinu'u and Walimanoanoa, and so were those related to Kanekua'ana and Lonowahine and the many other *mo'o 'aumakua* who, as has been said, acted as guardians that kept the land secure. When parents wished to change the bodies of their children into *mo'o*—or men their wives, or wives their husbands—it was with the hope that by giving them a supernatural body (*kino kupanaha*), the soul of the spirit body (*kino wailua*) would be strengthened and would return and possess a relative and tell them that it lived again in another body. As the Holy Scriptures say: "Every spirit that confesseth that Jesus Christ is come in the flesh is of God; and every spirit that confesseth not that Jesus Christ is come in the flesh is not of God" (I John 4:2-3). This was known before the coming of the Messiah, and was known afterward, as is shown by the Bible. Some things were the same—and some things were not the same—in the beliefs of the Hawaiian people.

When a chief was to be transfigured, the first thing was to erect a separate house, a *moku hale*, with a wooden fence around it, and to collect in it offerings of light yellow and dark yellow tapa wraps and skirts—tapas dyed with *'olena* or *noni*. The house was called a *hale puaniu*, and in it the offerings were made with *'awa*. Fires were lighted in the imus, and dogs and pigs put in to bake, at the *waihau* and *ko'a* houses of these *'e'epa* beings of many forms. Then the corpse or the bundle of bones, wrapped in yellow (*'olena*) tapa, was taken to be laid in the water at a suitable place for the transfiguring, together with a reddish-brown, brown, brindle, striped, or mottled dog (*'ilio maku'e, 'ilio 'i'i, 'ilio mo'o, hulu pe'elua, ulaia*).* By the time the pigs and dogs were cooked and the imus ready to be opened, there lay these fearsome beings in the water. All of them, large and small, were given *'awa* to drink and fed dog and other foods while the *kahu mo'o* prayed. Then he took the bundle and placed it in front of the *'aumakua* to whom it had been decided to offer it, and it was borne away. Not more than two or three days would pass before the spirit would return and "sit on" (*noho*) or utterly possess (*ke'ehi pa'a*) one of the relatives and say, "Drink *'awa* constantly, and call on my name; eat, and dedicate the food to my name. In your drinking and eating, we will be eating together, and this will strengthen my spirit. Then if you wish to see me, you shall see me." By doing this the relatives were able to see him, and this put an end to any doubting. The first appearance of the spirit was the time to begin ritual prayers (*kuili*). The *haka* whom the soul of the dead possessed drank *'awa* morning and evening, and he was the one who strengthened the spirit. Thus these many-bodied beings, the *kino lau 'e'epa*, became very strong, and would reward the living by bringing them prosperity, saving them from trouble and accident, giving them fish and other material things, teaching them what medicines to take to cure family illnesses, and instructing them in the knowledge of seers, *kilokilo*, and prophets, *kaula*, and teaching them to interpret visions and to call up the spirits of the *kupua* people and of ancestors and relatives.

The people in general, the *maka'ainana*, did not erect *puaniu* houses for the transfiguration of their dead into *mo'o*. These houses were built by chiefs to hold bananas, coconuts, *'awa*, yellow tapa wraps and skirts of *puaniu* and *halakea* tapa, and all the scented tapas. There the spirit was fed with constant offerings by the *kahu akua* to strengthen the souls of the dead persons. And they really did grow strong. Some of these spirits were of such great strength when they came back that the house shook as if in a strong wind, and great stones were broken into pieces without a sign of human hands. The spirits sometimes came to possess their *haka* in that way. Some came like the flash of a shot from the mouth of a cannon, or a lightning flash. It was perhaps because of the many kinds of spirits that returned to the *kahu akua* that Kamehameha I believed in having many *kahu akua* and a great number of gods.

Some of the *maka'ainana*, however, erected small *puaniu* houses for transfiguring their dead, and brought *'olena* sleeping tapas and *'awa* and a mottled brown dog (*'ilio 'i'i ulaia*) to transform their dead into one of the many-bodied *mo'o*. For some, all went well; but some were not accepted, and they drifted about in their bundles of tapa without being changed into *mo'o* bodies.

* April 28, 1870.

The dead were changed into the form of the *'aumakua* to whom they had been offered. If Kalamainu'u was the *'aumakua kino lau* to whom the body had been offered, it became a *mo'o;* it became a shark if offered to Kamohoali'i, and a volcanic manifestation (a *pele*) if offered to 'Aila'au. Some became thunder, some lightning, and some became signs (*ouli*) in the heavens; some were taken by Kukauakahi, and through his mana as an *akua,* they flew through the air as owls.

Human beings who entered into these many bodies issued the innumerable kapus of consecration (*kapu ho'ola'a*). That is why some things to eat are called "gods," which is not right; the gods are separate from these kapus. For example, take Kaneulupo, one of the gods that was worshiped. If he was not an ancestor of certain persons, but was related by blood to their ancestors, then he was related to them, too, as descendants (*mamo*) of these ancestors, even if they did not worship him or do him honor. These descendants, without a thought for the *'aumakua* of their ancestors, might transgress (*'ai ku, 'ai hele*) against the consecrated things of their god—the cock, *moa,* that crows for awakening,[9] or the *momoa wa'a,* or *pahu* fish, his kapu fish in the sea. It was kapu to even cross the smoke from a fire in which a cock or a kapu fish was cooking. If they did, they would get a *ma'i ho'opa'i* (a chastising illness inflicted by the ancestral *'aumakua*). Such a *ma'i kama'aina,* "native illness," cannot be cured by doctors or by just anyone with medical skill. It is extremely hard to cure when complicated by an introduced disease (*ma'i malihini*) with fever.

It is the same with Kaneikokala. The body of the god was separate from his body as a shark, but the *kokala* fish was consecrated to him in the ancient worship of him by the ancestors. Their descendants may have heard of Kaneikokala, although they do not worship him; but to this day, the whole district of Kahikinui, Maui, with the exception of *malihini,* will run away if they see a *kokala* fish cooking, or even the smoke from the cooking; and they will eat no "food" or "fish" that has come in contact with it. If they ate food, or crossed the smoke, or touched things that had been in contact with *kokala* fish, they might die. They have heard of, or perhaps seen, some of their own people dying from such things, and they are afraid of them even today. Kaneikokala was a shark famous for his good deeds. If a canoe was wrecked in the ocean and broken to pieces, and someone called for Kaneikokala, he would appear and save them; even though there were 10 or 20 people he would carry them all alive to shore, landing those from Hawaii on Hawaii and those from Maui on Maui. He thus saved a great many people. But no one except a relative had the right to call upon him; and only to descendants and offspring would he listen.

Not long ago a man, who is still living at Kipahulu, was walking along and saw a dead owl lying on the roadside. Only its wings and bones were left, held together by feathers. The man said to it, "Bird of mana that you are, O Owl, what was it that caused your death?" And he exposed his buttocks to it, saying, "Here is a head for you!" A part of the man's intestines slipped out, and a kahuna worked over him in vain to put it back in place. There it stuck out drying in the sun like an octopus tentacle while he wept night and day with pain, and there was such a stench that the flies gathered outside. Another kahuna came to him and said, "You exposed your buttocks as a head for the owl and treated the owl with contempt." The man answered, "Yes, I treated the owl with contempt. I thought those evil spirits had no power left, but they do still have power. I pray only to Jehovah and to Jesus and not to little worthless gods." The kahuna said, "Turn to them and pray. No kahuna can treat you or give you medicine to help you. You will get well by yourself if you repent of your fault." The man's intestines went in without any further treatment through repentance of his fault alone.

Punishment does not come to this man or that who is not related to those who had been consecrated as owls. The owl itself is a worthless thing; it is eaten by the people of Kula, Maui, and Na'alehu in Ka-'u, Hawaii,[10] and thrown about on the road. The owl itself is not a god—it has no mana. The god is separate. Kukauakahi is the main god (*po'o akua nui*) who is consecrated in the body of the owl and who shows his mana in the worthless body of the owl. The owl was famous in the old days for its mana, and for saving the lives of its *kahu* and averting danger. Lonokina'u, Kapo'i, Papa'a, Kapehu, Kahiuka, Ka'ahupahau, and many others were saved from death through the owl.

A short time ago a man at Lahaina named Napaepae had his boat broken up in the Pailolo channel. Most of the people aboard were drowned, but he swam all day and all night, and then an owl saved his life by flapping in front of his eyes, and he looked up and saw land and made shore at Kapa'akea near Kaunakakai, Molokai.

During the time of Alexander Liholiho, Kamehameha IV, when the country people had come in to Honolulu for the celebration of Restoration Day (*la ho'iho'i ea*), July 31st, a girl from Waialua was arrested for galloping her horse through the town. She was put into the prison (Halewai Ho'opa'ahao) with other prisoners to await trial. She cried violently. After midnight, when the other prisoners were asleep in the room, she heard a flapping sound at the door, and when she opened her eyes she found the door wide open. She went out and closed the door. Outside an owl was perched on a wooden fence. While the guard and the policemen were still awake, the owl guided the girl across the space between the prison house and the fence, then along the mauka side of King Street, keeping close to the fence, until they came to John Meek's yard enclosure. They entered, and came out on Maunakea Street; went on up through Ka'aione's yard at Kikihale, and reached the yard of William Stevens, who was called Po'omuku by the Hawaiians. There a horse was waiting, and a bundle of clothes. The girl mounted the horse, the owl turned its head toward Waialua and guided her to there, and then left her.

Is the owl a god? The writer of this history says that the owl is not a god—it is the form (*haili*) taken by a god. The owl is a humble bird among the birds of Hawaii, but it was consecrated, and was made kapu to certain people, but the *po'e kahiko* knew that the god itself was a different thing. The Holy Bible is new in Hawaii, but one can look there and see that God changed (*ho'olilo*) His Holy Spirit into a form that was visible to men—"And he saw the Spirit of God descending like a dove." The Hawaiian people have always known that God is in the heavens and everywhere in heaven and earth and that He fills all space.

Ka po'e kahiko said that their gods would save them from a death of misery and suffering—such as one caused by slander (*make 'ohumu*), or sorcery (*make ho'opi'opi'o*), or ill will of others (*make ho'opilikia*)—as well as from accidents. These were the *pilikia* that the gods would help with. Those whom the gods saved were those known as *kanaka hemolele,* "perfect" men. But if a *kanaka hemolele* was willing to die, the gods would avenge him by bringing a cruel death upon his murderers, and overthrow the rule of the chief who had condemned him to death. And so a *kanaka hemolele* might consent to die. His body was but one—those who joined him in death (*moepu'u*) would be many. For this reason the *kahuna nui* of Oahu, Ka'opulupulu, and his son Kahulupue agreed to die. Their god had revealed to them that they might escape by sailing for Kauai, otherwise they would be killed when they reached Wai'anae; but if they were killed, their murderers would meet with a terrible death, and there would be a great slaughter, and the kingdom would be overthrown and the ruling family and the chiefs of Oahu would be set aside and the ruler over the people would "belong to the sea," those who came from across the sea. Ka'opulupulu consented to dying, and prophesied what was to happen, and all this was fulfilled. Ka'opulupulu was killed at the edge of the sea at Pu'uloa, and his son Kahulupue at Wai'anae. Only a few years afterward the first part of the avenging came true—there was great slaughter and death, and the government was overthrown. Not a hundred years have passed since the death of Ka'opulupulu, and his famous prophecy for this kingdom of Hawaii is being fulfilled upon the Hawaiian race.[11]

THE KAPUS OF CONSECRATION

The kapus of the kingdom, *kapu aupuni,* were entirely separate from the kapus imposed upon individuals, the kapus of consecration, *kapu ho'ola'a.* The first applied to everybody and were set up by Wakea *ma.* Most of the others, the minor kapus, (*na kapu li'ili'i*) came much later. Here are their main divisions.*

The first division applied to those persons with shark, *mano, 'aumakua* and those whom they had transfigured and whose spirits (*haili*) had entered into *mano* bodies. Some fishes and all shark flesh were made kapu to them, and also some plant foods (*mea 'ai*) and some birds. The kapus of the second division applied to those with *mo'o 'aumakua* and transfigured *mo'o;* some sea fishes and some fresh-water fishes were made kapu to them, and some plants and some birds. The divisions of the *mo'o* and the *mano* kapus were large ones. The kapus of the third division, those with volcanic *'aumakua* (*'aumakua pele*) and those who had been changed into *pele,* had to be combined with the kapu of another *'aumakua.* A volcanic spirit, a *pele,* as I have said, had no kapu thing of its own; only a gift of a bit of salt was required. But if the *pele* was combined with Puna'aikoa'e, then the *koa'e* bird became kapu; if combined with the kapu of the *mo'o* Kalamainu'u, then the kapu was a very strict one, and several articles of food were forbidden.

---
* May 5, 1870.

There were a great many other kinds of *'aumakua,* but not many people were transfigured into their forms in order that their souls might live again within these *'aumakua.* Those who "lived again" would make themselves known by coming back to possess a parent or a relative, but there were not a great many of them—only those really related (*pili maoli*) by blood to the ancestral *'aumakua* (*kupuna 'aumakua*).

Some people wanted to make the souls of the beloved dead live again, and so they transfigured them. Other people were afraid of such transfigured souls and called them *'uhinipili* (deified spirits), *iwi nakeke* (rattling bones), or *nuku mane'o* (itchy-mouthed). Some *'uhinipili* spirits were well cared for by their *kahu,* or parents, or relatives, and were saviors in time of trouble who healed illness and warned of dangers to come. Turn to the story of Pamano and see the benefits he received through his *'uhinipili* sisters.[12] Not he alone, but thousands of other people have been saved through *'uhinipili* spirits, and they have helped to save the lives of relatives in times of great trouble from the old days until this day. But some people feared and despised *'uhinipili* spirits because they might do harmful things—even kill their *kahu* and relatives. They were a constant menace because if any of the things consecrated to these spirits, such as food, clothing, a water gourd, a calabash, a mat, or anything consecrated to or demanded by (*kauleo*) these spirits, were defiled with blood or treated disrespectfully, the wrongdoer would be severely punished (*ho'opa'i*). He would become humpbacked, or his eyelids would be drawn down, or he would fall lame, or suffer with chronic stomach ache (*nahu kau*) or consumption (*hoki'i*)—or he might be killed outright. No medical kahuna could heal these troubles; his only cure was to appeal to the *'uhinipili* spirit with many offerings and sacrifices. If the spirit heeded the plea, the person would recover. Because of these severe punishments inflicted by the *'uhinipili,* some people were afraid to offer their dead to the *'aumakua* to be changed into its form—and certainly not to the shark *'aumakua,* lest the dead become a man-eating shark. They were the fraction (*kekahi hapa*) of the Hawaiian people who were without gods—they were the skeptics and unbelievers.*

---

* May 12, 1870.

NOTES TO PART FOUR

¹ Kapapaialaka appears on Hawaiian cosmogonic genealogies as the wife of Laka, the son of Hulihonua and Keakahulilani (as in Kamakau, 1961, p. 433), or as the son of Li'aikuhonua and Keakahulihonua (*The Kumulipo,* line 1815, Beckwith, 1951, p. 233). See also Barrère (1961, pp. 422-423).

² "*Kaku'ai* is the term used to express the act of offering the body with sacrifice to become transformed and live again in some object, or it may be used in general to mean worshiping with offerings of food" (Beckwith, 1934, Chapter 9, Note 2. See Green and Beckwith, 1926, pp. 185, 186; Ellis, 1917, p. 271).

The present editor interprets *kaku'ai* as transfiguration. This transfiguration was into *'aumakua* and *kumupa'a* god forms; that is, manifestations of natural phenomena or legendary ancestral animal forms.

³ See Kamakau (1961, pp. 184-186) for a detailed account of this incident.

⁴ See *The Kumulipo,* lines 1981-1986 (Beckwith, 1951, p. 237) for Kuheleimoana, his wife Mapu'uaia'a'ala, and Maui-a-ka-malo, the son of Akalana. See also the 'Ulu genealogy, as in Kamakau (1961, p. 434).

⁵ See 'Ulu genealogy for Paumakua and La'amaikahiki, as in Kamakau (1961, p. 434).

⁶ Those who had control over a deified spirit sometimes forced it to do evil by threatening to feed it human filth instead of *'awa* [M.K.P.]. The implication here seems to be that those who worshiped through the buttocks used the spirit they controlled for harmful purposes.

⁷ "According to Mary Pukui, the saying is that when a shark acts in this way with its human victim it is not a natural shark but has been sent by sorcery to get rid of a person. The person sometimes calls to shore and waves his fingers in farewell to his relatives as the shark holds him, first tossing him up in the air, then hiding him under water" (Beckwith, 1934, Chapter 9, Note 12).

⁸ For the story of Punia, see Fornander (1918, pp. 294-301).

⁹ "*Kane ulu po* is literally 'Kane who wakens one at night.' *Kakala ho'oulu* is the spur that kicks at and wakens one. When a cock crows at untimely hours it is called *ulu po* or *ulu moku* and is a sign of illness, or of the arrival of strangers. The cock is supposed to crow in order to arouse one to meditate on some cause for illness, or to prepare for visitors" (Beckwith, 1934, Chapter 9, Note 25).

¹⁰ "Mary Pukui denies that the owl was ever eaten for food in Ka-'u district. She knew only a single family in Ka-'u who ate owls, and that family came from elsewhere" (Beckwith, 1934, Chapter 9, Note 28). See also Handy and Pukui (1958, p. 119).

¹¹ For the tradition of Ka'opulupulu, see Kamakau (1961, pp. 128-129, 134-136).

¹² For the story of Pamano, see Fornander (1918, pp. 302-313).

PART FIVE

PART FIVE

'Oihana Lapa'au —
Medical Practices

KAHUNA 'AUMAKUA

THE MEDICAL KAHUNAS, *kahuna lapa'au,* did not use real medicines in the ancient days. The illnesses they treated were those sent by the *akua* [*'aumakua*] to punish a man for doing evil, breaking oaths, and wrongdoing against consecrated things—eating the *akua's* animal form, or a kapu plant or fish, or wearing forbidden clothing—and all sorts of other errors. If the illness was a very serious one, one that a kahuna could not comprehend, and it was beyond the knowledge of the first kahuna who treated for it, then it was due to the *'aumakua.* It was very difficult to dodge the "smoke" (*uahi*) of the *'aumakua.* And they "entertained" introduced diseases (*a na ka 'aumakua i ho'okipa i na ma'i malihini*).

It was not well to treat a person whose illness had been sent by the *'aumakua,* a *ma'i 'aumakua,* with medicine, lest the force (mana) of the medicine cause his death. If the kahuna was an upright person he would be guided properly by true revelations of his spirit guides; the secret things of his ancestors would be revealed to him, and all the hallowed things about which he did not know. In order to rightly guide the kahuna, and for him to know the proper sacrifices and offerings and suitable prescriptions to use in treatment, he was commanded through *akaku* (apparitions), *hihi'o* (visions), *kahoaka* (phantoms), *kuaka* (shadowy forms), and by *'ike maka* (visual knowledge) through seeing and talking with an *akua* who had assumed human form. So it was in ancient times, and so it is now.

The [criteria of] uprightness of a *kahuna 'aumakua* were: the purity of his person and of his deeds, and his true piety. Then the *akua* would help him by revealing the cause of the trouble, the wrongdoings the patient had committed, and what offerings the patient must give to pay for his wrongs. *Kahuna 'aumakua* who did not keep their bodies clean and did not obey the laws of the land as well as those of the *akua* were likely to be led wrongly by their "angel watchmen" (*anela kia'i*), and their work be made erroneous. Evil spirits (*'uhane 'ino*) would aid them, and their work would be wrong.

Of the *kahuna 'aumakua*, the *kahuna po'oko'i* were the most notorious; that was because they demanded a great price of the patient in the way of sacrifices and offerings. However, the foods provided by the patient and his relatives were for their consumption, and not for that of the kahuna and his relatives; but if, through aloha, the patient's family wished it, the kahuna and his relatives would eat of them too.

The offerings were a black sow, eight *kala* fish, eight *kumu* fish, eight octopuses, a *weke* fish, a mullet, an *awa* fish, shrimps from the upland streams, shoots of *pohole* (*ho'i'o*) fern, a red chicken, a white chicken, a black chicken; a young coconut, tapa, a dog, sugar cane, spring water, a lei, some adornments for the body, and other things appropriate for a feast, such as sweet potatoes, taro, a pudding of sweet potatoes and coconut cream (*'uala palau*), and poi. When all these things were prepared, including bananas of the *popo'ulu* and *iholena* varieties, and *'awa* of the highest quality, then the feast was spread. This feast was the proper "remedy" for a deathly illness sent by the *'aumakua*. It was not well to treat such an illness with medicines. But if the illness was a combination of a *ma'i 'aumakua* and a natural one of the body, *ma'i kia'i kino,* then it might well be treated with medicines after the *ma'i 'aumakua* or *ma'i kumupa'a* had been cured.

If the patient was a wealthy chief, he gave many sacrifices and offerings, "several hundred" (*lau*) pigs, red fishes, dogs, coconuts, garments, *'oloa* tapas, and *'awa* roots. Then the feast was spread with much rejoicing in a *hale lau,* a house thatched with leaves, which was a *moku hale,* a house built just for this feast. The poor did not often make a feast; very few could afford one. A firestick, a little kindling, a taste of taro leaves, a few sacrifices and offerings, a bit of chicken or a bundle of fish—these were perhaps all they could afford. These humble offerings were for the little misfortunes that came to a person of small account, and were proportionate to the insignificance of the person himself. Sometimes such small offerings were acceptable if the *akua* had compassion upon the giver.

The kahunas of this class, the *kahuna 'aumakua,* have been called "pig-eating kahunas," *papa kahuna 'ai pua'a;* liars, *kahuna ho'opunipuni;* and deifiers, *kahuna ho'omanamana*—and so they are at times. But many times they are right, and they cure many who are sick unto death. The reason some of them are called liars and deifiers is because they call upon their ancestors and pray to the dead and offer up sacrifices which they throw into the sea or into fresh water, or bury at *ko'a* fish altars and at *Pohaku o Kane,* or at *waihau* or *unu* heiaus, according to the forms of the *'aumakua*. These might be sharks, fishes, *mo'o,* thunder, lightning, earthquakes, spirits of the volcano, the sun, the moon, stars, fire, or god forms of certain chiefs or ancestors, perhaps. That is why there were so many *kuahu* altars for the gods; and it was not right to trespass on someone else's altar. Those who were related to the *mo'o 'aumakua* of Kalamainu'u took a reddish-brown or a dark brown dog, a tapa dyed yellow with *olena,* and an *'awa* root, and took them to a deep fresh-water pond, tied them to a stone and lowered them into the water with appeals to the *'aumakua* to release their descendants from the *ma'i 'aumakua,* and that ended the trouble. The doings of such kahunas are to be seen to this day.

Illness caused by an *'aumakua* is familiar to the whole race. There is not one who has escaped from it, and it is an illness that is inherited in a family through generations, a *ma'i ku'una.* Medical kahunas should not treat a *ma'i 'aumakua* or *ma'i kumupa'a* with potions or medicines. When a laxative fails to work, and the disease becomes complicated, it is well to consider that a *ma'i 'aumakua* is the cause. If, however, the symptoms are those of an ordinary sickness, the *kahuna la'au lapa'au* (medical "herb" kahuna) can treat it.*

A sickness caused by an *'aumakua* or a *kumupa'a* ancestral deity is a very resistant one, as both medical kahunas and *haole* doctors know. It is beyond the power of their medicines or skill; it does not respond to medicines, and there are not many kahunas who are able to work on it. If the work is to succeed, there must be very burdensome offerings made by the family of the sick person. If he is a poor man and has no one to help him (*kanaka 'ole*), treatments involving so many offerings cannot go on. But if the sufferer is a wealthy man and has followers (*makaukau i ke kanaka*), then the work of the kahuna can be done immediately. The kahuna is worthless who does not then set his patient free and save him from death.**

Sacrifices and offerings to the *'aumakua* were not all the same. For minor punishments (*ho'opa'i li'ili'i*), such as illness suffered by a member of the family, a small fire [for a cooked offering] was made morning and evening for five times (*kualima*), and then a final offering (*pani*) of a few *lu'au* leaves or an egg (*kahi moa*), and the illness would be ended. If it was a serious illness, one that confined the sufferer to the house, then the final offering was an *'awa* plant (*pu'awa*) and a pig.

This was a customary thing to do, and was the work of the family; it could not be done by outsiders or strangers because their voices and appeals would not be heeded by the *'aumakua.* This work was known as *hana 'aumakua* or *hana kumupa'a.*

The chiefs made offerings and sacrifices to the *'aumakua* in proportion to the wrongs committed against the god. Sacrifices alone were not the atonement (*uku*) to the god. The first thing to do was to build the *moku hale.* This house was a *hale lau lama,* a house of *lama* wood; the posts, rafters, and thatching sticks were of *lama,* and the cords to bind it together were of *'ie.* The thatching might be of ti leaves (*lau'i*), banana fibers (*pa'a'a*), *lama* leaves (*lau lama*), or of *pili* (*pili maoli*). When all the material was in readiness, the house was built and thatched in one day, up to the roof top, and with a lanai and a fence. Some houses were large, and some small, with room enough for only four or five persons. When the *moku hale* was finished, it was kapu and could not be entered. The next day, the house was entered, and offerings were placed (*ua ho'olulu*) on the offering racks (*haka*). *Kahiki, popo'ulu,* and *iholena* bananas, many (*lau*) pigs, coconuts, red fishes, garments, and *ninikea* and *'oloa* tapas were offered, and *'awa,* pig,

---

* September 15, 1870.
** September 22, 1870.

banana, coconut, and red fish were given in sacrifice to the god. The god would heed the offerings and sacrifices (*alana a me ka mohai*), and death and troubles became as nothing.*

THE MEDICAL PROFESSION

The medical profession, *'oihana lapa'au*, is an ancient one in Hawaii, and there were many kinds of medical kahunas, *kahuna lapa'au*. However, medical practice was not widespread among the people. In the first place, there were infrequent destructive and contagious diseases and epidemics, and the native diseases (*ma'i kama'aina*) were few. In the second place, the people relied upon the skill of the *kahuna 'ana'ana*, the *kahuna kuni*, or the *kahuna huikala*. The *kahuna 'ana'ana* had a "healing jaw" (*he a ola*)—that is, he did his work by means of prayer— and he was superior to the *kahuna lapa'au* because he was learned in two arts: that of killing, and that of saving (*o ka make a me ke ola*).

These are the classes of *kahuna lapa'au*:

CLASS 1.—*Kahuna ho'ohapai keiki* and *ho'ohanau keiki* [who induced pregnancy and delivered babies];

CLASS 2.—*Kahuna pa'ao'ao* and *kahuna 'ea* [who diagnosed and treated childhood ailments of] puniness and fretfulness (*'omali 'alalehe*);[1]

CLASS 3.—*Kahuna 'o'o*, who "held back" [kept closed] the fontanel (*ho'opa'a manawa*) [and practiced lancing];

CLASS 4.—*Kahuna haha*, who used a "table of pebbles" (*papa 'ili'ili*) and the ends of their fingers (*welau lima*) [that is, who diagnosed by "feel" (*haha*), or palpation];

CLASS 5.—*Kahuna a ka 'alawa maka* and *'ike lihilihi*, who could "see at a glance" (*'alawa*), or "through the eyelashes" (*'ike lihilihi*), dislocations (*uwai*) and sprains (*anu'u*) [and who diagnosed by insight (*'alawa maka*) or critical observation (*'ike lihilihi*)];

CLASS 6.—*Kahuna 'ana'ana* and *kahuna kuni*, who used *'ana'ana* and *kuni* magic in treatment (*ma ka lapa'au*);

CLASS 7.—*Kahuna ho'opi'opi'o*, who used [counteracting] sorcery (*ho'opi'opi'o*) in their treatment (*ma ka lapa'au*);

CLASS 8.—*Kahuna makani*, who "treated" (*ma ka lapa'au*) the spirits of illness.

All these classes of *kahuna lapa'au* differed in their practices. [The work of the kahunas of Classes 6, 7, and 8 will be explained later.] For two, Classes 4 and 6, the procuring of a remedy was much work. In olden times only, perhaps? Yes, in olden times, for that is what this account is about. Some other classes had a few medicines—as much as could be put into the flap of a malo. Others had their remedies "at their fingertips" (*i ka maiu'u*), using words to explain what kind of disease the patient had, what kind of medicine to use, and how to treat the patient.

* September 29, 1870.

CLASS 1. KAHUNA HO'OHAPAI KEIKI AND HO'OHANAU KEIKI

In the old days the *kahuna ho'ohapai keiki* and *ho'ohanau keiki* had many ways to induce pregnancy among barren women who had ceased bearing (*'opu pa*), or who had never given birth (*hanau keiki 'ole*). The first way was that of the kahunas of the priesthood orders of Ku, Lono, or Kane; the second was that of the plant-using kahunas of Ku and Hina (*kahuna lau nahelehele o Ku a me Hina*). Although the second way was not without sacrifices, it was not by the sacrificing of a person, nor by the urging of others, that a child was obtained, but through the real desire of the husband and wife, and the harmony of their thoughts.[2] A child obtained thus, through entreaty or prediction (*me ka waha a ma ka wanana*), was entirely different from one born from natural pregnancy. He was not obtained from humans, but from the mana of the gods.

Ka po'e kahiko used to pray ritually (*kuili*) that the race might increase, and flourish, and sprout from the parent stock. "Thriving seedlings *ka po'e kahiko* bore; great gourds filled with seeds they were. But today they are poison gourds, bitter to the taste." Because of some wrongdoing, it is said. Well, now they pray to God in a congregation. What ruler of old would allow a mixed gathering of men, women, and children to pray together to the gods? None! A pure and faultless time this is, indeed!

A man and a woman might live together from the time they were young and strong and full of hope until old age approached without having a child or children.* Then they would sigh because they had no children, and their longing would grow for the children they had not wished for in youth because the wife would have been ashamed to have sour-smelling breasts; to have been called an old woman; and to have had children tagging along behind her. Parents, grandparents, and husbands would help (*kokua*) the young good-looking women to prevent pregnancy; but this was not general. In later years, when the desire for a child came to the woman, and the husband helped, then they had a child. They induced pregnancy, if they had relatives who knew what to do—grandparents of the wife, perhaps, or of the husband. It was better if they were of the side of the husband, because then his side would have no sorrow because of the suffering of their child. They had only to ask one of the family who knew how to induce pregnancy, and, without a doubt, they would have a child—there would be no failure. But there were some rules to be observed to induce pregnancy, and if the family was ignorant of these rules, then sacrifices and offerings were taken to the *kahuna lau nahelehele* of Ku and Hina, or to the kahunas of Ku, Lono, or Kane. The children begotten through such sacrifices and offerings called the gods their *'aumakua*. That is how the relationship was maintained between *'aumakua* and descendants, and how the Hawaiian people became actual children (*keiki ponoi*) of the gods.

The inducing of pregnancy was a hallowed act (*ua ho'ola'a 'ia*) when performed for high chiefesses and ruling chiefesses who were barren, so that they might bear

---

* August 11, 1870.

a chief to rule the kingdom. Some of the lesser chiefesses (*kaukauali'i*) were also prayed for ritually (*ua kuili pule 'ia*) in the *waihau* heiaus so that they might bear children.

Childbearing used to be induced in many barren women by their taking a concoction to produce pregnancy (*'apu ho'ohapai keiki*), or by making requests of kahunas, prophets, and *'aumakua*. That is one reason why the land was covered with people so that there were no waste lands—the whole land was peopled, from mountain to sea coast. There were a great many kinds of medicines and concoctions to bring on pregnancy. The best were the potions and fruits (*hua*) of Ku, the male *'aumakua,* and Hina, the female *'aumakua*. These were the *'aumakua* who increased mankind (*'aumakua ho'oulu kanaka*). The *po'e kahiko* believed strongly that they would bring on pregnancy and cause barren women to bear, and it really happened so.

The *kahuna lau nahelehele* of Ku and Hina had many methods. Their basic equipment consisted of calabashes, shallow bowls, and water gourds, in which they prepared plants, seeds, leaf buds, and things of that kind. The kahuna could foretell whether the child would be a boy or a girl, depending upon which sign he saw first when he went outside—an *'o'o* (digging stick) or an *i'e kuku* (tapa-beating mallet). When there were too many births, the women were given a concoction to stop births (*'apu ho'opa*). There were many women who were made pregnant in the old days. Was this true of the old days only? Perhaps so, but fulfillment always comes to those who have faith. So it is recorded in the Holy Scriptures. I know some people who received fulfillment of their faith.

A certain woman, a cousin of mine, had been married for 25 years without bearing a child. She and her husband had been among the first to be married by the Reverend H. Bingham, and they lived under proper marriage conditions. They observed the rules of marriage until they approached old age and feebleness without having a child. When they were about 45 years old they asked their old folks for a child, and were told they would have a child, a daughter, and they did have a daughter. In appearance, the woman was elderly, and so was her husband, yet they had a child begotten in their old age.

Here is another case that I have witnessed. At Waihe'e on Maui was a couple who had been married for some years and had no children. The wife was determined to have a child, and spoke of it to one who knew how to bring on pregnancy. She was given a concoction to drink to induce pregnancy, *ia Ho'ohuakawowo* ("to cause to give birth to progeny"). That was in 1852. The first child was a boy; the second, a girl; and so it went on each year until the woman had over 10 children, some of whom lived, and some of whom died. She became tired of being pregnant year after year, and appealed to the kahuna who had made her fruitful to give her a potion to make her stop giving birth. The kahuna consented to treat her after the birth of the child which she was then carrying. When it was born the kahuna examined the child and the afterbirth (*'iewe*) and said, "I cannot give you any medicine to make you stop bearing. You are going to bear over 20 children, and no kahuna can put a stop to it."[3] The woman, however, insisted that the kahuna give her a potion to drink to make her barren, but it had no effect. After that, she sometimes killed the unborn child by piercing (*'o'o*), and sometimes she let it be born properly. This last year, she pierced the child, and died together with the child. She died because of excessive childbearing, and the difficulty they had in making a living because the government will give no help to parents with many children. These are not the only women I have known to be made fruitful.*

Another thing in which *ka po'e kahiko* were skilled was in delivering babies from the wombs of their mothers. When chiefesses or favorite daughters became pregnant, care was taken to prevent suffering in childbirth. After the seventh or eighth month of pregnancy (*ku*) they were given a potion of some *ho'opahe'e* ("that which makes slippery") to drink frequently. This was water and sap (*wale*) from the *mamaki* tree, or *kikawaioa* (*kikawaio*) fern, or *palau* yam, or *hau* tree. The reason for giving this "slipperiness" (*pahe'e*) to pregnant women was so that there would be no pain at the time the child was born if it was born in the eighth or ninth month, before the end of the pregnancy. Then the child would be born without the mother straining with labor pains and having to bear down. With children born easily (*ho'opahe'e;* literally, "made slippery"), the mother does not know the pain of childbirth, nor does she raise her voice in lamentation and distress.

Here is another thing they did. Just before the reddish discharge (*'ina'ina*) came, the woman would be given a "birthing" potion to drink (*la'au ho'ohanau keiki*). Then the *kahuna ho'ohanau keiki* would assume the birth pains. The woman carrying the child would not feel any pain, but would just give birth to the child. All she had to do was to prepare herself for the birth, and the contractions and straining of childbirth were assumed (*aia maluna*) by the kahuna. This is a very difficult thing to do. I have seen kahunas and midwives (*po'e pale keiki*) who could do this, but they are few and far between. Most of the *kahuna ho'ohanau keiki* give potions and plants (*lau nahelehele*) to help delivery, but do not transfer the pain to others.[4]

In these ways the *kahuna ho'ohanau* assisted at childbirth.**

CLASS 2. KAHUNA PA'AO'AO AND KAHUNA 'EA

The *kahuna pa'ao'ao* were skilled in examining newborn babies and their parents to discover signs of *pa'ao'ao*. *Pa'ao'ao* ailments (*ma'i pa'ao'ao*) cling to (*pili pu*) the parents. When their children are born, they pass on (*pili aku*) the *pa'ao'ao,* as well as physical disabilities (*ma'i lolo*) and inherited diseases (*ma'i ku'una*). *Pa'ao'ao* and *'ea* are symptoms of widespread illnesses (*he mau kulana ma'i nui ke pa'ao'ao a me ke 'ea*).[5] If the father or the mother had a *pa'ao'ao* ailment, the parent was given the *pa'ao'ao* treatment, and the child was spared. If it were an ailment that had afflicted (*pili*) the ancestors, coming down from

---

* August 18, 1870.
** August 25, 1870.

them and afflicting the parents and then the child, if it were not treated in childhood, the child would have a more severe ailment in maturity.

Such *pa'ao'ao* ["predispositions"] as *'opu lauoho* ("hair stomach"), *ha'alele makua* ("parent deserter"), *papa ki'i* ("bound bowels"), *mapele manawa* ("soft [depressed] fontanel"), and many others, if not treated in childhood would develop in maturity into severe ailments—*ninole* (emaciation), *hoki'i* (tuberculosis), *nae* (consumption), *hano* (asthma), *'ohemo* (dysentery), *pehu* (swelling), or *'ohao* (swelling of the abdomen). There are many ailments that result from *pa'ao'ao* and *wai'opua* ("cloudy secretions").

The signs and symptoms in a newborn infant that reveal the presence and kind of *pa'ao'ao* are: first, the cuttlefish, *muhe'e;* second, the cuttlefish with the swaying head, *muhe'e pulewa;* third, the red cuttlefish, *muhe'e makoko;* fourth, the white cuttlefish, *muhe'e kea;* fifth, the multicolored cuttlefish, *muhe'e lehua;* and sixth, the flattened cuttlefish, *muhe'e papaki'i.*[6] These signs and symptoms show what kind of *pa'ao'ao* are within the child, such as *ha'alele makua, 'opu lauoho, 'omino* (general unhealthiness), or *'alalehe* (fretfulness).*

PA'AO'AO REMEDIES

There are many remedies, gathered from the sea to the top of the mountains, which are good to rid children of *pa'ao'ao*. Hair, *lauoho,* is a *pa'ao'ao* remedy, used for *'opu lauoho,* "hair stomach." The remedy must be suitable for the ailment. It is not right just to fill the child with medicines; the ailments of children and young people must be studied and the proper remedies applied. Proper diagnosing (*'ike kupono*) by the *kahuna pa'ao'ao* and *kahuna 'ea* is by observation (*'ike lihilihi*), insight (*'ike a ka 'alawa*), and experience (*'ike hana*).**

Medicines for *pa'ao'ao* should be taken while the child is in the womb, or when it comes forth. If a man or woman reaches maturity and approaches old age and has a tendency to a *pa'ao'ao* ailment which had not been removed in childhood or in youth, it will take a new form (*loli*) and become severe or fatal, and the legs will become bloated (*'ukakai,* or *'u'ulukai*) and wrinkled (*papa'akai*). There are a great number of characteristics of diseases that can come to the person.†

Kupele is a very good remedy for *pa'ao'ao* and for *'ea*. It is made of mashed sweet potatoes (*poi 'uala*) mixed with *pa'ao'ao* medicines. Some taros (*kalo*) are also good to use for *kupele*. The sweet potatoes or taro are not mashed (*ku'i*) with water, but with the juices (*wai*) of the *pa'ao'ao* medicines. When the *kahuna pa'ao'ao* is satisfied that the medicines are suitable, then the *kupele* is given; and after that, a purgative (*la'au ho'onaha*) made of ingredients suitable to go with the *pa'ao'ao* or *'ea* medicines in the *kupele*. When the cause of the *pa'ao'ao* or the *'ea* is under control (*aia a hina ke kumu*), then leaf buds or leaves are given to the infant from the body of the parent who feeds it—through the milk of the mother, the *pa'ao'ao* medicine enters the child. If it is a leaf bud, then [the medicinal

---
* August 18, 1870.
** August 25, 1870.
† September 15, 1870.

property of] that leaf bud comes out in her milk; and so it does also if it is a leaf, or a root, or a fruit. This is accompanied by prayer (*a me ka pule*). The sign that shows that the *pa'ao'ao* is over (*ua pau ke pa'ao'ao*) is when there is no more yellow, greenish, or blackish discharge [meconium] (*ua pau ka wili pu ana o ka lena, ke pakaiea, ka mea 'ele'ele, a me ka wekaweka o kamali'i*). Then, if the tongue is "coated" (*pala ka waha*), and the infant's head is hot, an *'ea* medicine is given. Those who are skilled say that *'ea* is male, and that *pa'ao'ao* is female, and that they are entwined (*huipu*), one above and one below, so it is best to treat both at the same time.*

Here are some *pa'ao'ao* medicines. Any one of them may be chosen by the parents to feed to their infants. The same medicine is given to either loosen or to tighten the bowels. They are, leaf buds (*mu'o*), leaves (*lau*), roots (*mole*), and bark (*papa'a*) from which *kupele* is made.

The *makou* is the finest of all *pa'ao'ao* medicines.[7] It is used from leaf bud to root, and may be eaten plain (*'ai maoli*) or in *kupele*. The *puako'olau* (*ko'oko'olau*) with its leaf buds, leaves, and roots is used in *kupele* or "eaten dry," *'ai malo'o* [used as a tea]. Other plant medicines are: the flowers of the *aloalo, koki'o, 'auhuhu,* and *'ilima* (also called *kanaka maika'i*); the *mohihi, lemu o makili* (*'okole-makili*), *hinahina ku mauna* (*hinahina-kuahiwi*), and *pulihilihi* with their flowers; the fleshy part of the key (*pua*) and [tips of] the aerial roots of the *hala;* the new red leaves, *liko,* of the *lehua* and the *lama;* the *liko* and fruit (*hualewa*) of the *'ohi'a* or *'ohi'a 'ai;* leaves of the *makolokolo* and the *palaholo;* the ripe fruit (*hua pala*), *liko,* and bark of the *kanawao;* the *kauno'a* (*kaunao'a*) and its seeds (*hua*); the *laukahi* with its leaf buds (*mu'o*); the *popolo,* and its berries called *pu'ili;* the flowers and tubers (*hua*) of the *haloakea* (*lauloa*) taro; *uhauhako* (*pawale*), *iliau, hinahina, pa-'u o Hi'iaka, pahekili* (*huahekili*), the large- and small-leafed *pamakani* (*pamakani lau nui a lau li'ili'i*); and the *limu 'ekaha* of the mountain (*limu 'ekaha o ke kuahiwi*).

Ashes, hair, the *walu* fish, *niho* (the Aristotle's lantern of sea urchins), the *'ea* turtle shell, *'ana* (a "stony sponge"), the *'ekaha ku moana* (a "kind of coral"), and many other medicines were also used for *pa'ao'ao* and *'ea*.**

'EA

There are two kinds of serious ailments (*ma'i ikaika*) that children and youth get; they are passed down from the grandparents to the parents, and from the parents to the children. The first is *pa'ao'ao*, and the second is *'ea*.

There are two kinds of *'ea*: the *'ea huna*, "hidden" [latent] *'ea*, or *'ea mahani*, "vanishing" [evanescent] *'ea*; and the *'ea ho'ike*, "revealed" [manifest] *'ea*, or *'ea wawaka*, "flaming" [acute] *'ea*. The *'ea ho'ike*, or *'ea wawaka*, can be seen by the untrained eye and can be removed in childhood. The *'ea huna* does not show itself in childhood, but if nothing is done about it then, in maturity it shows itself by

---
* August 18, 1870.
** August 25 and September 15, 1870.

kua wawaka, "flaming back," and turns into *pala* ("yellow rot"), *kaokao* ("red rot"), *'ala'ala* (scrofulous sores), *puhi kaokao* ("red puffiness"), *kua puhi* ("burst back"), *kua 'o iwi* ("back pierced by bone"), *kua nanaka* ("back split open"), or some other severe disease. *'Ea* will attack the soft palate (*e pau ana ke kileo o ka pu'u*), and erupt (*hua'i*) on the head, face, nose, and all over the body if not treated in youth. It is the cause of *po'o hua'i* ("erupted head"), *ihu 'ole* ("no nose"), *maka 'ole* ("no eyes"), *po'o pilau* ("stinking head"), *po'o lehu* ("ashy [scaly] head"), *umauma naha* ("cracked chest"), and other serious diseases.[8]

'Ea is the condition (*ma'i*) that "played host" to the introduced diseases (*o ka 'ea ka ma'i nana i ho'okipa i na ma'i malihini*) *kaokao* (syphilis), *pala* (gonorrhea), and *pu'upu'u hebera pake* (leprosy). So declared a certain *kahuna pa'ao'ao* and *kahuna 'ea* in 1821. Kama was his name, and he was skilled in treating *pa'ao'ao* and *'ea* in young people and in adults. He diagnosed by critical observation, by insight, and by "feel" [palpation] (*ua 'ike ma ka lihilihi, a ma ka 'alawa, a ma ka haha*). He would choose the age when persons should be treated with medicines for *pa'ao'ao*, as well as the proper medicines for *'ea huna*, or *'ea mahani*. When the persons took the proper medicines—at the age the kahuna had chosen—they would not get a "sudden" illness (*ma'i ulia;* such as a stroke), or an introduced disease.*

As *'ea* used to kill one man with its "poison" (*'awa'awa*), so now the race is being killed by *'ea,* through its playing host to "poisonous" introduced diseases—*pala, kaokao, pu'upu'u hebera pake,* and *ma'i pu'upu'u hebera* (smallpox).

'EA REMEDIES

There are many suitable medicines for *'ea* diseases. One is the medical potion (*la'au 'apu 'ea*) made from the *limu kalemakapi'i* (*makole-makopi'i*), a moss that looks like the leaves of the dark pine tree (*paina uliuli*). It is found in damp mossy places—near waterfalls in the mountains, beside a spring or a never-failing stream, and along the edge of a wet taro patch (*lo'i*) in the rainy season. It has a "flower" (*pua;* a spore case) that is like sugar cane stem braid (*he pua ko lu*) in color—some are yellow (*lenalena*), and some are white (*ke'oke'o*). Gather a large quantity of this *limu* and twelve unopened young shoots (*mu'o 'opiopio*) of the *'ahu'awa* sedge. Shred the *'ahu'awa* into fibers—like those used for straining *'awa*—and put in the *limu,* the young shoots of the *'ahu'awa,* and powdery scrapings of *'ea* turtle shell and of *'ana.* Wrap these in the *'ahu'awa* fibers and put ti leaves around, making two bundles of the same size. Broil them in a fire with little pieces of sweet potato. When they are cooked, waft (*ho'okololio*) the steam of the first bundle at the eyes, nose, and mouth of the child, then suck out the liquid from this bundle and feed it (*pu'a*) to the child, and then a mouthful of sweet potato (*mana 'uala*). Do the same with the second bundle. Do this five times (*e hana a kualima*), and the *'ea huna* will be gone—the *'ea kakua* ("back" *'ea*),[9] or *'ea mahani,* as well as the *'ea wahi* ("erupted" *'ea*), or *'ea ho'ike.* If it is the parent who has the *'ea,* the best thing to do is to make a potion of all of these things and drink it like tea,

---

* August 18, 1870.

morning and evening. Or make a *kupele* concoction of them with mashed sweet potato.

The bark of the *'ohi'a 'apane*, the young shoot (*'opu'u*) of the *iholena* banana, the root of the *'ala'alapuloa* (*'uhaloa; hialoa*), and many other things, are suitable medicines for *pala kea* ("white rot"), *pala* ("yellow rot"), *pala hao* ("hard rot"), and sore throat (*'eha o ka pu'u*). They are good as a gargle (*ke ho'olaola*) or as a "mouthwash" (*ke kale*). *Kohu kukui,* the sap of the green kukui nut, is also good to check (*komi ai*) *'ea* (thrush) and to harden the lining of the mouth.*
The *'ohi'a, 'uhaloa,* and *iholena* are used for the *'ea ho'ike,* or *'ea wahi* (eruptions). These medicines are not taken for the *'ea huna;* medicinal potions (*'apu*) and steaming (*mahu*) are proper treatments for *'ea huna.***

SMALLPOX

In 1853, smallpox (*ma'i pu'upu'u hebera*) came to Hawaii.[10] This writer entered the houses and himself saw the many people who had been overcome by the destructive disease (*ma'i luku*), and the many dead. It was heartbreaking. People got rough with very fine eruptions (*ua ho'omanunu 'ae me ka hunehune makali'i loa*), and after five or six days they turned "yellow" (*pala*)—like the yellow-brown of the *'ohi'a* (*uliuli*). On the seventh or eighth day came the itching and the scratching. Then they turned red, like someone toasted (*'olani*) with fire. From the day the sickness first started, not ten days would pass before they were dead.

A person would be full of pimples from the crown of the head to the soles of the feet—no spot had respite. His mouth was full of them; they were in the nostrils, on the face, in the ears—only the teeth and nails had none. The house stank like poison gourds (*lauhue 'awa'awa*); the stench was "beyond words" (*'a'ole o kana mai*). Those who died before the skin broke open were not so bad—they did not stink so much.

Of the people who got the smallpox, if the pimples were pointed (*kiokio 'o'oi*) these were "good" pimples (*pu'upu'u maika'i*)—pimples that it was possible to cure—and the patient could be told so; in 10 to 15 days he would be well. When the throat became sore from the growing of the pimples on the palate, *kohu kukui* and *'ohi'a* bark were the remedy. With a single gargling, the pimples coming to a head in the palate and throat would be healed (*ua ola ka kiokio o ka pu'upu'u*). When the pimples began to decrease, to hasten the healing [the cores of] those that were left after seven or eight days were pressed out (*poke ana*), and the pimples well daubed (*pala maika'i ana*) and smeared with medicine and left overnight; the scabs (*papa'a*) would fall off and the pimples would be healed. There remained those on the head—because of the hair—and those in "pinched places" (*wahi haiki*) that were not smeared with the "pimple ointment" (*la'au kapili pu'upu'u*). They took longer to heal. If the pimples were just left alone and not daubed with the healing medicine they would remain a long time; the scabs would stay on, and the bases of the pimples would pit (*po'opo'o*) underneath

---
* August 25, 1870.
** September 15, 1870.

the flesh. That is what scarred (*manumanu*) those who got smallpox, and made the features ugly.

The writer is well acquainted with smallpox. He cured more than a hundred persons, and some are now alive because they were healed by his treatment in Kipahulu and Hana, because the government did not take care of those who got the sickness there.*

CLASS 3. KAHUNA 'O'O

To remove weakness and sickliness and to clear up itch and scale on children, the lance was the remedy. Children with *pa'ao'ao* of the kinds revealed by the markings of the *muhe'e pulewa,* the swaying-headed, and the *muhe'e makoko,* the reddish cuttlefishes, are sickly (*'omino*) and fretful (*'alalehe*). They have lumps (*pu'upu'u*) and boils (*palapu*) on the head, and have a crusty fontanel. For them the proper remedy is the point of the lance, the *koholua*. They need to be lanced but twice, and the ailment will be gone, the lumps clear away, and the sickly condition disappear.

To force open (*ho'onaha*) the fontanel of the child is the duty of those who rear the child. If the fontanel closes too soon, and becomes solid like a coconut shell, it will cause the temperature to rise. It is good to keep a poultice of *kopili* tapa on the fontanel, dampened frequently with milk or with *'olena* or ti sap; otherwise the child will hiccough frequently.

This is how *ka po'e kahiko* took care of their youngsters and newborn babies.

CLASS 4. KAHUNA HAHA

The *kahuna haha* belonged to the order of Lono—that is, Lonopuha. It was a very ancient order of medical kahunas. The work of these kahunas was to "feel" for the disease, to locate it, and to prescribe for it. The original kahuna (*po'o kahuna mua*) of this order was Kamakanui'aha'ilono. He showed his skill and knowledge in the treatment of Lono, a chief of Ka-'u, Hawaii, who had pierced his own foot through the sole with an *'o'o* digging stick. *Popolo* was the ointment he applied, and when it was removed after a short while, the foot was healed; the hole made by the *'o'o* could not be seen. That very day Lono became a follower of Kamakanui'aha'ilono, and he became a *kahuna lapa'au*. Lono, that is, Lonopuha, was called the *po'o mua,* the first head, of the medical profession, and he was the first *'aumakua* of the *kahuna haha*.

There were kapus connected with learning the art of healing by the *haha* method. An apprentice must first release (*huikala*) any kapus that he was under pertaining to his own *'aumakua* before entering the Lonopuha profession (*'oihana* Lonopuha). The training was given under kapu, and sometimes in a special house, such as an *ulu hale,* a *moku hale,* or a *hale lau*. The pupils were taught the laws and rules of the practice until they obtained knowledge and skill, and if they had listened to

* September 9, 1869.

and observed these laws, the 'aumakua of this medical art ('aumakua lapa'au) looked after them at the time of the 'ailolo, the ceremony at the completion of their training.

In learning the medical arts, including that of Lonopuha, the first thing was to learn the prayers. These were the foundation and the guide to knowledge and skill whereby a man learned to heal and to recognize the mysterious things inside a sick man. The god was the guide to all things, the giver of boundless life; therefore every person who was learning the arts depended upon the god. The god did not give the same gifts to all the hosts of heaven. As there were different gifts to men on earth, so there were different gifts for the hosts of heaven and for the hosts of darkness, na pu'ali ma ka lani, a ma ka po. There were hosts that brought destruction, and hosts that brought life.

In some countries of the world, medical practitioners are not like the Hawaiian ones. In other countries they rely on their own skill, and on the lessons taught in medical schools. Human bodies are cut up and studied; flesh, ligaments, parts of the muscles, the position of tendons, the blood vessels that branch out from their source—the heart—and the circulation system. Also the nerves that go through the bones and come out fine and thin under the skin of man from their source—the brain; also the bones, tissues, cartilage, protuberances, glands, liver, and intestines. A body is cut to pieces, inside and out, and sections of intestines, stomach, and bowels are examined to find out what remedies to use to heal diseases. Some are medical experts, not through the mana of God, but through their being guided by visual proof (ma ko lakou alaka'i 'ikemaka) in their search for knowledge. In the Hawaiian school of medical kahunas, the god was the foundation, and secondly came prayers. Third came schooling in the kinds of diseases; fourth, in the kinds of remedies; fifth, in the art of killing; and sixth, in the art of saving.*

The foundation of the knowledge and skill of the *kahuna lapa'au* was the god. It was he who knew without error the treatment; it was he who pointed out the nature of the ailment and the things that pertained to this or that disease of man.

Second came prayer. Those who prayed to Lonopuha recited and used the Kumuhonua prayer. In it is revealed the mana of the god in creating heaven and earth and in creating the first man from soil.

O Kumuhonua, O Mehani,	Kumuhonua, Mehani,
O Kupuanu'u, O Kupualani,	Sprout-out-of-earth, Sprout-out-of-heaven,
He ko 'ula, he ko lei, he ko kea. . . .	A red sugar cane, a light sugar cane, a white sugar cane. . . .

After the prayer of thanksgiving (*pule ho'omaika'i*) for the mana of the god came the prayer of remembrance (*pule ho'omana'o*) for those who had belonged to the order of the medical kahunas of Lonopuha and for the long-time kahunas (*kahuna mo'i*) of the medical profession. That was the first basic learned by the pupil, and the prayers were memorized by the pupil until he could say them without hesitation while making offerings of food and praying ritually.

---

* August 25, 1870.

Third came [the diagnosing of diseases by means of] the *papa 'ili'ili*, the "table of pebbles." This was an arrangement of pebbles in the form of a man, from head to foot, until there was an outline of an entire man. The study of the pebbles began at the feet. There began the showing of the basic causes of the diseases that men get from the balls of the feet to the crown of the head. There are 100 to 1,000 diseases that snuff out the life of man, and a *kahuna haha* must know everything about the body of man, from the soles of the feet to the crown of the head, when he is in "full leaf" (*lau nui*) and the blood is circulating freely [in the prime of life]. Those who had studied until they were well grounded in knowledge and skill could predict when a man would die, and a death so forecast could be averted if the man listened to advice.

While the teacher taught, the pupils sat alert and remembered carefully everything that was taught them. When the teacher came to the torso (*kino*) of a man, he began with the disorders (*ma'i*) from the *mons pubis* (*pu'ukole*) to the navel (*piko*). These were: *pou* ("a ridge," "a lump;" "a hard, long substance lying perpendicularly above the umbilicus"*); *pou pa'a* (an immovable "ridge" or "lump"); *pou lewa* (a movable "ridge" or "lump"); *wai'opua* ("cloudy secretions"); *papaku* ("a disease attended with entire costiveness and always fatal"*); *haikala* (severe cramps); *iki'alamea* (ulcers); *ponaha* ("a round swelling with a soft middle"); *kaukihi* ("a swelling on the side"); *ane* (tiny pustules); *honokoi* ("a hard lump beside the *mons pubis*"); and *hu'ilele* (darting pains). From these beginnings of diseases develop *pu'u holo* ("moving protuberance"), *'ohao* (bloating of the abdomen), *pehu* (swelling), *pehu kumu niu* (swelling of the lower limbs), *pehu kala'e* (swelling of the body as far as the head), *pehu holoku* (swelling of the entire body), *pehu pauku* (swelling of part of the body, or on one side of the body). In these, the back turns dark (*pi'i ke kuawehi*; the skin turns a purplish color), and panting and hiccoughing follow.[11]

Kumulena (jaundice) was a disease looked for in man. Its origin is back of the navel, by the liver. The source of it is the gall bladder, which secretes a fluid and mixes with the liquid food of the stomach and turns it yellow, like the yellow of the bile. It is not a serious disease, according to the *po'e kahiko*. It is a disease that comes when a man is in his prime, when his body is strong and takes in large quantities of food. When the man becomes feverish and ill, the bile flows freely and cleans out the blood and the remnants of food in the stomach. That is what the yellow bile in a man's stomach is for, to clean out the body. However, in the opinion of some people, the bile is a cause of disease.

By the time the instruction with the *'ili'ili*, the pebbles, was finished, the pupils knew thoroughly the symptoms and the "rules" (*na kulana ma'i a me na loina*) for treatment of the diseases from the crown of the head to the soles of the feet. Then the teacher would bring in a man who had many disorders and would call the pupils one by one to go and "feel," *haha*, for the diseases. If the diagnosis (*'ike haha*) was the same as that of the teacher, then the teacher knew that the pupil had knowledge of *haha*.

---

* Andrews (1865).

If it was a disease that was curable (*he ma'i ola*), the pupil would say so; if the man was halfway between life and death, then the pupil would tell what he found in his diagnosis, in accordance with his knowledge of *haha*. If the man were close to death, he might have *papaku* (obstipation) or *kua'eho* ("tumor;" lipoma); his abdomen would be bloated (*'ohao*). If not these, there might be swelling (*pehu*), and his back would turn purplish (*kuawehi*). However, if it were *iki'alamea* (ulcers), he would gasp for breath (*nae 'owaiku*) and have severe cramps (*haikala*). If there were a chance for him to recover, the pupil would say so, and if it were evident that he was going to die because there were complications (*ua komo iloko o ka pe'a*) [from *'ana'ana*], the summation of the diagnosis would be that the man was dying because someone had obtained his "bait." If the symptoms of all the diseases were in accordance with the knowledge learned from the "table of pebbles," then the pupil had learned how to diagnose by palpation (*ka 'ike ma ka haha*).

Sometimes a diagnosis by *haha* was erroneous. A "structural defect" (*ke'e*), or a bit of hard fecal matter (*pauku 'eka*) might be mistaken for a *pou pa'a* or a *pou lewa* (rigid or movable "lump"), or for *hoaka* (a disease of the abdomen, perhaps appendicitis), or *papaku* (obstipation), or *'eho* (lipoma), and a mistake made in predicting death. But not by those who were extremely skilled.*

THE REMEDIES OF THE KAHUNAS OF LONOPUHA

In very ancient times many people observed the rules of the art of healing (*'oihana kahuna lapa'au*), but in later times most of them abandoned medical practices because there was not much sickness within the race. Foreigners (*malihini*) had not yet come from other lands; there were no fatal diseases (*luku*), no epidemics (*ahulau*), no contagious diseases (*ma'i lele*), no diseases that eat away the body (*ma'i 'a'ai*), no venereal diseases (*ma'i pala a me ke kaokao*). Therefore, the *kahuna pa'ao'ao* and the *kahuna 'ana'ana* were always victorious. *Ho'opi'opi'o* sorcery was a later practice, more than a century later. In the time of Kamehameha I the practices of the Lonopuha kahunas were revived. Kua'ua'u was a kahuna of the order of Lonopuha, and he taught this art of healing to the chiefs. That was the beginning of the spread of this medical art, one which was famous in the time of Kamehameha I.**

Pa'ali'i is the *koali*, morning glory, and is much used by the *kahuna lapa'au*. The fleshy root of the *koali* (*koali ho'i'o*) is given, either baked (*kalua*) or mixed with other things. The unmixed *koali* root is favored; it burns the throat like fire and is preferred by the preparer of remedies (*kumu lapa'au*). Mixed *koali* is fit for women and children, for it is not very strong and is easy to take by those who are weak. The trouble is that it works but slightly on the bowels.

Ho'oilo, a bitter (*'awa'awa*) medicine, is a very strong purgative (*la'au naha*); and *peka'a*, also called *kukapihe* (a mixture of *koko* bark and kukui-nut sap), if diluted until it is a weak solution, is a good laxative.

---
* September 1, 1870.
** September 15, 1870.

Kulukulu'a consists of drops of green kukui-nut sap and drops of *'akoko* sap. The drops must be counted, for the potion purges blood too and is extremely strong.

Lumaha'i is easy to take, but it does act on the bowels. *Moa* also works on the bowels as a purgative. It is a pleasant and delicious drink to take and can be drunk as a tea with crackers or bread, but it gives gripes (*nahunahu*); and although it does act on the bowels, it does not cure the sickness. There are very many other purgatives used by the *kahuna lapa'au*, the last to be mentioned being the *waiki* [or *waiiki*, an enema concoction].

Waiki was a chiefs' remedy and a famous one, and was administered by a kahuna chief. Forty or more people helped him prepare for the *waiki* treatment. The *waiki* [concoction] was made from two young *ipu 'awa'awa* gourds; each was cut in half, two pieces were used, and two thrown away. Some salt was added, and the juice squeezed into a small cup, to a depth scarcely enough to cover a fingernail. This was used as an enema (*holoi malalo me ka hahano*).

When an *ali'i* or a *kaukau ali'i* or a *kanaka* [a relative of the chief who served or supported the chief] was to be given the *waiki* enema, many "rules" were observed before administering it. The *kupele* treatment came first. There are many kinds of *kupele;* tender taro leaves and coconut, poi and coconut, sweet potato and coconut, small taro offshoots and leaf stalks and tender leaves combined with coconut, or the fleshy part of the *hala* fruit and coconut mixed with mashed sweet potatoes might make up the *kupele*. *Kupele* was given in order to build up flesh on the body, and to create an appetite for "food and fish." After this, a little purgative was taken, [made from] *moa*, or *pilikai*, or *pa'ali'i* perhaps, then *halehau* [*hau* bark soaked in water until the water is "slippery"] to give relief to the body and to tempt the appetite for "food and fish." When the body felt well and comfortable and no longer ill, it was the right time for the *waiki*. The preparation for the *waiki* treatment was a well-publicized day, and "cousins," relatives, and friends gathered. When the day set for the *waiki* treatment came, the *kahuna lapa'au* and his helpers made ready the reviving lotions (*ehu*), the drinks of *hau* water (*'apu hau*) and *pala* water to be taken as an after-drink to give relief, and a milder *waikea* enema [juice of fresh kukui nuts mixed with water], with heated stones to warm it, was prepared. Stones were heated for a steam bath, and *'awapuhi* ginger was pounded up with *maile* and other wild plants of the mountains for reviving the patient when he fainted after the *waiki* had acted on his bowels. When everything was ready, the only voice to be heard was the kahuna's.

Two young *ipu 'awa'awa* gourds were divided into halves, two halves were pounded with salt and strained into a small cup, scarcely to the depth of a fingernail, and the concoction injected into the rectum (*aia ma ka 'olemu e hahano ai*). The *waiki* was a burning concoction, and the milder *waikea* enema, and the potions of *hau* bark, *pala* fern, or *palau* yam were given to relieve the burning sensation when the bowels began to loosen.

After the *waiki* had been injected, there came discharges of yellow, then green, then fibrous, then whitish substances (*o ka lena, o ke pakaiea, o ka maka'upena, o ka 'oliko kaikea*); the patient became feverish (*pi'i ka wela*); a *waikea* enema was given, and a drink of the *'apu hau* (*kaomi ka 'apu hau maluna*); flecks of blood appeared in the discharge, and then bloody discharges (*hakiakoko*). That was the difficult moment, and the kahuna and his helpers got ready for it. After two or three gourds had been filled with blood, the patient was revived, and a *waikea* enema given. The blood was "sooty" and dark (*a pa'uhale, a 'ele'ele*), and the patient fainted and was restored (*a ola*) several times. When the blood turned pinkish (*'ohelohelo*), the patient was revived, warmed over the heated stones, and washed clean. The patient now looked like an old man, and one would think that the *waiki* treatment had indeed killed him. Sometimes it did, but those who survived enjoyed vigorous health afterward, up to extreme old age.

Here is another way of giving the *waiki* treatment: a dried gourd, which had been kept in the house until needed, was put to soak in water; a well-flattened stone was heated in fire until it was red hot, then a hole was dug and the red hot stone laid in it. The hole was covered by the gourd, or half of the gourd, that had been soaked in water, with a hole made in it so that the steam might rise through and be of the proper warmth. Then the steam was directed (*kololio*) into the rectum. This treatment was an emptying (*he puhaka*), and blood appeared, as in the real *waiki* treatment; this was also a *waiki* treatment.

A remedy much thought of by this class of kahunas was the saltwater enema, *kaiku*. Two scoops of salt, making two handfuls, were left overnight in a container [with a little water] and the next morning given as an enema.

The *kaiku* treatment was a "gravy train," (literally, "pig gravy," *he kai pua'a nui keia o ke kaiku*) for the unscrupulous kahuna. Seeing a man with no illness at all, a kahuna might say, "You are a very sick man; you have high blood pressure (*koko lana*)." When the man heard this he would have the kahuna give him a *kaiku* enema. Its action is strong; it gripes mightily; and the intense pain would make him writhe. But the kahuna would not come near him until the man could no longer stand it and would offer to give him a pig an *anana* in length, and several sets of sleeping tapas. Then the kahuna would come and give him a *kaikea* enema. This *kaikea* enema was real salt water with one mouthful (*mana*) of masticated kukui nuts or *koali* stirred into it. This was given as an enema into the rectum, then a soothing potion of *palau*. The man would recover his health and be glad.

The enema was a treatment much used by this class of kahunas. Palaha was the first teacher to have thought of the benefits of the enema. This is how Palaha reasoned: When the water of a stream is stagnant, it is filthy; when a freshet comes, the water becomes clean—all the trash and filth are gone. So it is in filthy pools—when fresh water comes in, the filth is removed. Palaha meditated on this, and when he understood it, he gave an enema to a dog. Seeing the benefits of the enema, he thought of the illness of his father Puheke. By experimenting, he found the benefits of the enema given below (*hahano malalo*) and the purgative given above (*ho'onaha iho maluna*), and which illnesses to treat by means of loosening the bowels, and how to check the action of the bowels. When Puheke died, Palaha cut his father open, according to his father's wish that he look inside and see what the disease was and what its symptoms were. Because of his work,

Palaha became famous in the order of the *kahuna kapa'au,* and he and his father entered into the line of succession of Lonopuha kahunas (*papa mo'o kahuna Lonopuha*).

There are two serious illnesses that this order of kahunas considered important: *pehu* [edema] and *'ohao* [ascites]. There are four kinds of *pehu. Pehu kumu niu* is one that affects the legs. It goes upward twice, and goes down again to the feet, and at the third rising of the swelling, the patient dies. The abdomen swells (*pi'i pu ka 'ohao*), but the appetite for "fish and poi" remains, though death results. There is some relief if the patient heeds advice. In this kind of *pehu* a dire outcome may be predicted (*he pehu ho'oiloilo 'ia keia*). *Pehu kala'e,* extending from neck to feet, is a swollen condition of the whole body, with a dark coloration extending up the back (*ki'i kuaweli ma ke kua*) and the navel barely perceptible (*none iki ka piko*). From neck to head, however, the appearance is unchanged. Then, like a calm day when the mountains are cloudless and no one knows from where appear the mists to cover them but clouds and fog roll in, followed by rain and storm, so does death come to one who has the *pehu kala'e.* This *pehu* is called *pehu ale-'ai,* a "swelling that gulps down food" [the appetite remains]. It is one in which death can be predicted (*he pehu ho'oiloilo 'ia keia i ka make*), but there is some relief if the patient heeds advice. *Pehu pauku* is a swelling in only a portion of the body, and is curable (*he pehu ola*) if the patient heeds advice. It is one of the diseases that can be cured by the *kahuna lapa'au. Pehu holoku* is the swelling of the entire body; from head to feet no part remains unswollen. It is curable if the patient heeds, and this *pehu,* too, is among the diseases that can be cured by the *kahuna lapa'au.* The three remedies appropriate for *pehu* are: astringents (*liki*); ointments (*ehu*); and purgatives (*la'au ho'onaha*). One must be careful not to drink too much water, and to eat dry foods suitable for people who are in a bloated condition.

There remain many other medicines, from the sea to the mountains—as many as there are diseases in man. If a list of diseases were arranged with a list of medicines, and a Hawaiian "Book of Anatomy" (*Buke Anetomia Hawaii*) were made up, the diseases that attack the body, the symptoms, and the remedies for them would all be there.*

CLASS 5. KAHUNA A KA 'ALAWA MAKA AND 'IKE LIHILIHI

The kahunas who diagnosed by critical observation and by insight (*'ike ma ka lihilihi a ma ka 'alawa*), as well as by *haha,* had superior knowledge and skill. In their discernment (*nana maoli*) and interpretations (*koho*) they were like *kaula* prophets, perhaps [divinely directed]. When one was called to come and look at a patient who lay between life and death, he could tell what had caused the illness just by pressing a hand on the crown of the head, or by touching the tips of the toenails, and he would begin by telling the cause of the illness, if it had begun in the stomach, and was *pou,* perhaps. Or he might say that the temperature had risen, the back had become pained, the feet cold, the loins heavy, the chest gripped

---
* September 22, 1870.

with pain, the eyes weak, the head dizzy, and the ears ringing [symptoms of influenza]. All this the kahuna would tell, and also the time when the illness had begun, without having been told beforehand. When he told the patient the characteristics (*'ano*) of the illness, the patient would assent—in amazement that the kahuna would know these things—for usually it was the sick man who would first tell his symptoms to a kahuna, or the kahuna would *haha* and find the source of the illness in the "stomach" (*'opu*) and would then understand it. This diagnosing from critical observation, *'ike ma ka lihilihi,* was a very great art and it required truly great skill.

In diagnosing by insight, *'ike a ka 'alawa,* the kahuna might be in one place and the patient in another, and yet the kahuna could tell what the sickness was (*ke 'ano o ka ma'i*), the symptoms of the sickness from head to foot, and whether the patient was going to live or die. Now, if the kahuna could diagnose death before death occurred, he could use this skill for profit, or perhaps he would sympathize with the dying man in order to gain his aloha. Such kahunas were called deceivers, *he po'e ho'opunipuni,* because they knew beforehand that death was imminent. Some of them did not learn medical lore (*'oihana kahuna lapa'au*), and they, too, were called deceivers. They were led blindly by other things (*ma ke 'ano 'okoa*) [signs and omens]. Some kahunas, though, really knew whether or not a man was going to live or die when a messenger came to the house to fetch them, but they could not know this unless they had observed all the laws and rules [pertaining to the art of diagnosing by insight, *'ike a ka 'alawa*].

THE UNIVERSAL REMEDY

For *ka po'e kahiko* the sea was the remedy upon which all relied, from Hawaii to Kauai. When people took sick with stomach upsets (*'ino'ino ma ka 'opu*), griping stomach aches (*nahu*), fever (*wela*), grayish pallor (*hailepo*), squeamishness (*nanue na 'opu*), nausea (*polouea*), or dizziness (*niua*), the usual ailments caused by a change of regular diet from sweet potatoes to taro—or from taro to sweet potatoes—a drink of sea water was the universal remedy employed. Those who live on lands that grow sweet potatoes have foul stools (*ua 'eka ko lakou lepo*) when they change to taro lands, and are subject to worms (*ua ulu ka ilo maloko*). It is the same with those from lands where taro is grown when they go to lands where sweet potatoes are grown. Their custom therefore was to drink sea water.

In the early morning they lighted an imu for sweet potatoes and put them in to bake with a chicken and a dried fish. Then they fetched a large container full of sea water, a container of fresh water to wash away the salty taste, and a bunch of sugar cane. They would drink two to four cupfuls of sea water, then a cupful of fresh water, and then chew the sugar cane. The sea water loosened the bowels, and it kept on working until the yellowish and greenish discharges came forth (*puka pu no ka lena a me ke pakaiea*). Then the imu was opened, and the sweet potatoes and other foods eaten [without resulting discomfort]. The stomach felt fine, and the body of the elderly or the aged was made comfortable.

Another good use for sea water was to secure forgiveness (*huikala*). When someone in the family broke an oath sworn against another (*ho'ohiki 'ino*)—a man against his wife, a mother against her children, relatives against relatives, "cousins" against "cousins" (*hoahanau*), and so on—then the *pikai*, or sprinkling with salt water, was the remedy to remove [the repercussions from the breaking of the oath]. This is how it was done. A basin or bowl of real sea water, or of water to which salt had been added, in which were placed *'awa* rootlets (*huluhulu 'awa*) and *olena*, was the water to absolve and cleanse (*kalahala e huikala*) the family for the defilement (*haumia*) caused by the one who had broken his oath.

Any defilement pertaining to the house, to fishing, tapa printing, tapa beating, farming, or *wauke* cultivation, from which trouble had resulted, could be cleansed with *pikai*; it purified and caused an end to defilement. Implements of labor could also be cleansed of their defilement by *pikai*.

Another way to purify the family was this. In the evening, after dark, a "canoe procession" was formed (*wa'a huaka'i*, in which the participants lined up in single file, as in a canoe). The person at the head of the procession had a pig, another had tapa garments and *ninikea* tapas, and another held in his hands bunches of *kohekohe* grass. The last person in the line offered the prayers for forgiveness and carried the basin for the ritual procession to cleanse the defilement (*ka po'i ka'i huikala*). The ritual procession (*ka'i*) had to be perfect, with the voices responding in unison in the prayers for forgiveness and purification, and their steps exactly alike as they went in the procession and entered the *mua*, the "family chapel." They lighted the imu for the pig and continued their praying until the pig was cooked and eaten. The rewards (*uku*) they received were health, blessings, material prosperity, and other benefits of this kind to them all.*

NOTES TO PART FIVE

[1] This definition applies to Kamakau's discussion on child care. See also Notes 5 and 8.

[2] "Mary Pukui tells a true story of a family in which such a sacrifice was demanded. In this family firstborn daughters for generations had been unable to bear children alive. A certain firstborn daughter of the family had eight stillborn infants. She consulted a kahuna and was told that only by the death of one male in the family could she have a child that would live. One of the uncles of the family consented to offer himself and in a short time he was, as they say, 'prayed to death that others might live.' The firstborn was a girl. She lived, and the five children born after her, but she never bore children. She died in 1933." (Beckwith, 1934, Chapter 11, Note 2.)

[3] The kahuna's sign was the presence of little bumps, called *kukae'iole*, on the *'iewe*, which told how many more children were to come. [M.K.P.]

[4] For a modern account of transference of labor pains see Pukui (1942, pp. 360-361).

[5] *Pa'ao'ao* and *'ea* as medical classifications appear to have included predispositions to ailments and diseases as well as the ailments and diseases themselves. Kamakau's remarks and examples indicate that, in general, *pa'ao'ao* was a classification for malfunctionings of

---

* September 22, 1870.

the body, and *'ea* a classification for certain diseases now recognized as infectious. For an account of diseases prevalent in Hawaii in historic times, see Chapin (1954).

[6] "The cuttlefish markings which determine a child's future health were real blotches on the infant's abdomen supposed to resemble the shapes of cuttlefish. The disease was diagnosed by studying these markings. They were especially prominent on the fifth day" (Beckwith, 1934, Chapter 11, Note 4).

[7] Where the same Hawaiian name is applied to more than one plant, the botanical name given in Appendix I is that which is assumed to be the plant referred to by Kamakau. For specific prescriptions using many of the medicinal plants he mentions, see Spencer (1895) and Kaaiakamanu and Akina (1922).

[8] O. A. Bushnell, professor of microbiology at the University of Hawaii, and Frank Tabrah, M.D., of Kohala, Hawaii, were consulted for clarification of Kamakau's remarks on diseases. To them the editor is indebted for many helpful suggestions, including that of giving literal translations of Kamakau's descriptive terms except for those already established—that is, found in Andrews (1865) or in Pukui and Elbert (1957). The following comment on Hawaiian diseases was written by Dr. Tabrah in this connection:

> Translation of many of the Hawaiian terms for disease in early times cannot be certain, because accurate differentiation between afflictions had not yet been made by either Hawaiians or Haoles.
>
> By a comparison of Kamakau's descriptive Hawaiian terms with known diseases and signs, it is engaging from the vantage point of 100 years to attempt diagnoses of some of the diseases he lists. From Hawaiian descriptions, or other sources, the following translations seem reasonable:
>
> *Pala*—gonorrhea
> *Kaokao*—syphilis
> *'Ala'ala*—tuberculous adenitis
> *Puhi kaokao*—secondary syphilis
> *Kua puhi*—boils or abcesses
> *Kua 'o iwi*—inanation
> *Kua nanaka*—confluent lesions on the back
> *Ihu 'ole*—syphilitic "saddle nose" or damage from leprosy
> *Make 'ole*—blindness
> *Po'o pilau*—impetigo or eczema
> *Umauma naha*—inanation, starvation.

[9] "*Ea kakua* may refer to secondary lues with its 'serpiginous' lesions, most prominent on the back" [Dr. Tabrah]. Similar prescriptions using *limu kalemakapi'i* are given by Spencer (1895, p. 14), and Kaaiakamanu and Akina (1922, p. 60).

[10] See also Kamakau (1961, pp. 416-418). Kamakau's description of the disease was omitted from that published account; it is included here as a matter of record.

[11] "An excellent description of congestive heart failure," says Dr. Tabrah. His translations of some of the disorders treated by the *kahuna haha* follow:

> *Pou*—diastasis recti
> *Pou pa'a*—fixed ridge-like mass in epigastrium
> *Pou lewa*—movable ridge-like mass in epigastrium
> *Papaku*—bowel obstruction
> *Iki'alamea*—gastric or duodenal ulcer
> *Ane*—scabies
> *Honokoi*—enlarged inguinal lymph node(s)
> *Pu'u holo*—movable or moving mass; visceral tumor
> *'Ohao*—ascites
> *Pehu*—edema
> *Pehu kumu niu*—edema of legs
> *'Eho*, or *kua'eho*—lipoma.

PART SIX

PART SIX

O ka 'Ana'ana a me ka Hana 'Ino — Magic and Sorcery

'ANA'ANA MAGIC

THE ART OF *'ana'ana*[1] is very old, although it does not date back to the time of Wakea *ma*. It spread after their time—from the time of Huanuikala'ila'i, chief of Oahu about 39 generations later. Hua's son was Kuheilani, and the sisters of Kuheilani were Uliiuka and Uliikai. Uliiuka was the one who reared Kana in the uplands of Wahiawa, Oahu; Uliikai lived with a fisherman down at Kualaka'i [Kaluako'i, Molokai].

Uliiuka became an *'aumakua* for the *kahuna 'ana'ana* [who prayed people into illness or death]; for the *kahuna 'ana'ana kuni* [who divined the source of death from *'ana'ana* and who retaliated in kind]; for the *kahuna kuni 'o* [who healed one afflicted by illness from another's *'ana'ana*]; the *kahuna kuni ola* [who also divined the source of the *'ana'ana* illness and who saved and avenged the victim]; and for the *kahuna 'ana'ana kalahala* [who freed one from his "sins of commission and omission" that had been the cause of being a victim of *'ana'ana*]. These were different branches of the *kahuna 'ana'ana* profession, and there were distinct prayers (*kulana pule*) for each, up into the hundreds. Most of them were offered to the *'aumakua*, and they enumerated those of the heavens; of the east, north, south, and west; of the mountains, the sea, the water, and the land—from those below of Milu's company (*ko lalo o Milu ma*) to those of the heavens and of the earth. The prayers were the foundation to be learned.

'Ana'ana can be the most evil of evil deeds (*hana 'ino*); evil spirits of darkness become friends of men, and devils and demons (*diabolo me na daimonio*) and "ghosts of the night" (*lapu o ka po*) empower them. But to a humble man who is pure in thought, *'ana'ana* is a virtuous profession (*'oihana hemolele*); it is a means of absolution (*he pu'u kalahala*) and of dispelling troubles. The gods will help such a man until he "walks with a cane, has eyes blurred like a rat's, and

grows white as the sugar cane tassel," *a kani koʻo, a haumakaʻiole, a ulu ko kea.*

When a person wanted to be instructed in *'anaʻana,* this is what he did. He took a fine fat sow, black all over, and 40 sets of sleeping tapas (*hoʻokahi kanaha kuʻina kapa*) to the kahuna, and offered the gifts in the name of the *'aumakua* and the gods of *'anaʻana,* and in the name of the kahuna who was to be his teacher. Then he released the pig and laid it down before the kahuna. This was the correct thing to do. Some people, however, only wanted to learn *'anaʻana,* how to pray to death, and brought gifts for the prayer of Nihoʻaikaulu, one of the *'aumakua wahine* appealed to in *'anaʻana* prayers. Hers is the famous prayer of Oahu called *O kini Kailua, he mano Kaneohe* ("A host of Kailua, a multitude of Kaneohe"). After receiving his offerings and gifts, the kahuna would give him the words of the prayer to be learned.

The work (*'oihana*) of learning the magical prayers, the *pule 'anaʻana,* was a laborious undertaking, filthy and deadly and dangerous (*poʻokoʻi*); one that required the eating of disgusting and poisonous foods. It was carried on under kapus and great consecration. It kept a man in isolation—apart from women and children, and from the houses of others. He must not covet the big fishes of others, or their clumps of sugar cane, or bunches of bananas, mounds of taro or potatoes, or their pigs or dogs, or their sleeping tapas. He must not take another's wife, nor lust after another's daughter. In learning the *pule 'anaʻana* a man had to control his temper; if someone hit him he must not retaliate. It was for the gods to take care of him and to avenge him upon his enemies. When death came to the very door of the house, he was to remember the gods and the things that he had been taught which had wearied his body and cost him the material wealth of the world. He must not send forth his death-dealing prayers first (*mai lele mua*). He must not look upon a heap of wealth brought to his door as the payment for healthy blood (*waiwai koko ola;* that is, for causing the death of an innocent person); he must not take it, lest his life in this world be shortened. The wealth he might accept was that which was brought for the detection of one whose blood was foul (*waiwai koko pilau;* that is, one who had prayed a victim to death).* This is how he did it. In broad daylight he would light a fire and *kuni*[2] (burn some part of the victim's body and pray for a divination of the perpetrator of this death). He would say aloud before the whole assembly the name of the person whose spirit, *kahoaka,* was revealed to him. Whether it was that of a chief or of a commoner, he said the name before them all; and predicted the day on which that person would die, and the affliction (*maʻi*) of which he would die. He had now accomplished the first lesson taught by the kahuna.

Next, a *moku hale,* a house set apart for this training, was built, and there his course of instruction began. His hair was kapu, and must not be cut, and his hair and beard became snarled and tangled. His water gourd was kapu, his food calabash was kapu, his sleeping place was kapu. It was kapu for him to carry food, or anything else, on a carrying stick at his neck. His body was consecrated, and was kapu; his malo became foul, for it was kapu to bathe in water. And it was kapu

---

* July 21, 1870.

to touch a woman with his hands. The only time he was free to carry things was when friends brought food and stood outside the wooden fence surrounding the *moku hale* and called to those within. All he did was to learn the prayers, and to pray continuously (*kuili*) night and day until the prayers were so memorized that they would slip from his mouth as easily as an *olioli* or *mele,* without hesitating or stammering.

Each teacher had from three to five pupils. The teacher, too, lived under kapu. When he saw that the pupils were skillful, he had each of them prepare a fat pig, three *iwilei* (cubits) in length, for the *'ailolo* ceremony, with the tip of the snout, the tips of the ears, and the spleen wrapped separately. If the back of one of the pigs split open in the cooking, the teacher would say that it would not be well for the pupil who had brought that pig to practice (*malama*) what he had been taught, or he would become a *kahuna 'aihamu*—a murdering kahuna—and that would result in his death. If a pig was all right, but an eye had fallen out or the throat was cracked, that, too, was a bad sign. That pupil should not practice what he had been taught, for he would have an insatiable greed for other people's property [literally, a "scarred throat," *pu'u po'aka*], and the teacher would advise him to abandon the art in order to escape death. If the *lolo* ritual went well (*i maika'i ka lolo ana*), from the cooking of the pig to the eating of the food consecrated for the ceremony, he would tell the pupil whose pig it was that he had been chosen by the gods; he was to practice the prayers. Thus the teacher gave advice according to all the omens and signs of the pig.

At the end of the first *lolo* ceremony, another set of prayers was taught, and the rituals that accompanied them, and then another ceremony performed. This went on until 10 or even up to 20 such ceremonies had been held. When there had been many ceremonies and many regulations laid down for the various sets of prayers to all above and below, until the pupil knew as much as his teacher, then the teacher would say to the pupil, "Concentrate your prayers (*E kia ko pule*) on that solid cliff and make it slide," and the pupil would concentrate on the cliff until it crumbled. He would concentrate his prayer on a hard rock and it broke up as if nothing, just as if a roll of powder had been inserted into the rock and had broken it to fragments. He would concentrate his prayer upon a grove of trees and the trees would wither. He would concentrate his prayer upon a whale and it would be cast up on land. He would concentrate his prayer upon a shark that had eaten a man, and the wicked shark, and the man, would land on shore. The mana of the *'ana'ana* prayers was his, and the mana was made manifest. Another thing he could do was to make fire come out of a rock, or out of a green, growing tree. The kahuna *'ana'ana* could drink cups of poison (*'apu koheoheo*) as if they contained nothing but water; earthworms and lizards did him no harm; the poisonous *'auhuhu* and the bitter *ipu 'awa'awa* were as nothing; *kumimi* crabs and *'opihi 'awa* were as nothing.

When the fire was lighted and the flags for the *kuni* ceremony (*lepa kuni*) were set up on some important day when there was a dead king or a high chief whose cause of death he was to divine, an audience would gather to listen to the kahuna's words of prophecy and divination (*'olelo wanana a me na 'olelo hoakaka*). Before making his divination, he prayed and threw in the *maunu*, the personal "bait," of the dead chief into the fire, and as he continued praying, he fought with the "devil" (*diabolo;* the spirit of the person who had caused the death). It was the spirit of the living person, his *kahoaka,* that was fighting with the kahuna. He fell on the ground and rose again, still praying; fell down again, and rose up—and so on it went. If it was the *kahoaka* of a high chief, the crowd would see gashes on the head of the kahuna, and blood flowing. There are perhaps some still living who witnessed the *kuni* ceremony of Kalawai'amilu for Ka'oleioku at Napuoko's fireplace at Honokohau, Hawaii. [Ka'oleioku died in 1818.]

At the fireplaces for the *kuni* ceremonies—the *kapuahi kuni*—of Kahekili Ke'eaumoku for his wife Kuaiaea (Kekuaiaea), Kahakauila was the kahuna at the one at Waimea, Kauai; and Lokai and Pu'ali were the kahunas at the *kapuahi kuni* at Waialua, Oahu. These were the kahunas who detected her killer (*oia ka po'e i 'a'e kino ke kahoaka*), and when the fires in the *kapuahi kuni* were extinguished, he was roasted whole (*kalua pa'a*) in the *umu* at Waikele in Ewa, Oahu. The kukui trees of Waipahu were dried up by the prayers of Pu'ali. [This was in 1822.]

Such kahunas spoke out openly, without fear of a kapu chief, even if he was a ruler. That was always the way of the *kahuna kuni.* There was mana in the old days, and those people who were correctly taught had real mana; eyewitnesses could not say that their mana was false (*wahahe'e*). But the way in which kahunas are taught in these days is perhaps not correct. Most of them are murdering kahunas, *kahuna 'aihamu;* they do not come out in the open. They have perhaps just taken the form (*'ano*) of the prayers and mixed them with Molokai ways; the ancient ways have been mixed with the newer one of *ho'opi'opi'o* sorcery.

THE DIVISIONS OF 'ANA'ANA

There were many divisions within *'ana'ana* magic. The methods and the prayers were separate, and the forms of the prayers and the rituals were different. The *kahuna 'ana'ana kuni* performed in the light of day. One of his duties as a *kahuna 'ana'ana* in his practice of *kuni* (*iloko o kana 'oihana kuni*) was to *kalahala*—remove the grounds for offense within the victim, and so remove (*wehe*) the affliction (*make*) sent by another. It was one of his duties also to practice *kuni ola*—to cause the death first of the one using *'ana'ana,* and so release (*ho'oku'u*) the intended victim. This was an important work of the kahunas who learned *'ana'ana,* and one famous among the people. It was performed openly, not in secret. It was for this *kuni ola* that the *kahuna 'ana'ana* in the old days prepared their *imu loa,* their "long ovens," for the treatment of a patient to remove the influence of *'ana'ana* upon him.

The *kahuna kuni 'o* was similar to the *kahuna kuni.* He was a kahuna well skilled in his rituals, but he had only half as many of these as the *kahuna kuni.* His main work was to heal (*ho'ola*), and he shunned praying another to death;

he used the mana of his prayers only upon those enemies who had first used *'ana'ana* on others. This kahuna could free (*kala*) those who were being prayed against (*'ana'ana 'ia*).

The *kahuna 'ana'ana 'aihamu* were spoken of as being very evil. They were called *kahuna po'oko'i,* "adz heads," perhaps because kahunas of this type were frequently beheaded, or perhaps because they were so frequently pointed out as death-dealing kahunas. These were the kahunas who took another's *maunu;* these were the kahunas who robbed others of their possessions—of their "fish," and "poi," their wealth, their handsome husbands or beautiful wives, and favorite children. Because so many families and their friends were put to grief for those who died from the doings of these murderous kahunas, they treated them harshly, cutting off their heads and dragging their bodies along the highway.

Was it only in Hawaii that there was magic incantation, *pule 'ana'ana?* The Holy Scriptures say, in Deuteronomy 18:10,11: "There shall not be found among you anyone that maketh his son or his daughter to pass through the fire, or that useth divination (*kahuna 'ana'ana*), or an observer of times (*mea nana i ke ao*), or an enchanter (*mea nana i ka mo'o*), or a witch (*mea kilo*), or a charmer (*mea ho'owalewale i na nahesa*), or a consulter with familiar spirits (*mea ninau i na 'uhane 'ino*), or a wizard (*he kupua*), or a necromancer (*po'e ninau i ka po'e make*)."

There were two types of prayers, the *pule kaholo,* and the *pule 'umi.*[3] Here is a *pule kaholo,* one of the *'ana'ana* prayers which is a *pule kuni* for one who is already dead. At the beginning of the praying, the most important thing is to appeal to the *'aumakua* gods of the *kahuna 'ana'ana,* and enumerate those of the heavens, the firmament, the four directions, the ocean, and earth—those in every place whatsoever—and then to invoke Uli. After that, the prayer begins, invoking Uliiuka, Uliikai, Ulinanapono, and Ulinanahewa.

PULE KAHOLO

Arise, O Kama! Break open the front!
Arise, O Kama! Break open the head, O Kama!
Seize the victim, O Kama!
The maggots crawl in your head, O victim!
Seize the victim, O Kama!

Maggots bunch together in your eyes, O victim,
Your mouth is eaten by maggots, O victim,
Your mouth rots away with maggots, O victim;
Disease breaks through your throat, O victim,
It is broken through by maggots, eaten by maggots;
Maggots itch in your throat, O victim!

Disease cracks your chest,
The chest ulcerates, eaten away by maggots,
By many maggots; is eaten away by maggots, O victim!

Disease breaks open your back, splits open your back;
Maggots crawl in your back, the maggots crowd;*
The maggots move around, the maggots keep your back raw;
You are broken open by maggots, disemboweled by maggots,
Maggots dig open your back, O victim!

Disease eats out your stomach,
Disease rots your stomach,
Disease multiplies in your stomach,
Maggots crowd in your stomach,
Maggots crawl in your stomach,
Maggots move about in your stomach,
Maggots take root in your stomach,
Flies buzz in your stomach,
Flies hum in your stomach,
Flies swarm in your stomach,
Flies that produce many maggots, O victim!
You are killed in the night, O victim, by Kama!

Disease starts in your loins (*i ko leu*),
Disease grows in your loins,
Disease festers in your loins,
Disease rots your loins,
Disease multiplies in your loins!
Disease cracks open your groin (*i ko hola*),
Disease comes out through your groin,
Maggots squirm in your groin,
Maggots crowd in your groin;
Flies swarm in your groin,
Flies hum in your groin,
In your groin touched by Kama!

Disease breaks through your thigh (*i ko 'uha*),
Disease bursts out of your thigh,
Eaten by disease until it splits, O victim!
Crawl, O maggots, with a drawing-up motion,
Break through, O maggots, your thigh bones,
Root, O maggots, in your thigh bones,
And disease break out in the calves of your legs!

Crawl, O maggots; itch, O maggots;
Eat, O maggots; root, O maggots;
Disembowel, O maggots, the victim!
You are rotten with maggots,
O victim who is seized fast!
You are slow, O victim,
You are rotten; you are changed!

Heaha ka i'a—what is the food?
A *kumimi* crab, an earthworm, a dragon fly grub;
'Akia, ho'awa, and *'auhuhu,*
Ipu 'awa, and *'ilie'e.*[4]

---

* August 4, 1870.

When the first part is finished (*'Amama i ka lele mua*), eat an eyeball, the slimy part, and continue with:

> This is a death I inflict (*ka'u make*): he is to go and lie in the roadway, and his back split open (*nanaka ke kua*), a stench arise, and he be devoured by dogs. A death I inflict is to start in him while he is in his own place, and when he goes elsewhere he is to vomit blood, and die, and his grease (*hinu*) is to flow on the road, and he be eaten by dogs. This is a death I inflict: he is to go to the ocean, and when he returns to shore, his grease is to pour out of him as he goes. This is a death I inflict: he is to fall off a cliff and break his bones, and his grease pour out on the highway. This is a death I inflict: he is to be buried in the earth five *anana* deep, and be dug up by dogs. Such is the death I inflict.

In from five to fifteen days they [your victims] will be dead. When you see the characteristic signs of these deaths (*'ike 'oukou i na aouli o keia mau make*) on your relatives and friends, do not go and wail for them, or the prayer will return upon you, and you yourselves will die.

PULE KAHOLO

For a life, a death,
A great *ka'upu* bird is calling,
Sounding nearby, calling out.
What is the food it is calling for?
A man is the food it is calling for.
Thunder cracks in the heavens,
The earth quakes.

Your legs bend,
Your hands become paralyzed,
Your back hunches,
Your neck is twisted,
Your head breaks open,
Your liver rots,
Your intestines fall to pieces.

You have crawled by, O land shell,
O great shell chirping on the ridges of the mountain,
Chirping, calling out.
What is the food it is calling for?
A man is the food it is calling for.
Thunder cracks in the heaven,
The earth quakes, the lightning flashes.

Your legs bend,
Your hands become paralyzed,
Your back hunches,
Your neck is twisted,
Your chin is crooked,
Your eyes are sunken;
Disease has broken into the brain,
Your liver rots,
Your intestines fall to pieces.

A great owl calls out,
Whistling as it calls.
What is the food it is calling for?
A man is the food it is calling for.
Thunder cracks in the heavens,
The earth quakes, the lightning flashes. . . .

PULE 'UMI HO'ANO

Numbness, numbness, numbness, numbness,
Spreads, spreads, spreads, spreads,
Stiffens, stiffens, stiffens, stiffens;
Your head droops, droops, droops,
Bends over, bends over,
It droops, droops.

His eyes droop,
His nose droops,
His mouth droops,
His neck droops. . . .

In the praying of the *kahuna 'ana'ana* and the *kahuna kuni* for the *kuni make* or the *kuni ola* ritual, when they came to this prayer, they removed their malos and "took the bait of the victim" (*ka lawe maunu ka'ameha'i*). The *kahuna 'ana'ana* and the *kahuna kuni* acted insanely (*he pupule*) amid the people there in the open. The *kahuna 'aihamu* did not—he worked in secret. But in their devilish deeds (*'oihana diabolo*), they were alike.

In preparing for the prayer ritual of a *kuni* ceremony, the *kapuahi kuni*, the ritual fireplace, was set blazing with *ho'awa* and *'akia* with stalks and leaves still green. The firesticks were rubbed (*hi'a ke ahi*), and the fire lighted with green leaves serving as kindling and green wood as fuel, and it sprang into a blaze. Only by prayer can fire be lighted in water. The *kahuna kuni* continued with his *kuni* ritual, and when the fire was blazing in the *kapuahi kuni* he threw the bait of the dead person into the fire. A rainbow would arch overhead, misty rains would fall, and lightning would flash about the *kapuahi kuni*. Thunder would peal with a rattling sound, like a fluttering sheet of tapa, and the vibrations would strike down into the fireplace and scatter the ashes—[signs that the forces of nature were responding to the prayers]. Then the kahuna began the prayer for the burning of the bait.

PULE KUNI KA'AMEHA'I

Coming around corners, coming straight forward,
Here they come, exposing themselves;
Coming around corners, coming straight forward,
Here they come, exposing themselves.
Here is So-and-so, going down there,
And that woman, coming this way,
To that grove of trees, to that grove of trees. . . .

And so on until the bait was entirely gone. As the *kahuna kuni* did this, the devils fought with him. As they smote him with clubs, he fell down beside the fireplace, and blood flowed from his head and body. The assemblage would say, "This is a kahuna of mana, a kahuna of knowledge." The kahuna would say (*wanana*), "I feel regret for my ritual today. There are about 40 persons, men, women, and children—some of them chiefs—whom I have detected in my fireplace (*i 'a'e iloko o ku'u kapuahi kuni*); the number who have been exposed grows to the hundreds." At this time in the burning (*kuni*) and the praying (*'ana'ana*), the *kahuna kuni* and the *kahuna 'ana'ana* drank down poisonous potions of earthworms, lizards, dragonfly grubs, *'auhuhu, 'akia, ipu 'awa,* and other poisons that kill men. Wondrous indeed are the works of devils. The ashes from the *kapuahi kuni* were taken and thrown into the sea, and some were taken to the source of a stream. Such were the practices of the *kahuna kuni,* the *kahuna 'ana'ana,* and the *kahuna 'o.*

An adz was the first gift to be given to a *kahuna kuni;* and an *'o'o,* a digging stick, the first gift to a *kahuna 'o.* But if the *kahuna kuni* or the *kahuna 'ana'ana* felt that the payment for the service was meager, he might skip through the prayers. However, if the kahuna saw a relative of his own in the apparition (*ma ke kahoaka*), and skipped through the prayers so that there was some bait left [rendering the prayers ineffectual], or if he freed (*kala*) the perpetrator in his prayers, then his prayers returned upon himself. Thus did Uli regard his act (*a pela iho la o Uli e nana mai ai*).

I have seen a *kuni* fireplace lighted with green wood. This was in 1822, at Waialua, Oahu. The *kuni* ceremony had been ordered by Kahekili Ke'eaumoku, a brother of Ka'ahumanu, because of the death of his wife Kekuaiaea (Kuaiaea) on Kauai. *Ka'ameha'i* of Kekuaiaea was given to be burned (*kuni*) openly by all the kahunas of Waialua, to reveal who had prayed her to death (*e ho'ike i ka mea nana i 'ana'ana o* Kekuaiaea). All the kahunas saw the same apparition, and said the name of a certain chief. Some of the kahunas felt regret for their master (*haku*) when they saw him as the *kahoaka,* but because of the number of people who performed the *kuni* ceremony from Kauai to Hawaii, that chief died. I saw with my own eyes the great number of *kuni* fireplaces.

Here is a good thing I have seen. There was a great fish-poisoning day (*la holahola nui*) from Waialua to the fishing grounds at Mokuleia, called a "*hola moku,*" a district poisoning. A woman named Kihewakeoho was with a man at Waialua. One of them caught a *manini* fish, and the other an *aholehole,* and bit their heads. The fishes wriggled down into their throats, and stuck. The two struggled about on the surface of the water, and, as there were many people there, they were pulled ashore. They were almost dead. The fishes were too big to push in or to pull out, and their fins stood upright. The two were so near death that wailing began. A man named Kaloulu arrived, who was a *kahuna 'ana'ana* and *kahuna kuni.* He forecast life or death thus: "As I pray, if my prayer does not go well [literally, goes obliquely, *a'e ka pule*], they will die; wail for them. But if my prayer goes well (*lele wale*), they will not die." Then he called upon all the *'aumakua,* and then began his prayer, a prayer to heal.

PULE HO'OLA

Choke and live; strangle and live.
Soften, O fish, cook through, O fish,
Fall to pieces, O fish, grow soft, O fish;
Let the bones decay, let the bones turn to ash.

You ate the *manini* fish,
You are strangled and choked; life draws out fine;
You are doubled up; life draws out fine;
You are doubled over, helpless; life draws out fine.
You ate the *aholehole* fish,
You are strangled and choked; life draws out fine;
You are doubled over, helpless; life draws out fine. . . .

And so on he went. As the kahuna prayed, the fishes became as soft as fishes cooked in a fire and they came out, and the persons got their breaths again. *Pomaika'i ke ola na ke Akua*, "Blessed is life from God."*

THE SORCERY GODS OF MOLOKAI

The Kalaipahoa were poisonous and death-dealing tree gods (*mau akua la'au 'awa'awa keia a me ka make*). The trees themselves would have been harmless if they had not been combined with something else [*spirits*] that caused death, or if they had not been worshiped (*ho'omana 'ia*). From ancient times until today people have known these trees to be harmless, and have used them as firewood to cook *pao'o* fish at Kala'e, on Molokai. It is a wondrous thing how these trees became poisonous, since nonpoisonous trees of the same species (*'ano*) grow all over the islands, from Hawaii to Kauai. The first of these poisonous trees was an *a'e*, a reddish tree like the *koki'o*, with a brownish bark the same thickness as the *koki'o;* with the second was a *nioi*, a tree with thin bark; the third was an *'ohe*, a tree with white wood and brittle white bark. Its wood is not very tough; the branches break easily; the leaves are rounded and fade quickly, and are sometimes yellowed and drooping like the leaves of the *kauila*. These three trees were called Kalaipahoa because they were cut down and hacked with stone axes (*ke ko'i o ka pohaku*), the *pahoa* axes of Kaluako'i, Molokai. It was only after they had acquired mana, and their mana was known, that they were worshiped. The basis of their mana was in their power to kill. If anyone were fed a small fragment of their trunks (*kino*), even the smallest bit, or if it was rubbed against his skin, or if it had been beseeched for his destruction (*kalo ho'ola'a 'ia*), the person would die.

THE COMING OF THE KALAIPAHOA GODS

A certain man of Kalaupapa, named Kaneiakama, some of whose descendants are still living, went to play *puhenehene* at Haleolono in Kaluako'i. He bet success-

---
* August 11, 1870.

fully, and he and his people were going home laden with his winnings, when they reached Kapohako'i on the windward (*na'e*) side of Maunaloa. Here there was a *maika* playing ground just above Kaluako'i, to which all the players of Molokai, chiefs and people from Waikolu, Kalaupapa, Kala'e, and all the other places, resorted to roll *maika* stones, slide *pahe'e* sticks, and play all kinds of sports. In a sliding contest (*koi*) of Kaneiakama and one of the chiefs, Kaneiakama lost all his winnings to the chief, and then offered the household property belonging to his wife and children—a sow (*a kuhi i ka waiwai o ka hale a pili i na keiki me ka wahine, he kumulau pua'a*). For three nights he had stayed at the playing site and played, until his body was the only thing he had left, and this he was afraid to bet lest he be killed. He stayed another night at the playing ground, and, while dozing (*hihi'o*), someone spoke to him and said, "Beaten, eh?" (*Make ea?*) "Yes, beaten," he answered. The other said, "Not yet beaten. These are his days to win; yours are to come. You will win back what you have lost, and all of his possessions, and he will sneak away from you." "I have nothing left to put up," said Kaneiakama. "Bet your own body, and fear nothing," said the man.

When Kaneiakama awoke from this dream (*moe 'uhane*), he began by staking his body to be put to death against a very great counterwager (*kumuku'ai*). They played, and he won the wealth; they played wealth against wealth, and luck (*laki*) was with him all that day. Kaneiakama therefore resolved to take the man whom he had seen that night to be his god, and to worship him, and to offer the pig he had won as a sacrifice to this god.

That night as he slept the man spoke with him again, and revealed his name—Kaneikaulana'ula—and told him about himself and his companions and of their nature as gods. He said they would reveal their nature as gods (*'ano akua*) by coming with a grove of trees that would appear below the head of the *maika* playing ground of Maunaloa. On the appointed night Kaneiakama was led (*alaka'i*) to see these gods with his own eyes. His soul (*'uhane*) saw them, while he himself was hidden, lest he die. The soul of Kaneiakama watched a great number of spirits (*akua*) approaching with the trees until they reached Maunaloa. Kaneikaulana'ula was their leader, and it was he who had the mana. The first god commanded by him to enter a tree was Kahuilaokalani, who, although himself a god of great mana, obeyed and entered the red tree called *a'e*. The goddess Kapo, who led the female spirits, went into the *'ohe* with her mana, and Kaneikaulana'ula himself entered the *nioi* tree. The next day this grove of trees was seen standing at the head of the *maika* site of Maunaloa,[5] and so strange a thing was it for these tall trees to be standing there that everyone, from chiefs to commoners, came from all about to see the sight. Everyone said that these trees must be gods; they must be trees with mana, like the tree of Haumea [out of which were made the images] Kuho'one'enu'u and Kukalani'ehu; like Kaloakaoma's tree, Kahaiki, [out of which was made] Kukeolo'ewa. Another tree with mana was the breadfruit tree into which Haumea entered, and which then became the kingdom-seeking god Kameha'ikana. These were all trees with mana, and gods who sought kingdoms (*mau la'au mana, a he mau akua 'imi aupuni;* that is, they were all gods in tree form who helped their worshipers to attain kingdoms).

The chiefs of Molokai were all agreed to the cutting out of god-images from these trees, and a proclamation was sent out all over Molokai to fashion *pahoa* axes to carve them out. When they began to cut the trees, if a chip of wood flew out and hit a man, he died; and where the sap splattered, that, too, brought death.* If they wrapped themselves in mats and tapas it made no difference. But the spirit of Kaneiakama was taught what to do by Kaneikaulana'ula, and he then taught the others the *kanawai* for the cutting down of these trees. They were to take to the trunks of the trees an offering of many (*lau*) pigs, coconuts, dress tapas, red fishes, and bunches of *kohekohe* grass and offer them in sacrifice, then bathe themselves all over the body with the water of coconuts and with urine, and the trees could be cut without harm.[6] This was done just as he directed, and thus the woods were obtained. Not the whole of these trees was taken, however, but only a few pieces not quite an *anana* in length, and some shorter than others. Kahuilaokalani was one, Kaneikaulana'ula was another, and Kapo was the third. These three god-images (*po'e*) were called Kalaipahoa because of their being carved with *pahoa* axes (*no ke kalai ana i ka pahoa*). The stumps (*kumu*) and branches (*lala*) were thrown into the sea, for they would have brought death to the race if all men had them, and the people were deathly afraid of them.

Each tree was carved into an image (*ki'i*), with head, eyes, mouth, nose, and chin, just like other images. People were terribly afraid of these three images. They were not set up, nor were they displayed to the people or the chiefs. The ruling chief of Molokai had charge of them, and Kaneiakama became the kahuna, or priest, for these gods. The people were strictly prohibited from taking any part of the trees; branches, trunks, sprouts, and leaves were kapu. It is said, however, that the stump of one tree was left by the spring at the *maika* ground of Ka'akeke, and that people and animals were poisoned by drinking the water there; hence that spring at 'Ualapu'e was filled in (*kanu 'ia*). The chiefs pronounced a *kanawai* in the ancient days, prohibiting any man from taking a piece of wood from these trees and making a god for himself to work sorcery (*hana 'ino*) against any man or to do him to death. Anyone who became known for sorcery (*po'oko'i ana*), and was known to have harmed (*pepehi*) others, would be killed and his body dragged along the highway or burned with fire. So the people were protected. No man skilled in sorcery (*kanaka po'oko'i*), or any other *kanaka*, was known to harm others by this means. The chiefs carried out the penalty, and some kahunas who became known for sorcery (*kahuna po'oko'i*) were beheaded and their bodies dragged on the highway and burned with fire. The lives of the chiefs and people were therefore protected.

In the ancient days Molokai did not have a reputation as an evil land; the chiefs did not foster gods imbued with the mana of the Kalaipahoa (*'a'ole i hanai akua kumuhaka*). Kalaipahoa *ma*, the god-images, were kept very restricted through the time of the rule of the chiefess Kane'alai on Molokai. She did not give even the least piece of Kalaipahoa to her husband Keaweikekahiali'iokamoku, ruler of Hawaii, nor to any other chief. The care of Kalaipahoa *ma* was left to the descendants

---
* May 12, 1870.

of Kaneiakama. After the death of Kane'alai and Kumuko'a, her son by Keawe, and all the other children of Kane'alai, these gods became the property of Kahekili, ruler of Maui. He also kept them under rigid restriction. While Kahekili was still alive, Kamehameha I asked for a Kalaipahoa god for himself, and Kahekili gave him a little Kalaipahoa god in the shape of a small wooden image about a foot high; he was named Kanemanaiapai'ea. That was the first Kalaipahoa god obtained by a chief of Hawaii island.

After the death of Kahekili, and after his son Kalanikupule and the chiefs of Maui had died in the battle of Nu'uanu, which gave Kamehameha victory over the land from Hawaii to Oahu, all their gods became the property of Kamehameha, the Kalaipahoa among them. Kane'alaikane and Keli'ikukahaoa then became the kahunas of Kalaipahoa *ma*. Kalaipahoa did not kill them because they were also the *kahu* of Ma'iola, the antidote to the Kalaipahoa poisons. Ma'iola had a thick white bark which, if simply touched to the lips of one who ate some scrapings of Kalaipahoa, caused him to recover. Kalaipahoa woods were the most powerful and poisonous of woods. They were not bitter or anything, nor did they eat the internal organs like opium and other poisonous mixtures made by *haoles,* but they caused death. There was no antidote that compared with Ma'iola, which, if only touched to the lips, brought recovery.

PUA MA

It was less than a hundred years ago that sorcery, *hana 'ino,* began on Molokai. Peleioholani was ruling on Oahu, Kamehameha-nui on Maui, and Kalani'opu'u on Hawaii when sorcery, *ho'opi'opi'o, hi'u, kaina,* and *lelopu'u,* had their start on Molokai, and at first it was not widespread. The hereditary chiefs *na'li'i nona pono'i)* of Molokai were still living at that time; Kane'alai was still alive, and her children, and most of the chiefs of Molokai. It was kapu to use Kalaipahoa for sorcery or for praying to death (*hana 'ino a me ka 'ana'ana*). But one man, and only one, on Molokai was taught sorcery by the gods, and he did not spread his knowledge. Let this writer of Hawaiian history explain a little about the origin of the spread of sorcery, *ho'opi'opi'o, ho'ounauna, kaina,* and *pahi'uhi'u.*[7]

Kaiakea, a prominent man of Kala'e and its vicinity, was said to have been a man without a god. He built a large new household below Kahanui and provided all kinds of food, such as poi, pig, 'awa, bananas, fish, and everything else necessary for a "house-warming" (*o ka hale komo*). When the day came, Kaiakea's wife and the other women were at the *hale noa,* the common house, and Kaiakea and the other men and the servers were at the *hale mua,* the men's house. The *hale noa* was apart from the *hale mua,* which was surrounded by a lanai. Kaiakea was in the doorway of the *hale mua,* and while the feast was being prepared, he saw a long procession of women coming over the plains of Ho'olehua to Pala'au. They were dressed in yellow tapa skirts and yellow tapa shoulder coverings (*kihei*), with variegated (*papahi*) leis of *ma'o* and *'ilima* crowning their heads. There was one man among them. The procession went down to the spring, named Piliwale, and left their things (*he ukana*) there. These were a *puniu hulihuli,* or coconut-shell container, and the women's *'alae* bird bodies. When Kaiakea saw the many beautiful women in that company, he called out to them to come in on the lanai, but they remained outside. Only the man who was with them approached and stood at the door of Kaiakea's house and talked with him. Kaiakea offered them food, but the spirit man (*kanaka anela*) said they would not eat his food unless a leaf-thatched house, a *hale lau,* was built for them; then they would eat of his food. This man revealed that they were not humans, but "angels," and he told Kaiakea their names. Pua was his name, and Kauluimaunaloa (the-grove-at-Maunaloa, that is, Kapo) was the name of the chiefess who led the procession. He said they would become Kaiakea's gods if the *hale lau* was finished that day, and would give into his charge the *puniu hulihuli,* their visible form (*ko lakou kino 'ike maka 'ia*), and all the paraphernalia to do their work (*ka lakou mau hana a pau*), which was inside it. The *'alae* birds were their bodies which they showed abroad (*kino ho'ike 'ia iwaho*). After revealing these things to Kaiakea, the being vanished. Kaiakea went to the spring to look for the *puniu,* and got it; the *'alae* birds were resting there at the spring. That very day Kaiakea erected the *hale lau* and filled it with poi, *'awa,* bananas, and tapas appropriate to these gods; that same evening it was dedicated (*ke kapu no 'ia*). The food offerings (*ka 'ai me ka i'a*) and the *'awa* were all consumed by the *'alae* birds, and they were well content with the food provided for them.*

It was in this way that Kaiakea became the *kahu* of gods, and he became known as a man who had gods. He was the *kahu* of Kapo (Kauluimaunaloa) and Pua. Kaiakea, however, just took care (*malama pono*) of these gods. He did no harm to others, and did not send his gods to bring death (*ho'ounauna e make*) to any man or to any chief. He just took care of his *akua ho'ola'a* (the spirits who had been made gods by his consecration and offerings). Upon his death he commanded his children to take care of the gods against the days of trouble; the gods would repay them with life (*ola*). But they were not to seek wealth from the gods through sorcery.**

Before Kaiakea died he strictly warned his children not to spread the knowledge of sorcery, nor to give it to outsiders. But after his death his daughter Ka'akaumakaweliweli set up kapus (*kukulu i na kapu*) and built some houses for these gods, and made offerings to the *'alae* bird (*ho'olulu i ka manu 'alae*). Kapualei, and all the lands where the daughter of Kaiakea lived, became famous on account of the houses erected for these gods. This art of *ho'ounauna,* the sending of spirits on malicious errands, did not come from Kaneiakama; this was a different art, although the gods were the same kind (*ma ke 'ano akua ua like*). The two sides, *'ao'ao,* [that is, the side that sent the spirits to do harm and the side that counteracted their harm] would conflict; one or the other of the *kahu* of the gods would be defeated, or victorious, and the contesting (*ku'e*) goes on between them to this day.*

---
* May 19, 1870.
**July 14, 1870.

After Kaiakea's death the chiefs of Molokai were slain by the chiefs of Oahu, and Molokai became a dependency of Oahu. The country was in turmoil. Some of the people of Molokai helped the chiefs of Oahu, and some helped those of Maui and Hawaii. During these times the worship of sorcery gods increased, and so did the number of such gods. At this time Kaiakea's daughter Ka'akaumakaweliweli was inspired (*uluhia*) by the spirits of Pua and Kapo to prophesy the loss of Oahu to Kahekili. When the kahuna Ka'opulupulu—the prop that supported Oahu—died, her prophecy was fulfilled, and she was given the lands of Kapualei and 'Ualapu'e on Molokai and Pu'uho'owale at Lahaina, Maui, by Kahekili.

Up until the time Kahekili, the ruler of Maui, came to Oahu, Ka'akau lived with Puhene in the gulch at Kapualei, on the easterly (*na'e*) side of Molokai. Men and women dreaded to go along the highway there when the women were dressed in fine *pa'u*, skirts, and the men and women had on *papahi* leis. One annoying incident (*hana ku'e*) after another would arise, and they would have to send for Ka'akau and Puhene to clear up the difficulties; then all would be well (*ua ola*). [They were being molested by the spirits in the vicinity, and Ka'akau and Puhene were sent for so as to quiet the spirits and make it safe for them to go on.]

It was in Kahekili's time, and in that of Kamehameha, that Molokai became known as an *'aina ho'ounauna*, a land where spirits were sent on malicious errands.

When Pua *ma* became gods who destroyed human beings (*po'e nana e 'ai a humuhumu*), some people took the corpses of their dead and offered them to become transfigured into spirits of this nature (*kaku'ai iloko o Pua ma*). The corpses were divided into bits and went into the numerous gods of this type, such as Keawenuikauohilo, Kuamu, and Kaho'owaha, or into Kahili'opua, Ka'onohiokala, and others. They became "biting sharks" (*mano nahu*) of the land. As the shark gods Kapehu and Moanaliha were man-eaters in the sea, so these became man-eaters on land. This is the reason why the people of Molokai learned *ho'opi'opi'o* and *hi'u* sorcery—in order to counteract (*wehe*) *ho'ounauna* and *alelo pehu* sorcery. From these same gods, Pua *ma*, came inflicting, as well as counteracting, sorcery (*mai loko mai no o keia po'e ke wehe a me ka pa'a*) by brandishing a tapa, or by wielding a stick (*ma ke kuehu kapa a me ka ka'a la'au ana*).*⁸

The kahunas who practiced *ho'opi'opi'o*, *hi'u*, *kaina*, *ho'ounauna* or *alelo pu'u* sorcery were evil, like the *kahuna 'ana'ana 'aihamu*, but they used different methods to kill people. Death from a *kahuna 'aihamu* was slow, sometimes taking a year or more, but the prayers of the kahunas who used *ho'opi'opi'o*, *hi'u*, *kaina*, *apo leo*, or *alelo pu'u* sorcery killed quickly. Their prayers seemed to be just songs, *mele*, and seemed insignificant as they came from the mouth of the kahuna, but it was not from the songs that trouble came. It came from his command to the spirits of death (*kana kauoha ana i na 'uhane o ka make*)—that was where death came from.**

Ho'opi'opi'o sorcery was good for counteracting another's *ho'opi'opi'o*, *hi'u*, *kaina*, or *ho'ounauna* sorcery. These could be made ineffective (*hemo*) by it. But it was wrong to use *ho'opi'opi'o* to harm someone else—very wrong indeed. It

---
* July 14, 1870.
** August 4, 1870.

could kill a man by what seemed a trifling act—the hearing of a chant, or a gesturing of a hand or foot—that was when evil spirits of destruction were being sent to seek out and destroy the man (*eia ka e ho'ounauna 'ia mai ana i ka po'e 'uhane 'ino*). He might be an enemy, or perhaps just a man who was hated but who had done no wrong.

AKUA KUMUHAKA

Molokai became famed for *ho'opi'opi'o* sorcery, and at the same time arose the use of *akua kumuhaka,* gods who were imbued with the mana of the Kalaipahoa. Some people got bark, or bits of wood, of Kalaipahoa *ma* from where they had been carved at Maunaloa, and others got wood from the *kalaipahoa* grove, to ward off an illness (*ma'i*) or paralysis (*alelo pelu*) caused by *ho'opi'opi'o* or *ho'ounauna* sorcery. These had great power to save (*ho'ola*) from all sudden attacks of illness. Those who had large pieces of *kalaipahoa* wood (*na pauku la'au nui no ke kalaipahoa*) made them into *akua hanai, akua kumuhaka,* and *akua pepehi kanaka,* gods that injured men. They were carved into images and metamorphosed (*kaku'ai 'ia*), and they became imbued with the mana of Kalaipahoa. This was done secretly. A stone might also be carved into an image and, by being attached to *kalaipahoa* wood and metamorphosed (*ho'opili 'ia aku la me ka la'au kalaipahoa, a kaku'ai 'ia aku la*), the stone too would become a bitter destroyer of men. Just as a steel knife rubbed with a magnet itself becomes magnetized, they drew (*'ume*) their death-dealing mana from Kalaipahoa and became dealers of death themselves, strange as it may seem.

This was the beginning of the spread of these two evils, *ho'opi'opi'o* and *akua kumuhaka* sorcery.

In 1812, at the time of Kamehameha's return to Hawaii island, *ho'opi'opi'o* and *akua kumuhaka* sorcery became widespread. Those who had obtained *akua kumuhaka* kept them secretly in their knotted bundles (*hipu'u*). After the abolition of the kapus (*ke au 'ainoa*), and during the first years of learning letters (*ke au a'o palapala*), the *akua kumuhaka* were frequently seen flying from the houses where they were kept in their bundles. The people of Molokai were notorious for sorcery (*po'oko'i*), and when they went to other kingdoms, *ho'opi'opi'o* sorcery was frequently seen.

Akua kumuhaka could be seen flying through the air like the fire rockets of the *haoles*. It was the nature of the *kumuhaka* gods to fly great distances, and this is how it was done. When the *kahu* of a *kumuhaka* god wished to harm (*make*) a person, he would secretly take his god out in the evening and scratch the breast of the image on the left side. Even if the image was but the size of a hand, the *kumuhaka* god would fly from the house and stretch out, swelling and diminishing, swelling and diminishing, swelling and diminishing, and tapering off into a streaming tail. It would fly for miles in this way. The reason for its flying was that the *kahu* had treated it harshly (*hana na'aupo*), and when he scratched it harshly (*wa'uwa'u na'aupo*), the god was hurt, and it showed itself in its spirit form (*ho'ike ke akua i ke akua*). This flying of the *akua kumuhaka* was a common thing from the time of the abolition of the kapus until 1830;⁹ deaths were frequently known to have been caused this way. This is the way it was kept quiet. Coconuts and red fishes, pig and *'awa*, were procured, the god shut up in its coconut-shell container, and the offerings made. Then, if it were scratched, it would not fly.

The *akua kumuhaka* itself could cause death by being put into (*ho'okomo ana*) food, drinking water, or smoking tobacco; by being touched to a hand, or rubbed against the body—just so that it came in contact with the person being desired to die. Such a death gave no chance to leave a command for the disposal of his body (*he make kauoha 'ole*); it was sudden and instantaneous. After death, the place where the *akua kumuhaka* had touched the body was visible. If the forehead was the place, the print of fingers would be seen on the forehead of the dead; if on the shoulder, the prints would be there—anywhere on the body where it had been touched. It was evident to everyone that So-and-so had been killed by an *akua kumuhaka*, a god who had been fostered (*akua hanai*), and that his destruction had been beseeched (*a ua make i kalo ho'ola'a*).

KAMEHAMEHA'S CARE OF THE KALAIPAHOA AND PUA GODS

When Kamehameha returned to Hawaii in 1812, at the time of the return called Kani'aukani, he settled at Kailua on Hawaii for a period of seven years. He built several houses for his own gods (*na akua ona*), and for the keepers of his own gods. He also built houses for the many other gods, and for the *malihini* (newcomer) gods he had obtained from his dependencies (*panala'au*), that is, Kukeolo'ewa, Kuho'one'enu'u, and Ololupe ('Olopue)—the god who led souls, and who was also called Kapapakahui. For the Kalaipahoa and the Pua gods, *hale 'ili mai'a*, houses lined with banana fiber sheathing were built. Ka'akau, the daughter of Kaiakea, was the *kahu* of Pua, and Ma'alo and Moeluhi were the *kahu* of Kalaipahoa. Kane'alai and Keli'ikukahaoa were the kahunas of Kalaipahoa *ma*. The house for Pua was separate from the *hale 'ili mai'a* of Kalaipahoa *ma*.*

The *hale 'ili mai'a* for Kalaipahoa *ma* was where their *kahu* lived, and Kamehameha went there morning and evening to pray over a broiled banana (*e pule ahi ai i ka mai'a pulehu*). He would sit on the threshold, facing outward. The *kahu* of Kalaipahoa would take up a broiled banana, peel it, and bring it to him with some words of prayer. Kamehameha would exclaim, "O-ho-ho," and pick up the words of the prayer. The *kahu* would take up the last words, and the ruler would utter the *'amama*, the concluding words. Then he would bite into the banana and eat it up.

The mana of Kalaipahoa could be seen, and everybody saw it—including the *haoles* who lived with Kamehameha. They saw that in some mysterious way harmless wood had become deadly poisonous. It was not through fear of death, or any misgiving, or terror, that it caused death to pigs, or dogs, or birds. The wood had no bitter taste or yellow color like the *'auhuhu*, or the *ipu 'awa*, or the *'akia*, or

---
* July 14, 1870.

the *'opihi 'awa* or *kumimi* crab. Their poisonous (*'awa'awa*) qualities were known, their bitter taste recognized, and they themselves used in poisonous concoctions (*'apu koheoheo*).

The marvelous thing was that Kalaipahoa caused instant death, without giving time to leave a command for the disposal of one's body (*mea make kauoha 'ole*). Not only was Kalaipahoa fatal to eat or to touch, but it was also fatal if one carelessly went in and out of the house in which the god-images were kept without going out backward, with the face toward the house. A person would drop instantly at the door of the house if this rule was not observed. A bird that flew over the ridgepole of the house died; rats, cockroaches, and all creeping things died—all except the *mo'o kaula* lizard, and Kamehameha. They alone went in and out unharmed. When Kamehameha did not feel well, these gods were sent for and laid beside him, and he recovered. When he was seriously ill and enfeebled, these gods were fetched from the *hale 'ili mai'a* and laid down beside him so that he could sleep against Kalaipahoa *ma,* and he did not die; the illness left him [counteracted by their mana, which was greater than that of any other god-spirit that could be sent to inflict illness upon him].

Why was not Kamehameha killed by Kalaipahoa? Because of the righteousness (*pono*) of Kamehameha. His offerings of many (*lau*) pigs, coconuts, tapas, and red fishes were seen by the gods, and they looked upon him with favor. But if he had not respected their kapus (*'aiahulu*), or had sent the gods to destroy the life of some chief among them, he would have wronged the gods, and they would not have helped to protect his life. Blood for blood; life for life. All the symbols of a god left with man as visible tokens will not help to save the life of a wrongdoer. There have been signs of gods constantly, from ancient times down to the time of Christianity. A person who looks after (*malama*) a god, without doing wrong against holy things, the god will take care of and help; but the person who disregards the things made holy and set down by the god's laws, the god will not help. In this time, those who tread upon the laws of God are the wrongdoers. When the Kalaipahoa god-images (*po'e akua Kalaipahoa*) were to be anointed (*poni*) it was necessary to secure many coconuts, chew the coconut meat, pour off the coconut water, and with it fill as many containers as there were Kalaipahoa images; and also roast fine fat pigs, and prepare (*mama*) a large quantity of *'awa.* The *po'e akua* were then anointed and wrapped up well in tapas. These *po'e akua* were never kept on display nor set up like most of the images in the heiaus. Kalaipahoa *ma* were not images of gods, *akua ki'i*—they were themselves the gods, *he akua.* They were kept wrapped up in long bundles and laid on a shelf (*olo'ewa*) until the time came for their anointing. Then they were fetched and anointed with the masticated meat of coconut. When the anointing and the bathing with coconut water were through, then they were adorned with tapas and set up for the feast for the anointing of the gods, the *'aha'aina poni akua. 'Awa,* pigs, fishes, and other things were provided for the feast.

At that time one of the *kahu* ate some scrapings from the body of Kalaipahoa, which had been scraped into a cup of *'awa;* the other *kahu* drank the rest of the 'awa. The *kahu* who drank the cup of 'awa into which the body of Kalaipahoa had been put recited the prayer for the offerings, the prayer for the dedication of the food to the gods, and the prayer for the life of the king, the chiefs, and the people. He ended the prayer with the *'amama,* and then drank the cup of poison, while all the *kahu* of the gods drank their cups of *'awa.* The one who drank the poisoned cup took it hurriedly, the mark of a person about to die by Kalaipahoa. He turned red and his sight grew dim, and he gasped as if with his last breath. Then the healing bark of Ma'iola was applied to his lips, and he recovered like a man who has plunged into water and has come up to breathe fresh air again. Only last year a man died who was accustomed to eating the scrapings of Kalaipahoa when Kalaipahoa *ma* were anointed.

Kalaipahoa *ma* were wonderful things, and Ma'iola was a wonderful thing. It was said of Ma'iola that it was a *"kahu"* of Kalaipahoa. Any Kalaipahoa death could be saved by the *"kahu."* It was one of the trees that had stood among those *malihini* trees at Maunaloa on Molokai. What a pity that the Ma'iola tree is unobtainable. It is said that, if all the trees, including the Kalaipahoa, were to grow again they would be restorers of the people (*he po'e ho'oulu kanaka*); all their former destructive power would become a power for good. They would become healing trees for the race, and there would be no more poison in them. How would Ma'iola act upon opium? Perhaps it might counteract the effects of opium and of the poisonous drugs (*la'au make*) of the *haole* doctors.*

In the old days, and down through Kahekili's time, there were no conspicuous god-houses built for Kalaipahoa *ma*. The gods were kept very restricted lest the people imitate them and get out of control, and worship these gods in order to take the lives of other people or to menace the lives of the chiefs. But some of the chiefs acquired *kalaipahoa* (*kumuhaka*) gods, and their *kahu* kept them hidden away inside the house.

It was a cause of fear among the people in the old days when it was heard, and perhaps known, that a certain man had been killed by a *kumuhaka* god, and when a *kalaipahoa* god was seen flying from the house in which it was kept. A complaint was brought before the king at once against the person who had such a god. Then the king would send the *kahu* of Kalaipahoa with the god-image to the house, or to the place where this god who menaced the lives of people was hidden away. When this ravaging god (*akua 'aihamu*) saw the true Kalaipahoa being borne hither, it would flee in the form of a flock of white chickens, the body form (*kino maoli*) of this particular *kalaipahoa*. The place where it had been hidden was thus revealed, and its kahuna would be beheaded with an ax (*'oki 'ia ke po'o i ke ko'i*). Kahuna *'aihamu,* kahunas who destroyed people, were put to death in that way in the old days. For fear of being put to death, people in that time took their gods to the mountains, to hollows of trees, or to secret caves in the mountains. But when they saw that Kamehameha I openly built houses for his Kalaipahoa and Pua gods, then these evil ways of killing men grew. Kalaipahoa has vanished, but Pua still persists.

* July 21, 1870.

To Pua belong *ho'opi'opi'o, kaina, hi'u,* and *ho'ounauna* sorcery. These are the works of Pua (*oia ka Pua mau hana*).* People who are made ill by these means of sorcery do not have the symptoms of real diseases. The illness cannot be diagnosed by the *haha* method of the school of the medical kahuna Kua'ua'u, nor can the *kahuna kuni* divine its source. The ways of Pua are the ways of men, "men with teeth" (*he 'ao'ao kanaka no 'ia a me ka niho*). It only takes a "trivial remedy," a *la'au kilihune,* to save one; not remedies of offerings or medicines [the "trivial remedy" being countersorcery].**

REMEDIES FOR ILLNESS SENT BY PUA MA

For an illness caused by *ho'opi'opi'o, ho'ounauna,* or *kaina* sorcery, a piece of kauila wood, from three to six feet long, rolled, whirled, and set upright (*he ka'a a he 'oniu a he kukulu*), or a white tapa or a ti leaf passed over the patient (*kuehu*), was used to exorcise (*wehe*) the evil spirits (*na mea*) which had been made slaves of by devils and wicked souls.[10] The victim of *ho'opi'opi'o* sorcery was made well by such a treatment. The prayers used were *oli* or *mele*. Such an illness could not be cured by the medical kahunas of Lonopuha, nor by the kahuna *pa'ao'ao,* nor did the symptoms respond to medicines or purgatives. Such remedies would result in *pilikia* and eventually in death. However, such an illness was but a mere trifle (*ma'i palau'eka*) to those who knew *ho'opi'opi'o* [counter] sorcery. Such kahunas did use some remedies as medical potions (*'apu*), such as *'ohe* (bamboo), stripped of its leaves and grated; grated *olona* and *'awa* rootlets; "*uhau;*" "*kuka'i makani;*" root of *malena* [*manena?*]; bark and key of the *painahala* (*hala*); leaves and blossoms of *kanaka maika'i* (*'ilima*); tuber of the *haloakea* (*lauloa*) taro; bark of "*puhilani,*" "*ma'iola,*" "*ki'ikea,*" and "*ki'i'ula;*" bark and trunk of "*pua,*" "*kapo,*" and "*kahuilaokalani,*" bark and fruit of the "*hualewa*" (*'ohi'a 'ai*); and some others.[11] The kahunas of this sort went into metaphors and hidden meanings (*nanenane a me na 'olelo huna*) in their important work of expulsion (*kaiehu a'a*), and some of them were truly gifted.

The basis of the cure and saving lay in inducing (*uluhia ana*) the spirits who had brought the illness to enter into the patient. Even if the patient were near the grave, if the spirits could be persuaded to possess (*ulu*) him, the kahuna would rejoice and be happy and would tell everybody that the patient was saved from death and would recover; and it would indeed be so. [If the kahuna could induce the spirits to enter, he could gain control over them and effect a cure.] However, if the spirits could not be made to possess the patient, then the case would be a stubborn (*pa'akiki*) one, and recovery would be uncertain.

The kahunas who counteracted Pua sorcery were experts in *ho'opi'opi'o, ho-'ounauna, hi'u,* and *kaina* sorcery, and so were the *kahuna makani,* the kahunas who could induce spirits to enter the patients. They were often called "deifiers," and "deceivers" (*po'e kahuna ho'omanamana, a he po'e ho'opunipuni*). Some of

---
* July 14, 1870.
** July 21, 1870.

them, perhaps, did seek wealth by deceiving and lying, but there were others who did not—they really did have medical knowledge and they did heal many people. The medical profession was dual-natured (*he 'ano papalua ka 'oihana kahuna lapa'au*); [it combined physical and spiritual treatment].

REMEDIES OF THE KAHUNA 'ANA'ANA

Prayer was the one great "poultice" (*popo la'au lapa'au*) used by the *kahuna 'ana'ana*. Prayer availed to bring about either death or life. If there were a mistake in the utterance of the prayer, death was quite certain; if the utterance of the prayer went well, it was plain that life and blessings were assured. Prayer was the first ground (*eka*) covered by the *kahuna 'ana'ana*. When an illness brought on by a sorcerer appeared (*ma'i ku o ka pilikia ia waho*), a prayer to release the fault in the patient, a *pule kalahala,* was the prayer to utter. This would release the fault (*kala*) and remove (*uweke*) the evil influence. If the wrongdoer, the one who had sent the illness, were one who was resentful of others, or jealous, or suspicious, or who coveted the property of others, or who sought means of seizing the property of others, or plotted harm without cause, or carried on "black magic" (*lawe aku 'ana'ana*), he was a murderer, *he 'aimahu ia;* the *pule kala* would remove his influence.

If not, a *kuni ola* ceremony was performed for the patient by one versed in counteracting an illness caused by man. Very few prayers could save a man who "took bait" to cause another's death, or who stole from others. But only when the prayers for death were equally strong (*kulike ka make*)—when the prayers for freeing and release (*ka pule uweke a me ka pule kala*) were equal to the wrongdoer's prayer for strangulation (*pule 'umi*)—could the evil influence be removed (*hemo*). The same was true of the prayers at the *kapuahi kuni,* the ritual fireplaces for detecting and avenging the evildoers. But if a *kahuna kuni* thought only of the riches that he would receive, the mana of his prayers would return and be concentrated upon himself, and the wrongdoer and "sinner" would go free. The kahuna's prayer would "bite" him, just as a *kapa* eel held by the tail with its mouth and teeth left free turns sideways and bites.

Another important remedy used by the *kahuna 'ana'ana* was the long oven, the *umu loa,* for *kuni ola*. This was a large, red-hot *umu* in which were put plants from the mountains to the depths of the sea, and upon this matting (*kauwewe*) the patient lay for ten days to a month. Four or five men went to the summit of the mountains and four or five went to the sea, and they gathered many kinds of leafy plants, enough for a load for each man. If the patient were a chief, the preparation of the *umu loa* was even more elaborate. The *umu loa* was an *umu kala hala,* an oven to remove causes of grievances, and an *umu wehe,* an oven to counteract the deadly effects of another's *'ana'ana*. It could also counteract a death from *kuni,* that is, from the *kuni 'ana'ana* prayers of a group (*hui kuni*) who had taken "bait" for this purpose from the dead person (*lawe ka'ameha'i*), or who had taken his "bait" to pray him to death. If the prayers to absolve him of his offenses, the *pule kala,* were as strong as the *kuni* prayers for his death, he would live; otherwise he would die.

Here is another "poultice" used by the *kahuna 'ana'ana*—the *haihaia*.¹² When all other methods of healing had failed, the kahuna sought to cure his patient by acting "insanely" (*'imi ke ola ma ka haihaia*). There were several ways of doing this. He would eat with relish all manner of harmful things, drink potions of *'auhuhu, ipu 'awa'awa,* and *'akia,* and eat *'opihi 'awa* limpets and *kumimi* crabs; or he would go naked, exposing his private parts; or go naked in a circuit around the house, and on out onto the highway; or he would sleep at the crossroads of a highway at night. He would concentrate bitter thoughts (*ho'awahia*) against the other—the enemy who had sent the evil—on the highway, and at the crossroads, and at the enemy's house.

There were many diabolic things done by these *kahuna 'ana'ana,* and their works were terrifying. Lightning and flames of fire and columns of smoke would issue from their mouths. If they were in the right, the gods helped them; if they were in the wrong, they would die a cruel death without getting any help from the gods. To be the first to do a wrong was a great fault which the gods would not forgive.*

NOTES TO PART SIX

¹ *'Ana'ana* was true magic, a manipulation of the spirits in natural forces by means of magical incantation and prayer.

² See also Malo (1951, Chapter 28).

³ *Pule kaholo: 'Ana'ana* prayer spoken in a moderate or natural voice. *Pule 'umi:* "A black magic prayer which was uttered without drawing breath" (Pukui and Elbert, 1957, p. 326).

"The *pule 'umi,* or prayer of strangulation, was one in which the kahuna prayed in a special way over an object belonging to an intended victim before burning it. He drew a long breath and began to pray in a loud voice, growing gradually fainter and fainter until the voice died away to a whisper. Then he took another long breath, and so on, until finally he writhed in imitation of his victim" (Beckwith, 1934, Chapter 11, Note 8).

⁴ The crab and the plants were considered poisonous, as was *'opihi 'awa;* the earthworm and dragonfly grub were self-inflicted potential destroyers of his body. The taking of these things with impunity by the kahuna demonstrated his mana. The Kama called upon in the prayer was the particular god-force which, acting as "agent" for all the natural forces, did the actual destroying of the victim.

⁵ In the pineapple fields (1963) north of the road, on the northeast side of Kaka'ako Gulch, at an elevation of about 1,300 feet.

⁶ "Sprinkling with urine is still used as a means of warding off evil spirits, according to Mrs. Lahilahi Webb. A poultice of *popolo* leaves or other medicinal herbs applied to cure a sprain is moistened with urine" (Beckwith, 1934, Chapter 10, Note 2).

⁷ These, and others to be named, were all forms of sorcery—the manipulation of spirits created and controlled by men. They required some physical act besides praying on the part of the kahuna.

Ho'opi'opi'o: See Pukui and Elbert (1957, p. 306); Emerson (1918, p. 18); Fornander (1919, p. 74).

---

* September 15, 1870.

Hi'u: "consists in motioning with the hands in a certain way destructive to the person to whom the sorcerer is speaking" (Beckwith, 1934, Chapter 10, Note 3; from Daniel Ho'olapa of Kona, Hawaii).

Kaina: See Pukui and Elbert (1957, p. 109); the description of manipulating a hand kahili or shoulder wrap by Ii (1959, pp. 124-125); "depends upon the way the sorcerer sits" (Beckwith, 1934, Chapter 10, Note 3).

Ho'ounauna: See Pukui and Elbert (1957, p. 343); Emerson (1918, pp. 18, 30); Fornander (1919, pp. 110-112).

Alelo pu'u (synonyms, *lelo pu'u, alelo pehu*): a method of causing a paralysis of the tongue; [depends] "upon a strange way of using the voice" (Beckwith, 1934, Chapter 10, Note 3).

Apo leo: a method of causing the loss of voice; Pukui and Elbert (1957, p. 27); Emerson (1918, p. 19).

Pahi'uhi'u as a method of sorcery is undescribed.

[8] "In sorcery by the *kuehu* tapa, says Daniel Ho'olapa, the sorcerer shakes his tapa garment in a way that seems innocent but in reality brings a curse upon the person to whom the motion is directed. The 'twisted stick' (*ka'a la'au*) refers to the sorcerer's method of sending a curse by playing with seeming carelessness with four or five sticks held together in his hand" (Beckwith, 1934, Chapter 10, Note 4).

[9] "In Puna district on Hawaii some twenty years ago belief in Kalaipahoa sorcery still terrorized some communities. 'Although the keepers are dead, the gods still fly,' said my informant. Death by consumption was attributed to this cause. The Kalaipahoa was kept in the form of a bundle of small round blocks of wood graduated in size from large to small. When sent out by the sorcerer it was seen passing through the air from the house of the sorcerer to that of his victim in the form of a large ball of fire dwindling away into a tail. This was called the *puali* shape" (Beckwith, 1934, Chapter 10, Note 5).

[10] "The kahuna, or someone qualified, takes ti leaves, salt water, white tapa, bamboo stalks, or any other object and, beginning with the head of the sick person, draws the object down over the right arm, then shakes it in the air with an outward motion as if to expel something, then down the left arm, the front of the body, the right leg to the toes, the left leg, each time shaking the object as if to shake off the disease which has been transmitted to the object. If it is to be a *kuehu kane hekili,* the patient sits upright with the tapa draped over his head to his knees. The kahuna gathers the tapa up over the head with a prayer, then replaces it. He takes up a corner and draws it away from the right side with a certain prayer, then from the left side in the same way, then in front, then behind, each time with a particular prayer" [Mary Pukui, informant] (Beckwith, 1934, Chapter 11, Note 9).

[11] The names in quotes are medical terms, "trade names," for certain plants, just as *kanaka maika'i* is the "trade name" for *'ilima,* and not all are identifiable. *"Uhau"* is perhaps the *uhauhako (pawale); "hualewa"* is the *'ohi'a 'ai. "Ma'iola," "pua," "kapo,"* and *"kahuilaokalani"* are *kinolau* (plant body forms) of the Kalaipahoa gods of the same names, but not necessarily the trees the gods "entered." For instance, the *manele* (also called *a'e*) is a *kinolau* of the god Ma'iola, as is the *panini,* the common wild cactus.

[12] *"Haihaia.* To court the favor of the gods, or rather perhaps to use various arts, as by getting herbs and medicines and offerings to prevent the gods from hearing another's prayers" (Andrews, 1865, p. 132).

Pukui explains that the kahuna "prevents the gods from hearing another's prayers" (of destruction) by diverting them to himself by rash and "crazy" actions. In thus taking upon himself the curses that had been directed against the victim, the victim is freed; the kahuna does battle against the forces of destruction sent by the "enemy" and, by his superior mana, overcomes them and turns them back against his rival.

Compare *haihai* (Andrews, 1865, p. 132, verb 2), and *ho'omanewanewa,* Pukui and Elbert, 1957, p. 219).

APPENDIX I

GLOSSARY

Identifications of plants and animals listed here are in general limited to the genera or species indicated by the context in which they are mentioned.*

a'e. Soapberry tree (*manele*), *Sapindus saponaria* form *inaequalis*. Also, *Fagara* (*Zanthoxylum*) sp. [Kamakau's description of *a'e* does not conform to a description of either the soapberry or the *Fagara,* but does conceivably match that of the *maua* (*Xylosma* sp.) which John Ii names as a *kalaipahoa* tree.**]
'ahi. Tuna fishes, especially the yellow-fin tuna, *Neothunnus macropterus*.
'ahinahina (*hinahina ku mauna*). A shrub, *Artemisia australis*. Used medicinally.
aholehole. Young of *ahole* fish, *Kuhlia sandvicensis*.
'ahu'awa. Sedges, *Cyperus laevigatus* and *C. javanicus*. Leaf buds (*mu'o*) of *C. javanicus* used medicinally.
'akia. Shrubs and trees, *Wikstroemia* spp.
'akoko (*koko*). Trees and shrubs of the genera *Euphorbia*. *E. multiformis* used medicinally.
'ala'alapuloa ('*uhaloa*). Shrubby plant, *Waltheria americana*. Used medicinally.
'alae. Mud hen or Hawaiian gallinule, *Gallinula chloropus sandvicensis*.
aloalo. Hibiscus, *Hibiscus* spp.
'ana. A siliceous sponge, *Leiodermatium* sp. (class Demospongia, order Lithistida [Schmidt, 1870], family Scleritodermidae. Identified for Bishop Museum by G. J. Bakus, University of Southern California, November, 1963). Used medicinally.
'anae. Full-size mullet, *Mugil cephalus*.

---

* Major references used: Bryan (1958); Edmondson (1946); Gosline and Brock (1960); Handy (1940); Kaaiakamanu and Akina (1922); Neal (1948); Pukui and Elbert (1957); Rock (1913).
** *Ku'oko'a,* March 12, 1870.

a'ua'u. A small *a'u* fish. *A'u* comprise any billed fish, including the marlin, swordfish, sailfish, and spearfish (family Istiophoridae), broadbill swordfish (family Xiphidae), needlefish (family Belonidae), and halfbeak (family Hemiramphidae).

'auhuhu. Perennial herb, *Tephrosia purpurea*. Flowers used medicinally.

awa. A milkfish, *Chanos chanos*.

'awa. Shrub, *Piper methysticum*.

'awapuhi. Herb, *Zingiber zerumbet*. Used medicinally.

'aweoweo. Red fishes of the genus *Priacanthus*, especially *P. cruentatus*.

'ea. Hawkbill turtle, *Chelone imbricata*. Shell used medicinally.

'ekaha ku moana. "Black coral," *Antipathes grandis* (class Anthozoa, order Octocorallia (= Zoantharia), suborder Antipatharia, family Antipatharidae). Used medicinally.

hala. Tree, *Pandanus odoratissimus*. Used medicinally.

haloakea. Poetic name for *lauloa* taro, *Colocasia esculenta* sp. Used medicinally.

hau. Tree, *Hibiscus tiliaceus*. Used medicinally.

hilu. Some wrasses of the family Labridae: *hilu*, *Coris flavovitata*, *Anampses cuvieri*; *hilu lauwili*, *Coris lepomis*. See also *hinalea* and *'opule*.

hinahina (*hinahina ku kahakai*). Beach heliotrope, *Heliotropium anomalum*. Used medicinally.

hinahina ku mauna. See *'ahinahina*.

hinalea. General name for wrasses, family Labridae. Specifically: *hinalea lauwili*, *Thalassoma duperreyi*; *hinalea luahine*, *T. ballieui*; *hinalea 'aki-lolo*, *Macropharyngodon geoffroyi* and *Gomphosus varius*; *hinalea 'i'iwi*, *G. varius*. See also *hilu* and *'opule*.

ho'awa (*'a'awa-hua-kukui*). Tree, *Pittosporum hosmeri*. Used medicinally.

ho'i'o. See *pohole*.

'ie. Aerial root of the *'ie'ie*, *Freycinetia arborea*.

'ie'ie. Woody branching climber, *Freycinetia arborea*.

iholena. Banana, *Musa* sp. "Its name 'yellow core' describes the salmon-pink color of the ripe flesh. The bunches are small and the fruits are angular, plump in the middle, arranged loosely on the stem and stand out at right angles to the stem." (Handy, 1940, p. 175.)

iliau. Kauai silversword, *Argyroxiphium gymnoxiphium* syn. *Wilkesia gymnoxiphium*. Used medicinally.

'ilie'e. Wild plumbago, *Plumbago zeylanica*.

'ilima. Shrub, *Sida fallax*. Used medicinally.

ipu 'awa'awa (*ipu 'awa*). Bitter gourd, *Lagenaria sicericia*. Used medicinally.

kahiki. Banana, *Musa* sp. "The fruit is long, skin ripens yellow, meat white and edible cooked but not raw. It grows tall." (Handy, 1940, p. 175.)

kala. Unicorn fish, family Acanthuridae; usually applied to *Naso unicornis*, but often applied to other species of the genus.

kalo. See taro.

kanawao. Trees, *Broussaisia arguta* and *B. pellucida*.

kapa eel. See *puhi kapa*.

kauila. Trees of the buckthorn family (Rhamnaceae), *Colubrina oppositifolia* and *Alphitonia ponderosa*.

kaunao'a. See *kauno'a.*

kauno'a (*kaunao'a*). Dodder, *Cuscuta sandwichiana.* Used medicinally.

ka'upu. A large bird; no positive identification. Malo (1951, p. 40) describes it as "black [*'ele'ele*] throughout, its beak large, its size that of a turkey." Emerson says (Malo, 1951, p. 154, Note 4), "It was the gannet or solan goose" (family Sulidae). There are no over-all black or dark colored (*'ele'ele*) gannets (*Sula* spp.) in Hawaiian waters. Malo's description more nearly fits the black-footed albatross, *Diomedea nigripes.*

kawakawa. Adult stage of bonito fish, *Euthynnus yaito* (family Scombridae).

kawelea. A small barracuda, *Sphyraena helleri* (family Sphyraenidae).

ki. See ti.

kikawaioa (*kikawaio*). A fern, *Cyclosorus* [*Dryopteris*] *cyatheoides.* Used medicinally.

koa. Large native forest tree, *Acacia koa.*

koa'e. Tropic birds, *Phaeton rubricauda* and *P. lepturus.*

koali (*koali 'awa, koali 'awahia*). A morning glory; flowers open bluish-violet, changing to pink. *Ipomoea congesta.* Used medicinally.

kohekohe. Sedges; *Eleocharis* spp.

koki'o. A tree in the hibiscus family (Malvaceae), *Kokia rockii.* It has a thin grayish-brown bark which contains a reddish-brown juice; the wood is soft and of a reddish-brown color; the leaves resemble the kukui, and tint from reddish-yellow to green; the flowers are bright red (Rock, 1913, p. 307).

koki'o. Native shrubby hibiscus with red flowers, *Hibiscus kokio.* Used medicinally.

koko. See *'akoko.*

ko'oko'olau (*ko'olau*). Herbs, *Bidens* (*Campylotheca*) spp.

ko'olau. See *ko'oko'olau.*

kowali. See *koali.*

kukui. Tree, *Aleurites moluccana.* Used medicinally.

kule. Lizard fishes, family Synodontidae.

kumimi. A xanthid crab, *Lophozozymus intonsus* (Randall), syn. *Xantho eudora* Owen. Owen says, ". . . the native name is Kumimi."* Kumimi-maka'o, *Petrolisthes coccineus* (family Porcellanidae); kumimi-pua, *Lybia tesselata* (family Xanthidae).

kumu. Goatfish, *Parupeneus porphyreus* (family Mullidae).

lama. Tree, *Diospyros,* syn. *Maba.* Used medicinally.

laukahi. Plantains of the family Plantaginaceae. *Plantago major* most commonly used medicinally.

lemu o makili (*pulihilihi*). Herbaceous leguminous vine, *Vigna marina.* Used medicinally.

limu 'ekaha (*o ke kuahiwi*). No positive identification; perhaps a liverwort. "This limu grows on rotted trees. It is flat like a ribbon and is greenish in color. The limu is bitter both in green and dry state" (Kaaiakamanu and Akina, 1922, p. 59). Used medicinally.

limu kalemakapi'i (*makole-makopi'i*). A native moss, *Thuidium hawaiiense.* Used medicinally.

lumaha'i. Kaaiakamanu and Akina (1922, p. 24) say this is the Kauai name for *'ihi 'ai;* specimen was identified as *Portulaca oleracea.* [This portulaca is more commonly known as *'akulikuli kula,* and *Oxalis corniculata* as *'ihi 'ai.* Both the portulaca and the oxalis were used medicinally.] Also, a tree; unidentified. "This tree grows most abundantly on Kauai. The wood is very hard. The bark is light and very smooth. The bud and fruit of this tree are very useful for the cure of internal disorders" (Kaaiakamanu and Akina, 1922, p. 64).

---

* Richard Owen, "Crustacea." In F. W. Beechey, *Zoology of Captain Beechey's Voyage. . . ,* pp. 77-92. London: Henry G. Bohn, 1839, p. 78.

mahamoe. An edible bivalve; unidentified.
maile. Twining shrub with fragrant leaves, *Alyxia olivaeformis*. Used medicinally.
makolokolo (*honohono*). A weed, *Commelina diffusa*. Used medicinally.
makou. A perennial herb, *Peucedanum sandwicensis*. Used medicinally.
mamaki. Small native tree, *Pipturus albidus*. Used medicinally.
malena [*manena?*]. See *manena*.
mamo. Endemic Hawaiian honeycreeper, now extinct; *Drepanis pacifica*.
manena. A small native tree, *Pelea cinerea*, which was used medicinally.
manini. A surgeonfish, convict tang; *Acanthurus sandvicensis*.
ma'o. A shrub in the hibiscus family (Malvaceae), *Abutilon* sp.
maua. Forest trees, *Xylosma hawaiiense* and *X. hillebrandii*. Bark is smooth; young leaves reddish, older leaves dark green with reddish hue; leaves of the *X. hillebrandii* are crenate (Rock, 1913, pp. 313 and 315).
moa. Spore-bearing plants, *Psilotum nudum* and *P. complanatum*. Used medicinally.
mohihi. A variety of sweet potato, *Ipomoea batatas*. "The bulb is red on the outside while the interior is almost golden in color" (Kaaiakamanu and Akina, 1922, p. 35). Used medicinally.
momoa wa'a. See *pahu*.
muhe'e. Cuttlefish, *Sepioteuthus artipinnis*.

nahawele. Mussels of the families Isognomonidae, Pteriidae, and Pinnidae.
nehu. Anchovy fish, *Stolephorus purpureus*.
nioi. Tree; a native species of *Eugenia*, *E. molokaiana*.
noni. Indian mulberry, *Morinda citrifolia*.

'ohe. Bamboo, *Bambusa vulgaris*.
'ohe. Native tree, *Reynoldsia sandwicensis*.
'ohi'a 'ai. Mountain apple tree, *Eugenia malaccensis*.
'ohi'a 'apane. *'Ohi'a lehua* tree with dark red flowers; *Metrosideros collina*. Used medicinally. See also *'ohi'a lehua*.
'ohi'a lehua. Tree; flowers bright red. *Metrosideros collina*. Used medicinally. See also *'ohi'a 'apane*.
'o'io. Ladyfish, *Albula vulpes*.
'okupe. Bivalve; *Spondylus zonalis*.
'olena. Turmeric, *Curcuma domestica*. Used medicinally.
olona. Shrub, *Touchardia latifolia*.
'o'o. Endemic Hawaiian honeyeaters (family Meliphagidae), *Acrulocercus* spp.
'o'opu. General name for fishes included in the families Eleotridae, Gobiidae, and Blenniidae. Fresh or brackish water forms are found in the families Eleotridae and Gobiidae. See also *pao'o*.
'opelu. The mackerel scads (family Carangidae), *Decapterus pinnulatus* and *D. maruadsi*.
'opihi. Edible limpets, *Helcioniscus* spp.
'opihi 'awa. Nonedible limpet, *Siphonaria* sp.
'opule. Wrasse, family Labridae; *Anampses cuvieri*. See also *hinalea* and *hilu*.

pahekili (*huahekili, naupaka*). Shrub, *Scaevola* sp. Used medicinally.
pahu (*momoa wa'a*). Fish, *Ostracion lentiginosus*.
pala. Fern, *Marattia douglasii*. Used medicinally.
palaholo. The rolled-up frond of the *ama'u* fern, *Sadleria cyatheoides*. Used medicinally.

palai. Fern, *Microlepia setosa.*
palau. Maui name for yam (*uhi*), *Dioscorea alata.* Used medicinally.
pamakani. Native white hibiscus; *Hibiscus arnottianus* (large-leafed), *H. arnottianus* form *parviflora* (small-leafed). Used medicinally.
pao'o. A variety of *'o'opu* fish, *Istiblennius zebra* (family Blenniidae).
pa'u-o-Hi'iaka. Beach vine, *Jacquemontia sandwicensis.* Used medicinally.
pawale. See *uhauhako.*
pili. A grass, *Heteropon contortus.*
pilikai. A morning glory with rose-purple flowers, *Stictocardia campanulata.* Used medicinally.
pipi. Hawaiian pearl oyster, *Pinctada radiata.*
pohole. Fern; Maui name for *ho'i'o*, *Diplazium arnotti.*
popolo. Black nightshade, *Solanum nigrum* or *S. nodiflorum.* Used medicinally.
popo'ulu. Banana, *Musa* sp. Used medicinally. ". . . so called because the fruits, angular when young, mature as ball-like (*popo*) as breadfruit (*ulu*). The skin is fairly thin and yellow when ripe, flesh light salmon pink, edible raw but especially relished when baked (*pulehu*). The midrib is pinkish when young, and the petiole green. The trunk is low and green. The root of the young shoot (*pohuli*) may be substituted for the *Lele* [banana] in treating thrush ['*ea*]" (Handy, 1940, p. 177).
puhi kapa. Eel, *Echidna nebulosa.*
pulihilihi. See *lemu o makili.*

taro (*kalo*). *Colocasia esculenta.* Young leaves are called *lu'au.*
ti (*ki*). Shrub; *Cordyline terminalis.* Used medicinally.

'uhaloa. See *'ala'alapuloa.*
uhauhako (*pawale*). A vinelike plant, *Rumex giganteus.* Used medicinally.
uhi. Yam, *Dioscorea alata.* See also *palau.*
uhu. The parrot fishes, family Scaridae; most commonly, *Scarus perspicillatus.*
ulua. Jacks of the genera *Caranx, Caragoides, Gnathodon,* and *Alectis* (family Carangidae).

walu. Oilfish; *Ruvettus pretiosus.* Used medicinally.
wauke. Paper mulberry, *Broussonetia papyrifera.*
weke. Goatfishes (family Mullidae); *weke, weke 'a'a, Mulloidichthys samoensis; weke pueo, weke pahula, Upeneus arge; weke 'ula, Mulloidichthys auriflamma.*
wiliwili. Leguminous tree, *Erythrina sandwicensis.*

LITERATURE CITED

ANDREWS, LORRIN
    1865. *A Dictionary of the Hawaiian Language.* Honolulu: Henry M. Whitney.

BARRÈRE, DOROTHY B.
    1961. "Cosmogonic Genealogies of Hawaii." *J. Polynesian Soc.* 70(4):419-428.

BECKWITH, MARTHA WARREN
    1934. Notes. In Martha Warren Beckwith and Mary Pukui (Trans. and Editors), Moolelo Hawaii: Hawaiian Traditions by Samuel Manaiakalani Kamakau. Manuscript in B. P. Bishop Museum, Honolulu.

BECKWITH, MARTHA WARREN (Editor)
    1932. *Kepelino's Traditions of Hawaii.* B. P. Bishop Mus. Bull. 95. Honolulu.
    1951. *The Kumulipo: A Hawaiian Creation Chant.* Chicago: Univ. Chicago Press.

BRYAN, E. H., JR.
    1958. *Check List and Summary of Hawaiian Birds.* Honolulu: Books About Hawaii.

CHAPIN, ALONZO
    1954. "Excerpts from *Climate and Diseases of the Sandwich Islands* [1838]." In FRANCIS JOHN HALFORD, *Nine Doctors and God,* Appendix A, pp. 291-294. Honolulu: Univ. Hawaii Press.

DIBBLE, SHELDON
    1843. *History of the Sandwich Islands.* Lahainaluna: Press of the Mission Seminary.

EDMONDSON, C. H.
    1946. *Reef and Shore Fauna of Hawaii.* B. P. Bishop Mus. Spec. Pub. 22. Honolulu.

ELLIS, WILLIAM
    1917. *A Narrative of a Tour through Hawaii.* . . . (Reprint of London ed., 1827). Honolulu: Hawaiian Gazette.

EMERSON, J. S.
    1918. "Selections from a Kahuna's Book of Prayers." In *Twenty-Sixth Annual Report of the Hawaiian Historical Society for the Year 1917,* pp. 17-39. Honolulu: Paradise of Pacific Press.

FORNANDER, ABRAHAM
    1917, 1918, 1919. "Hawaiian Antiquities and Folk-Lore." *Mem. B. P. Bishop Mus.* Vols. 4, 5, 6. Honolulu.

GOSLINE, WILLIAM A., and VERNON E. BROCK
    1960. *Handbook of Hawaiian Fishes.* Honolulu: Univ. Hawaii Press.

GREEN, LAURA, and MARTHA WARREN BECKWITH
    1926. "Hawaiian Customs and Beliefs Relating to Sickness and Death." *American Anthropologist* 28:176-201.

HANDY, E. S. CRAIGHILL
    1940. *The Hawaiian Planter.* Vol. I: *His Plants, Methods and Areas of Cultivation.* B. P. Bishop Mus. Bull. 161. Honolulu.

HANDY, E. S. CRAIGHILL, and MARY KAWENA PUKUI
    1958. *The Polynesian Family System in Ka-'u, Hawaii.* Wellington: The Polynesian Society.

HANDY, E. S. CRAIGHILL, MARY KAWENA PUKUI, and KATHERINE LIVERMORE
    1934. *Outline of Hawaiian Physical Therapeutics.* B. P. Bishop Mus. Bull. 126.

II, JOHN PAPA
    1959. *Fragments of Hawaiian History.* (MARY KAWENA PUKUI, trans.; DOROTHY B. BARRÈRE, editor.) Honolulu: Bishop Museum Press.

KAAIAKAMANU, D. M., and J. K. AKINA
    1922. *Hawaiian Herbs of Medicinal Value.* (AKAIKO AKANA, trans.) Honolulu: Territorial Board of Health.

KALAKAUA
    1888. *The Legends and Myths of Hawaii.* (R. M. DAGGETT, ed.) New York: Charles L. Webster.

KAMAKAU, SAMUEL M.
    1961. *Ruling Chiefs of Hawaii.* Honolulu: Kamehameha Schools Press.

MALO, DAVID
    1951. *Hawaiian Antiquities.* B. P. Bishop Mus. Spec. Pub. 2. (2nd ed.) Honolulu.

NEAL, MARIE
    1948. *In Gardens of Hawaii.* B. P. Bishop Mus. Spec. Pub. 40. Honolulu.

PUKUI, MARY KAWENA
    1942. "Hawaiian Beliefs and Customs during Birth, Infancy, and Childhood." *B. P. Bishop Mus. Occasional Pap.* 16(17):357-381.

PUKUI, MARY KAWENA, and SAMUEL H. ELBERT
    1957. *Hawaiian-English Dictionary.* Honolulu: Univ. Hawaii Press.

RICE, WILLIAM HYDE
    1923. *Hawaiian Legends.* B. P. Bishop Mus. Bull. 3. Honolulu.

ROCK, JOSEPH F.
    1913. *The Indigenous Trees of the Hawaiian Islands.* Honolulu: Published under patronage.

SPENCER, THOMAS
    1895. *Buke Oihana Lapaau.* . . . (In Hawaiian). Honolulu.

INDEX

A'e Kuahu, a *kanawai akua*, 22
'Ahukini-a-La'a, 11
Ahukini-o-ka-lani, 31
Ahukiolani, a chiefess of Hana, 76
'ai ("food"), 44 Note 3
'Aila'au, 87
'ailolo, 121
Akahiakuleana, 6
Akahipapa, Honaunau, 18
akaku (kuaka); see visions
Akalana, father of Maui, 91
akua *'aumakua*
    of the *po'e kahiko,* 28
    [rationalization of], 55, 57, 59, 60
    see also *'aumakua*
akua *hanai,* 134
akua *haole,* 28
akua *ho'ola'a,* 28, 66, 69, 73, 75, 80, 132
    'uhane ho'ola'a, 54
akua *ho'oulu,* 28
akua *kaku'ai,* 28; see also *kaku'ai*
    (transfiguration)
akua *kanaka,* 80
akua *kapala 'alaea,* 20
akua *kumuhaka,* 130, 134-135, 137
akua *kumupa'a,* 28; see *kumupa'a*
akua *loa,* 20
akua *makemake,* 28
akua *malihini,* 28

akua *mo'o,* 82, 85
akua *pa'ani,* 20
akua *pepehi kanaka,* 134; see *akua kumuhaka*
akua *poko,* 20
akua *'unihipili ('uhinipili),* 28, 49, 54, 55, 73, 80, 90
'Alanapo, Ke'ei, South Kona, Hawaii, 67, 68
'Alealea heiau, Honaunau, 18
alelo pehu; see *alelo pu'u*
alelo pu'u (lelo pu'u, alelo pehu) sorcery, 131, 133, 141
Alexander Liholiho, see Kamehameha IV
Alia, Moanalua, Oahu, 48
Aliamanu, Moanalua, Oahu, 48
'Aliamoku, a *kanawai akua,* 14
ali'i ho'opilipili, 4
ali'i kapu, 4
Amala, 42
'ana'ana, 27, 29, 36, 37, 109, 119
    divisions of, 119, 122
'Anaha, a *kanawai ali'i,* 11
Anahua, a prophet, 7
Andrews, Lorrin, 42-43
Andrews, Dr. Seth, 42
"angels"
    of the *'aumakua,* 54
    guardian angels, 29, 50, 78
    of heaven, 55, 56, 58
    of *mo'o,* 83

"angels" (continued)
    of Pele, 69
    of thunder and lightning, 70, 71
    of sharks, 74
'Ao'ao'ele'ele, a *kanawai ali'i,* 11
ao 'aumakua, 47, 49, 49-51, 53; see also *kaku'ai* (transfiguration)
ao 'auwana (ao kuewa), 47-49, 53
ao kuewa (ao 'auwana), 47-49, 50, 53
ao o Milu, 47, 51-53; see Milu
apo leo sorcery, 133, 141
'aumakua, 28-32, 44, 54, 55, 66, 80, 91, 99; see *kumupa'a*
    acquiring and contacting of (*ho'aumakua*), 30-32, 59-60
    forms of: *mo'o,* 82-89; owls, 87, 88; *pele,* 64-69, 87, 89; thunder and lightning, 69-72; shark, 73-81, 87
    guides of spirits, 47-49
    ho'oulu kanaka (Ku and Hina), 99, 100
    Kane names of, 28, 57-58
    kapus of; see *kapu ho'ola'a*
    Ku names of, 58-59
    Lono names of, 59
    of medical arts, 99, 100, 106, 107
    o ka po, lights of, 80
    [rationalization of], 57-59, 80
    removal of bodies by, 50, 80, 81, 82
    rituals for; see *Pohaku o Kane*

"bait" (*maunu*), 35, 36, 37, 109, 122, 123, 126, 127, 139
Baldwin, the Rev. Mr., 76
betrothal (*ho'opalau*), 25-26
Bingham, the Rev. H., 100
[birthmarks]; see marks
breadfruit tree of Leiwalo, 47, 48, 49, 52
burial places, 38-43
    sites of: Aliamanu, 48; 'Iao, 39; Ka'a-'awa, 39-40; Ka'iliki'i, 41; Kaloko, 41; Kapalikalahale, 38; Nakoaka-'alahina, 38; Oloku, 40; Papaluana, 41; Pohukaina, 38; Pu'uwepa, 41; Waiuli, 39
burials; see disposal of corpses

calendar, 22
ceremonial days, 11, 13; see ritual periods
chants and prayers, texts of, 13, 30-31, 31-32, 68, 123-124, 125-126, 126
chiefs from Kahiki, 68

childbirth, 101
    inducing pregnancy, 99, 100
    causing barrenness, 100-101
children
    aikane, 6
    chiefly ranks of, 4-6
    consecration of, 27
    hanai, 26
    keiki ali'i, 27
    keiki punahele, 8, 26-27
    makahiapo, 26, 44
    rearing of, 26-27
    training of, 27
Conde, the Rev. Mr., 78, 81
Cook, Captain (Lono), 54

death
    avenging of; see *kuni*
    causes of, 43-44, 89
    defilement at, 35
    disposal of corpses, 38-43
    mourning at, 34-35
    offering at, 33
    omens at, 35
    preparation of corpses (bones), 33-34, 43
defilement, 27, 32, 35, 114; see purification
disease(s), 115; see *'ea; pa'ao'ao*
    introduced, 75, 87, 95, 104
    smallpox, epidemic of 1853, 105-106
    see also *haha;* illness(es)
disposal of corpses, 38-43
dreams; see also visions
    hihi'o, 55, 56
    interpretations of, 56-57
    moe 'uhane, 55, 56
dying, 44, 50

'ea, 101, 103-104, 114-115
    kinds of, 103
    remedies for, 103, 104-105
'e'epa, 82, 83, 85, 86; see *mo'o*
'Ele'io, a chief of Hana, 76
'Ewa, Oahu, 83 [the four 'Ewas: 'Ewa-loko; 'Ewa-waho; 'Ewa-a-La'akona; 'Ewa-a-La'auli]
'Ewa-a-La'akona, 84; see 'Ewa

"fish," see *i'a*
    of Uko'a pond, 84
fishing, methods of, 75-76, 78, 82
fishponds, 82, 83, 84
"food"; see *'ai*

games and sports, 20, 129
gods
    creation of (*'unihipili*), 64
    kinds of; see *akua* listings
    names of; see individual god names
    see also: *'aumakua; kaku'ai*

Ha'alokuloku, child of Hina, 68
Ha'enakulaina, in Uluka'a, 50
haha, see *kahuna haha*
    diagnoses by, 108, 109, 113, 115
    method of diagnosis; see *papa 'ili'ili*
    training for, 106-107
haihaia, 140, 141
Hailikulamanu, Moanalua, Oahu, 38
Hakau-a-Liloa, 12
Hakipu'u, Ko'olaupoko, Oahu, 73
hakoko; see games and sports
Haku'alamea, a *kanawai ali'i*, 11
haku 'ohi'a, a heiau ceremony, 21
Halaki'i; see Lonowahine
Halali'i, Niihau, 49
Halawa, 'Ewa, Oahu, 83
Haleakala, Maui, 39
hale 'ili mai'a, 135, 136
hale lau, 96, 106, 132
hale lau lama, 97
Halemano [Helemano], Waialua, Oahu, 5
Halema'uma'u, Hawaii, 65
Hale-o-Keawe, 18
Haleolono, Kaluako'i, Molokai, 128
hale puaniu (*puaniu* house), 85, 86
Halewai Ho'opa'ahao prison, Honolulu, 88
Hamakuapoko, Maui, 78
Hana, Maui, 76, 78, 106
Hanauma, Honolulu, Oahu, 76
Haulani, a child of Hina, 68
Haumea, 28, 31, 44, 66, 67, 68; see Papa
    trees of, 129
Haunu'u, a child of Hina, 68
Hauwahine, a *mo'o*, 82, 84
Hawanawana, a *kanawai akua*, 14, 22
He'ea, a priest, 7
heiau(s)
    ceremonies and rituals: see *haku 'ohi'a; kapu 'ohi'a ko; kapu lama; kapu loulu; kapu luakini; kapu unu; ulu 'ohi'a*
    kinds of: see *ipu-o-Lono; luakini; ko'a; unu* (*unuunu*); *waihau.* See also *kuaha* altars

heiau(s) (continued)
    names of: 'Alealea, 18; Hale-o-Keawe, 18; Hekili's, 69; Moa'ula, 12; Mo-'okini, 41; Pu'ukohola, 15, 16
Hekili (Kanehekili), *kahu* of thunder, 69
[Helemano]; see Halemano
Heleipawa, 3
Hewahewa, the high priest, 7
hihi'o; see dreams
Hi'iaka, 28, 66, 67
Hiku, 53
Hina, daughter of Kamaunuaniho, 68
Hinanalo, a husband of Papa (Haumea), 25
hi'u sorcery, 131, 133, 138, 141
ho'ao; see unions, *ho'ao* marriages
Hoapili; see Ulumaheihei Hoapili
ho'aumakua, 30-32, 59-60
ho'i mating, 21
Hoku; see Ho'ohokukalani
Holoa'e, high priest, 7
Holoa'e, priesthood order of, 7
Holoialena, a priest, 7
Holy Scriptures, quotations from, 53, 85, 88, 123
Honaunau, South Kona, Hawaii, 18
Honokahua, Ka'anapali, Maui, 39
Honokohau, Ka'anapali, Maui, 39, 73
Honokohau, North Kona, Hawaii, 122
Honolua, Ka'anapali, Maui, 39
Honolulu, Oahu, town and district, 40, 88
Honouliuli, 'Ewa, Oahu, 83
Honuamea; see Pele
Honua'ula, Maui, 78
honuhonu; see games and sports
Ho'ohoku; see Ho'ohokukalani
Ho'ohokukalani (Hoku; Ho'ohoku), 14, 28
Ho'oikaika, a woman of Maui, 76
Ho'olehua, Molokai, 131
ho'opalau; see betrothal
ho'opi'opi'o sorcery, 29, 122, 131, 133, 134, 138, 140
ho'ounauna sorcery, 29, 131, 132, 133, 134, 138, 141
Huanuikala'ila'i, 119
Hulihonua, 21, 25, 91
    as "first man," 3; see Kanehulihonua, "first man"
hulihonua; see *papa hulihonua*
Hulikapa'uianu'akea; see Kapa'uanu'akea
Humu, a chief of Kahiki, 68

153

i'a
    of 'Ewa, 83-84
    "fish," 44 Note 3
    of Uko'a, 84
'Iao, burial cave in Wailuku, Maui, 39
Ihukoko at Uko'a fishpond, 83
ilamuku, 10, 12
illness(es); see *'ea; pa'ao'ao*
    inherited (*ma'i ku'una*), 97, 101
    sent by *'aumakua*, see *ma'i 'aumakua*
    see also: disease(s); *haha*
images, 12, 18, 20, 54, 85, 130, 131
imu loa (*umu loa*), 122, 139
Inaina, a *kanawai akua*, 14
instruction; see training
ipu-o-Lono heiau, 33

Ka'a'awa burial pit, Maui, 39
Ka'a'awa, Ko'olauloa, Oahu, 20, 38
Ka'ahumanu, 19, 80, 127
Ka'ahupahau, 88
Ka'ahupahau, the shark goddess, 73, 76
Ka'ahu'ula-punawai, 38
Ka'aikananu'u, a *kanawai ali'i,* 11
Ka'ai'ohi'a, a man of Kipahulu, 79
Ka'aione, a man of Honolulu, 88
Ka'akakai, a prophet, 7
Ka'akau (Ka'akaumakaweliweli), 132-133, 135
Ka'akaumakaweliweli, see Ka'akau
Ka'akauualani, a Lo chief, 5
Ka'akeke *maika* ground, 'Ualapu'e, Molokai, 130
ka'a la'au sorcery, 133, 141
Ka'alawai, Honolulu, Oahu, 74
Ka'ali'i, son of Malua'e, 51-52
ka'ameha'i; see "bait"
Ka'anapali, Maui, 70, 78
Ka'apuwai, 22
Ka'au, a Lo chief, 5
Ka'elepulu pond, Kailua, Ko'olaupoko, Oahu, 82, 84
Ka'ena, Waialua, Oahu, 48, 81
Kahahana, 9, 17, 54
Kahaiki, tree of Kaloakaoma, 129
Kahakauila, a *kahuna kuni,* 122
Kahakuakane; see Ka'oao
Kahakuloa, Maui, 39
Kahakumakapaweo, 11
Kahakauakoko, 28
Kahala, Honolulu, Oahu, 40
Kahaloa at Waikiki, Honolulu, 73

Kahamalu'ihi (Kalua-i-Ho'ohila), 9, 22
Kahanui, Molokai, 131
Kahawali, 31
Kahekili, 9, 11, 17, 41, 70, 74, 131, 133, 137
Kahekili Ke'eaumoku [Ke'eaumoku-'opio; George Cox], 122, 127
Kahekilinui'ahumanu, 70
Kahiki, 67, 68, 75
Kahikihonuakele, child of Hina, 68
Kahikinui, Maui, 87
Kahiki'ula, a chief from Kahiki, 68
Kahiko Luamea, 4, 25, 63
Kahili'opua, 28, 133
Kahinaaola, 31
Kahipa at Kahuku, Ko'olauloa, Oahu, 39
Kahiuka, 88
kahoaka, 36, 120, 122, 127
Kaho'ali'i, thunder god, 20, 28, 30, 50, 54, 66, 69, 71
    kanawai of, 14, 22, 72
    mark [birthmark] of, 70
Kaho'ali'i, the man-god, 14, 20, 54
Kaho'iho'ina-Wakea at Ka'ena, Waialua, Oahu, 48
Kaho'owaha, a sorcery god, 133
Kaho'owahaokalani, a chief of Oahu, 11, 22
Kahoukapu, a chief of Hawaii, 76
kahu
    of chiefs, 34
    kahu akua, 82, 86, 90, 135
    of Kalaipahoa, 135, 136, 137
    of *mo'o,* 82, 85, 86
    of owls, 88
    of Pele, 67, 69
    of sharks, 73, 74, 75, 76, 77, 81
    of sorcery gods, 132, 134, 135
    of thunder, 69, 71, 72
Kahuilaokalani, 30
    as Kalaipahoa, 129-130
Kahuku, Ko'olauloa, Oahu
    story of, 38-39
Kahulupue, son of Ka'opulupulu, 89
kahuna a ka 'alawa maka, 98, 112-113
kahuna 'ana'ana, 29, 98, 119, 121, 122, 123, 126-127
    remedies of, 139-140
kahuna ('*ana'ana*) '*aihamu,* 121, 122, 123, 126, 133
kahuna ('*ana'ana*) *kalahala,* 119, 122
kahuna ('*ana'ana*) *kuni,* 29, 36, 37, 98, 119, 122, 126-127, 139
kahuna 'aumakua, 33, 39, 95-98
kahuna 'ea, 98, 104

kahuna haha, 98, 106, 108
    remedies (medicines) of, 109-110
    training of, 106-107
    treatments of, 110-111
kahuna ho'ohanau keiki, 98, 99, 101
kahuna ho'ohapai keiki, 98, 99
kahuna ho'opi'opi'o, 98
kahuna 'ike lihilihi, 98, 112-113
kahuna kuni; see *kahuna ('ana'ana) kuni*
kahuna (kuni) 'o, 36, 37, 119, 122, 127
kahuna kuni ola, 36, 37, 119, 122
kahuna la'au lapa'au, 97
kahuna lapa'au, 29, 36, 95, 98, 109, 110, 112
    classes of, 98
    order of Lonopuha, 106, 107, 112, 138
kahuna lau nahelehele, 99, 100
kahuna makani, 98, 138
kahuna 'o'o, 98, 106
kahuna orders and professions
    'ana'ana, 27, 119
    lonomakaihe, 8
    kapala kua'ula, 27
    kilo hoku, 8, 27
    kilo honua, 8
    kilokilo (lani), 8, 27
    kilo 'opua, 8
    ku'ialua, 8
    kuhikuhi pu'uone, 8, 27
    Ku'ula, 27
    papa hulihonua, 8, 27
    papa kaula, 7
    papa kahuna pule, 7
    see also: *'ana'ana,* divisions of; *kahuna lapa'au,* classes of
kahuna pa'ao'ao, 98, 101, 104, 138
kahuna po'oko'i, 96, 123, 130
Kaiahua, a chief, 74
Kai-a-Kahinali'i, 13
Kai-a-Kahulumanu, 13
Kaiakea, a man of Kala'e, Molokai, 131-133, 135; see Pua ma, legend of
Kaiewalu, a *kanawai ali'i,* 11
Kaihehe'e, a chiefly decree, 9; see also *kanawai ali'i*
kaikea treatment, 111
kaiku treatment, 111
Ka'ili, Pu'uhaoa, Hana, Maui
    a *pu'uhonua* land, 19
Ka'iliki'i, burial cave in Ka-'u, Hawaii, 41
Kailua, Kona, Hawaii, 42, 73, 135
Kailua, Ko'olaupoko, Oahu, 15
    a *pu'uhonua* land, 18
kaina sorcery, 131, 133, 138, 141

Kai'okia, a *kanawai akua,* 13-14, 22
kai popolohua mea a Kane, 51
Kaka'alaneo, a chief of Maui, 70, 76
Kakahe'e at Ka'ena, Waialua, Oahu, 48
Kakahili, a husband of Papa (Haumea), 25
kaku'ai (transfiguration), 35, 64, 87, 90, 91
    kapus of the transfigured, 75, 89
    into *mo'o,* 85-86
    into sorcery gods, 133, 134
    into sharks, 76-78
    into thunder and lightning, 71
    into volcanic manifestations (*pele*), 64-66
Kakuhihewa, 6, 11
Kala'e, Molokai, 128, 129
Kalaeoka'o'io, Oahu, 20, 38
Kalahiki, a shark, 74-75
Kalahuipua'a, South Kohala, Hawaii, 67
Kalaimamahu, brother of Kamehameha, 15
Kalaipahoa, the god-images
    anointing of, 136-137
    houses for, 135, 137
    legend of, 128-130
    names of: Kahuilaokalani, 129; Kaneikaulana'ula, 129; Kanemanaiapai'ea, 131; Kapo, 129; see also Ma'iola
    trees, 128, 129
    see *kalaipahoa*
kalaipahoa, 29, 131, 134, 137, 141
Kalakahi, 'Iao valley, Wailuku, Maui, 39
Kalamainu'u, a *mo'o* goddess, 31, 67, 82, 85, 87, 89, 96
Kalananu'uikuamamao, a chief from Kahiki, 68
Kalanianoano [Kalanionaona], a chief, 4
Kalanikauiokikilo, a chiefess, 4, 10
Kalaniku'ihonoikamoku (Kekaulike); see Kekaulike
Kalanikukuma, a chief, 11
Kalanikupule, son of Kahekili, 17, 131
Kalanimakali'i, a chiefess, 18
[Kalanionaona], a chief, 4
Kalani'omaiheuila, a chiefess, 4
Kalani'opu'u, 5, 15, 18, 41, 131
Kalauao, 'Ewa, Oahu, 17
Kalaupapa, Molokai, 128, 129
Kalawai'amilu, a *kahuna kuni,* 122
Kaleopu'upu'u, a priest, 7
Kalepolepo, Waikapu, Maui, 83
Kalihi, Honolulu, Oahu, 38
Kalima, a man of Kipahulu, 78
kalo ho'ola'a, 29, 128, 135
Kaloko, Kekaha, Hawaii, 41

155

Kaloko pond and burial cave, Kekaha, Hawaii, 41
Kalola (nui), a chiefess, 4, 5, 41
Kalona, a Lo chief, 5
Kaloakaoma, 129
[Kalou]; see Kilou
Kaloulu, a *kahuna 'ana'ana*, 127-128
Kalua, Honua'ula, Maui, 78
Kalua'aha, Molokai
   a *pu'uhonua* land, 19
Kaluaahole, Honolulu, Oahu, 74
Kalua-i-Ho'ohila; see Kahamalu'ihi
Kaluako'i, Molokai, 119, 128, 129
Kama, a *kahuna lapa'au*, 104
Kamahana (Kumahana), a chief, 4, 22
Kamahano, a chief, 11
Kama'ipu'upa'a, a chiefess, 15
Kamakanui'aha'ilono, 106
Kamakaokeahi, 31
Kamalalawalu, 6, 43
Kamanawa, a chief, 15
Kama'oma'o, plain on the isthmus between East and West Maui, 29, 47, 49, 66
Kamapua'a, a chief from Kahiki, 68
Kamaununaniho, a chiefess from Kahiki, 68
Kame'eiamoku, a chief, 41
Kameha'ikana, 129
Kamehameha I, 4, 7, 9, 15-17, 17-18, 19, 21, 41, 54-55, 67, 74, 85, 86, 109, 131, 133, 134, 135-136, 137
Kamehameha II (Liholiho), 5, 43
Kamehameha III, 5, 41, 43, 80, 82
Kamehameha IV (Alexander Liholiho), 88
Kamehameha Kapuaiwa [Kekuaiwa, Moses; died Dec. 24, 1848], 83
Kamehameha-nui, 4, 131
Kamohailani, a goddess, 31
Kamohoali'i, a *kumupa'a* shark god, 28, 30, 50, 66, 73, 75, 76, 77, 81, 87
Kana, 119
Kana, a man of Hamakualoa, Maui, 71
Kanaha pond, Wailuku, Maui, 83, 85
Kanaka-o-kai, a *kumupa'a* shark god, 30, 50, 75, 76
Kanaloa, the god, 28, 30, 51-52, 67, 68
   kanawai of, 14
Kanaloaho'okau, Manoa, Honolulu, Oahu, 51
Kanaloakua'ana Puapuakea, a chief, 43
kanawai akua (gods' edicts), 4, 11, 13-14, 22, 58, 72, 73, 75, 76
kanawai ali'i (chiefs' edicts), 9, 10, 11, 14, 15, 17, 130
kanawai Kolowalu, 11; see also *kanawai ali'i*

Ka'uhuhu, a *kumupa'a* shark god, 75, 76, 77
Kane, the god, 13, 14, 21, 28, 30, 51-52, 57, 67, 68, 99
Kaneakaho'owaha, a chief, 74
Kane'alai, chiefess of Molokai, 6, 130-131
Kane'alaikane, a kahuna of Kalaipahoa, 131, 135
Kanehaka, a god, 28, 57
Kanehalo, 57
Kanehekili (Hekili), a *kahu* of thunder, 69
Kanehekili, the thunder god, 28, 30, 44, 50, 57, 66, 69, 72
   kanawai of, 14, 22
   mark [birthmark] of, 70
Kanehoalani, pali at Kalaeoka'o'io, Oahu, 38
Kaneholopali, 28, 58
Kanehulihonua, "first man," 21, 63; see Hulihonua
Kanehulihonua, the god, 57
Kanehunamoku, a *kumupa'a* shark god, 30, 50, 73, 75, 76, 77
Kaneiakama, 128-130, 132; see Kalaipahoa, legend of
Kaneikamakaukau, 28, 57
Kaneikamalamalama, 57
Kaneikamolehulehu, 57
Kaneika'onohiokala, 58
Kaneikapapahonua, 57
Kaneikapualena, 57
Kaneikapule, 28, 57
Kaneikauila, 28
Kaneikaulana'ula, 30, 57
   as Kalaipahoa, 129-130
Kaneikawaiola, 31
Kaneikawana'ao, 57
Kaneikokala, a *kumupa'a* shark god, 28, 57, 75, 76, 77, 87
Kaneikokea, 28, 57
Kaneikolihanaakala, 57
Kaneka'a, 57
Kanekapolei, a chiefess, 15
Kanekapu-a-Kuihewa, a chief, 11
Kanela'auli, a chief, 15
Kaneki'ei, 57
Kaneki'i, 28, 57
Kanekoa, 57
Kaneko'a, 33
Kanekoha (Kaneikoha), 28, 57
Kanekua'ana, a *mo'o*, 82, 83, 84, 85
Kanelele, 28, 57
Kaneluhonua, 31
Kanemakahi'olele, 57
Kanemakua, 57

156

Kanemanaiahuea, 28, 58
Kanemanaiapai'ea, 57
    as a Kalaipahoa, 131
Kanemilohai, 58
Kanene'ene'e, 58
Kanenuiakea, 13, 30, 49, 57, 59, 63, 67, 69
    kanawai of, 13-14
    see also Kane
Kane'ohi'ohi, 58
Kaneoneo, a chief, 4, 22
Kanepa'ina, 57
Kanepohaka'a (Kanepohakuka'a), 28, 58
Kanepua'a, 33, 58
Kanepuahiohio, 58
Kaneulupo, 28, 87, 91
Kanewahine, a priest, 7
Kanewawahilani, the thunder god, 28, 30, 44, 57, 66, 69, 70, 71
Kaniamoko, Hana, Maui
    a *pu'uhonua* land, 19
Kani'aukani voyage, 135
Kanikania'ula, 51
Kanikawa, 31
Kanikawi, 31
Ka'oaka, 71
Ka'oakaha'iaonuia'umi, 31
Ka'oao [Kahakuakane?], a chief, 11
Ka'oleioku, a chief, 16-17, 122
Kaomi, 74
Ka'onohiokala, 54, 133
Ka'opuaki'iki'i, battle of, 17
Ka'opulupulu, the high priest of Oahu, 7, 54, 89, 91, 133
Kapa'akea, Molokai, 88
Kapakule, fishpond at Pu'uloa, 'Ewa, Oahu, 83
kapala kua'ula, 27
Kapalaoa, North Kona, Hawaii, 67
Kapalikalahale, burial cave on Niihau, 38
Kapaliku, father of Pele, 67
Kapapaialaka, a "person," 63, 91
Kapapaialaka, a "place," 48
Kapapakahui; see Ololupe
Kapapakolea, Moanalua, Oahu, 48
Kapa'uanu'akea (Hulikapa'uianu'akea), 7, 28, 31
Kapawa, a chief, 3, 12, 21, 39
Kapehu, 88
Kapehu the shark; see Pehu
Kapihe, a prophet, 7, 54
Kapo, 28, 67
    as a Kalaipahoa, 129-130
    as Kauluimaunaloa, 132
Kapohako'i, on Maunaloa, Molokai, 129

Kapohauola, a chiefess, 70
Kapohinaokalani, 32
Kapo'i, 88
Kapokuakini, 47, 52; see Milu, realm of
Kapokuamano, 47; see Milu, realm of
Kapua in Waikiki, Honolulu, Oahu, 74
kapuahi kuni; see *kuni,* ceremonies
kapu 'aihamu; see *kapu ho'ola'a,* 81
kapu aupuni, 89
kapu days; see ritual periods
Kapueookalani, a chiefess, 4, 22
kapu ho'ola'a, 75, 80, 81, 87, 89, 90, 95
    divisions of, 89
    see also *akua ho'ola'a*
Kapukaki, Moanalua, Oahu, 48
kapu lama, 7, 21
kapu loulu, 7, 21, 59
kapu luakini, 59
kapu moe, 5, 9, 22
Kapualei, Molokai, 132, 133
Kapunakea, near Mala; Lahaina, Maui, 83, 85
kapu noho (kapu a noho), 9, 22
kapu 'ohi'ako, 7
kapu puhi kanaka, 9-10, 22
kapu unu, 59; see also *unuunu ho'oulu 'ai*
kapu wohi, 22
kapus, chiefs', 4, 5, 9-10, 12, 22, 85
kapus, gods', 10, 12, 29, 32, 63-64, 85
kapus of training; see training
Kauakahi'ailani, a Lo chief, 5
Kauakahi-a-Kaho'owaha, a chief, 11, 22
Kauaniani, in Uluka'a, 50
Kauilanuimakehaikalani, a lightning god, 28, 30, 44, 66, 69, 71
    mark [birthmark] of, 70
kaukauali'i; see *kaukau* chief
kaukau chief *(kaukauali'i),* 5, 6
kaula: see prophets
Ka'ulawena Konohiki Wawanakalana (Mapunaia'a'ala), 68
Kauluimaunaloa; see Kapo
Kaumaea, a man of Kipahulu, 72
Kaumakamano, a chief, 11
Kaumeheiwa, a chief, 22
kauoha (kauoha 'ole), 38, 40, 136
Kaupe'a (plain at Pu'ukapolei), Pu'uloa, Oahu, 29, 47, 49, 66
Kaupipa, Kipahulu, Maui, 78
Kaupo, Maui, 39, 40, 78
Ka'upukea, a *kanawai akua,* 14, 22
Ka'upulehu, North Kona, Hawaii, 67
Ka'u'ukuali'i, a chief, 72
kauwa, 6, 8-9

157

Kawainui fishpond, Kailua, Koʻolaupoko, Oahu, 82, 83, 84
Kawelu, 53
Kawiwi stronghold, Waianae, Oahu, 18
Keahiolalo, 31
Keakahulilani "first woman," 3, 21, 25, 63, 91
Keakaleihulu, 14
Keakamahana, 18
Keakealanikane, 18
Kealoha, a woman of Maui, 76
Keamoaliʻi, South Kona, Hawaii, 18
Keʻanae, Koʻolau, Maui, 39, 69
Keaoua (Keoua-kupu-a-pa-i-ka-lani or Keoua-kalani-nui-ahi-lapalapa), father of Kamehameha, 5, 15
ke au ʻainoa, 13, 34; see also *ke aupuni ʻainoa*
ke aupuni ʻainoa, 9
Keawe (Keawe-i-kekahi-aliʻi-o-ka-moku), 6, 18, 130-131
Keaweaweʻulaokalani, a god, 54
Keaweheulu, a chief, 15
Keawe-i-kekahi-aliʻi-o-ka-moku; see Keawe
Keawe-ku-i-ke-kaʻai, 18
Keawe-nui-a-ʻUmi, 22
Keawenuikauohilo, a sorcery god, 133
Keʻeaumoku, son of Peleioholani, 22
Keʻei, South Kona, Hawaii, 67
Keʻelanihonuaʻaiakama (Lonomahana), a chiefess, 22
Kehopu, a man of Hana, 78
keiki punahele, 8, 26-27
Kekaha, Mana, Kauai
 a *puʻuhonua* land, 17
Kekaulike (Kalanikuʻihonoikamoku), 11, 39
Kekauluohi, a chiefess, 83
Kekeleiaiku, child of Hina, 68
Kekio Pilakalo, a prophet, 54
Kekuaiaea (Kuaiaea), a chiefess, 122, 127
[Kekuaiwa]; see Kamehameha Kapuaiwa
Kekuʻiapoiwa Liliha, 5, 41, 85
Keliʻikukahaoa, a kahuna of Kalaipahoa, 131, 135
Keliʻimaikaʻi, 15
Keliʻiokahekili, a chiefess, 70
Keliʻiokalani, a chiefess, 18
Keokea, South Kona, Hawaii, 18
Keololani, a thunder god, 71
Keonekapu-a-Kahamaluʻihi, Waimea, Kauai
 a *puʻuhonua* land, 17
Keopuolani, 5, 85
Keoua, father of Kamehameha; see Keaoua
Keoua Kuahuʻula, a chief of Ka-ʻu, 15-16

Keoua Stone, 18
Kihawahine, the chiefess, 20
 transfiguration of, 85; see Kihawahine, the *moʻo* goddess
Kihawahine, the *moʻo* goddess, 20, 54, 82, 85
Kihewakeoho, a woman of Waialua, 127
Kiholo fishpond, Kiholo, North Kona, Hawaii, 67
Kihuluhulu, a man of Honuaʻula, 78
Kikaha, a priest, 7
Kikihale, Honolulu, Oahu, 88
Kikiʻi, a *kanawai akua,* 14, 22
Kilauea Crater, Hawaii, 65, 67; see also pit of Pele
Kilauea at Keawaʻula, Waianae, Oahu, 48
Kilohi, a prophet, 7
kilo hoku, 8, 27
kilo honua, 8
kilokilo (lani), 8, 27, 47
kilo ʻopua, 8
Kilou, 39 [now a place name, Kalou, in Waialeʻe, Koʻolauloa, Oahu]
kino wailua, 85
Kipahulu, Maui, 72, 78, 87, 106
Kiu, a prophet, 7
Kiwala-ʻo, 5
koʻa, 33, 73, 77, 80, 83, 86, 96
Kohola, a *kanawai aliʻi,* 11
koi; see games and sports
Kokoiki, Kohala, Hawaii, 16
Kokoloea, a Lo chief, 5
Koleana, the caterpillar at Kapapakolea, 48
Koleana cave in Moanalua, Oahu, 38
Konahuanui peak, Nuʻuanu, Oahu, 38
Koʻolau, Maui, 78
Koʻolauloa, Oahu, 20
Koʻolaupoko, Oahu, 20
Ku, the god, 14, 21, 28, 57, 99
 kanawai of, 14, 22
kuahu altars, 32, 33, 58, 64, 77, 96
Kuaiaea (Kekuaiaea), a chiefess, 122, 127
Kuaila, a man of Waialua, Oahu, 81
Kuaiwa, a priest, 7
kuaka (akaku); see visions
Kuakahela, a chief and priest, 7, 15
Kuakapuaʻa, a chief, 74
Kualakaʻi, Molokai, 119
Kualiʻi Kunuiakea Kuikealaikauaokalani, 9, 11, 14-15, 22, 54
Kualiʻi, priesthood order of, 7
Kualoa, Koʻolaupoko, Oahu, 20, 38, 73
 a *puʻuhonua* land, 18
Kualonoʻehu, a chief, 9, 22

Kualonowao, a god, 58
Kuamu, a sorcery goddess, 133
    kanawai of, 22
Ku and Hina (*'aumakua ho'oulu kanaka*), 99, 100
kuapala offering stand, 27, 69
Kua'ua'u, 109, 138
kuehu kapa sorcery, 133, 141
[Kuekaunahi]; see Kuka'iunahi
Kuhaimoana, a *kumupa'a* shark god, 58, 73, 75, 76
kuhaulua chiefs, 5, 6, 9-10
Kuheilani, 119
Kuheleimoana, 67-68, 91
Kuheleipo, 67-68
kuhikuhi pu'uone, 8, 27, 47
Kuho'oholopali, a god, 58
Kuho'one'enu'u, 7, 12, 31, 58, 129, 135
ku'ialua; see *lua* fighting
Kuihelani, H., 42
Kuihewa; see Kakuhihewa
Kuikaha'awi, a god, 59
Kuikaloa'a, 59
Kuikapono, 59
Kuikauweke, 58
Kuikealai, 58
Kuikekala, 58
Kuikepa'a, 59
Kuikepi, 59
ku'iku'i; see games and sports
Kukaha'ula, a god, 58
Kuka'ilimoku, 7, 12, 19, 58
    kanawai of, 14
Kuka'iunahi [Kuekaunahi], Waikiki, Honolulu, Oahu, 74
Kukalani, 12, 58
Kukalani'ehu, 7, 129
Kukalani'ehuiki, 12
Kukalaniho'one'enu'u, 31
Kukaniloko, a Lo chief, 5
Kuka'ohi'alaka, 58
Kukauakahi, a thunder god, 58
    kanawai of, 14, 22
    mark [birthmark] of, 70
    owl, a form of, 87, 88
Kukeaoho'omihamihaikalani, 58
Kukeaoloa, 58
Kukeaopoko, 58
Kukeolo'ewa, 7, 12, 33, 58, 129, 135
Kuki'iahu, battle of, 17
Kukuipahu, a chief of Hawaii, 76
Kukuipahu [Kukuipuka] Kahakuloa, Maui
    a *pu'uhonua* land, 19

Kukuipuka; see Kukuipahu
Kula, Maui, 40, 88
kulakula'i; see games and sports
kuleana, 49-50, 82
    in *mo'o* forms, 82
    in the sea, 76, 78
    in thunder, 72
    in volcanic forms (*pele*), 66
    to worship thunder, 69
Kulili'ai(ke)kaua, 58
Kumahana; see Kamahana
Kumauna, 58
Kumokuhali'i, 58
Kumuko'a, son of Kane'alai, 131
kumupa'a, 28-32, 66, 72, 80, 91
    Kamapua'a as a, 68
    mo'o as, 85
    Pele as a, 68-69
    sharks as, 74, 75, 76
    thunder gods as, 70
    see *'aumakua*
kuni, 36-37, 120, 139
    ceremonies, 121-122, 126-127
Kunuiakea, 7, 12, 57, 58, 59
Kupa'aike'e, 58
Kupalaha, Waikiki, Honolulu, Oahu, 74
kupele, 102, 103, 110
Kupepeiaopoko, 58
Kupiapia, a shark, 73
Kupou, a *kanawai akua*, 14, 22
Kupulupulu, 58
Ku'ula, profession of, 27
Kuwahailo, 58
kuwalawala; see games and sports
Kuwalupaukamoku, a chief, 11

La'a; see La'amaikahiki
La'amaikahiki, a chief, 11, 68, 91
la'au chief (*la'au ali'i*), 6
la'auli; see *la'au* chief
Lahaina, Maui, district and town, 39, 73, 76, 78, 88
Lahainalalo, Maui, 42
Lahainaluna, Maui, place and school, 42, 43
Laka, the hula goddess
    kanawai of, 22
Laka, son of Keakahulilani, 91
Laka, son of Wahieloa, 41
Lale, a Lo chief, 5
lama; see *kapu lama*
Lanikaula, a prophet, 7
Lanikepue, a prophetess, 7

159

lani kuaka'a, 49, 55, 57
Laniwahine, a *mo'o,* 82, 84
Laukahi'u, a shark god, 73
Laukupu, a *mo'o,* 84
Laulili'i, a *kanawai akua,* 14
Laupahoehoe, Hilo Paliku, Hawaii, 15
Leihulunuiakamau, 31
Leilono, Moanalua, Oahu, 47, 52
leina a ka 'uhane, 47-48, 49
lele altar, 12
lelo pu'u; see *alelo pu'u*
lepo popolo chief, 4, 6
Li'aikuhonua, 91
Lihau'ula, 3, 12, 63
Liholiho; see Kamehameha II
Lihue, Wahiawa, Oahu, 5
Liliha; see Keku'iapoiwa Liliha
Lo chiefs, 5
Loa, a *kanawai ali'i,* 11
Lokai, a *kahuna kuni,* 122
lokea chief, 5-6
Lono (Captain Cook), 54
Lono, a chief of Ka-'u; see Lonopuha
Lono, the god, 21, 28, 33, 57, 59, 99
Lonoikamakahiki, the god, 7, 20
Lonoikamakahiki, son of Keawe-nui-a-'Umi, 7, 20, 22, 43
Lonoika'ouali'i, the god, 7, 59
Lonoikiaweawealoha, 59
Lonoiki'eke, 59
Lonokahikini, a chiefess, 4, 22
Lonokina'u, 88
Lonokina'u, the god, 59
Lonomahana; see Ke'elanihonua'aiakama
Lonomauki, a priest, 7
Lonomakahi'olele, a god, 59
lonomakaihe, 8
Lonomakua, the god, 28, 30
Lononuiakea, 7, 57, 59
Lono'opuakau, 59
Lonopuha (Lono), 106, 107
  order of, 106, 107, 112, 138
Lonowahine (Halaki'i) a chiefess, 22
Lonowahine, a *mo'o,* 85
loulou; see games and sports
Lua, a husband of Papa (Haumea), 25
lua fighting, 8, 20
Luaho'omoe, a prophet and priest, 7
Luaipo, a thunder god
  mark [birthmark] of, 70
luakini heiau, 19, 33
Luanu'u, 3
Luhaukapawa, a prophet, 7, 12

Luia, a chief, 74, 75
Lumaluma'i, a chiefly decree, 9; see also *kanawai ali'i*

Ma, a prophet, 7
Ma'alo, a *kahu* of Kalaipahoa, 135
Maea, a *kanawai ali'i,* 11
Maeaea [beach], Waialua, Oahu, 80
Mahai'ula, North Kona, Hawaii, 67
Mahea, a prophet, 7
Mahi, a man of Ka'anapali, 70
Mahoe, a schoolteacher on Maui, 75-76
Mai'akuapu'u, a thunder god, 72
ma'ihi, 41
ma'i 'aumakua, 95-98
  ma'i ho'opa'i, 87, 90
  ma'i kama'aina, 75, 87
  ma'i ku'una, 97, 101
ma'i ho'opa'i; see under *ma'i 'aumakua*
maika; see games and sports
ma'i kama'aina; see under *ma'i 'aumakua*
ma'i kumupa'a; see *ma'i 'aumakua*
ma'i ku'una; see under *ma'i 'aumakua*
Ma'ilikukahi, a Lo chief, 5
ma'i malihini, 75, 87, 95
Ma'iola, antidote to Kalaipahoa, 131, 137
maka'aina chiefs, 6
maka'aina, the people, 8
Maka'alae, Hana, Maui, 81
Maka'alawa, a prophet, 7
makahiapo, 26, 144
Makahiki
  festival, 19-21, 22
  gods, 20
Makakuikalani, a chief, 43
Makawao, Maui, 40
Makea, a husband of Papa (Haumea), 25
Makuakaumana, a prophet, 7
Maku'uko'o, a magic cane, 52
Malo, David, 6, 21
Malokea, a *kanawai ali'i,* 11
Malua'e, tradition of, 51-52
Mamalahoa [Mamalahoe], Kamehameha's *kanawai ali'i,* 15-17, 22
Mamalahoe, 22; see Mamalahoa
Mana, Kauai, 49
manele litter, 26, 39
Manewa, a priest, 7
Manoheli'i, a woman of Waialua, 80
Manokalanipo, a chief, 6, 14
Manu'a, 51, 53, 60; see Milu
  po pau 'ole of Manu'a, 52, 53
Manuaha'i, 14

160

Manukiu, 14
Ma'ohelaia, Molokai, 49
Ma'onakala in Kanahena, Honua'ula, Maui, 75
Mapunaia'a'ala; see Ka'ulawena Konohiki Wawanakalana
Mapu'uaia'a'ala, 91
marks [birthmarks]
    of Kanehekili, 70
    of Kukauakahi, 70
    of Luaipo, 70
    of Kaho'ali'i, 70
    of Kauilanuimakehaikalani, 70
marriages; see unions
Maui-a-ka-malo, son of Akalana, 91
Maui-a-Wakalana, 68
Maunaloa [mountain], Kaluako'i, Molokai, 129, 134, 137
Maunalua fishpond, Maunalua, Honolulu, Oahu, 82, 83, 84
maunu; see "bait"
medical kahuna; see *kahuna lapa'au*
medical profession, 98, 139; see *kahuna lapa'au*
medicines; see remedies
Meek, John, 88
Mikololou, a shark, 76
Milipomea, kahuna line of, 63
Milu, 51, 53, 60, 119
    realm of, 47, 48, 49, 51-53
Moanaliha, a shark, 73, 76, 81, 133
Moa'ula heiau, Waipi'o, Hawaii, 12
Moeluhi, a *kahu* of Kalaipahoa, 135
moepu'u, 34
moe 'uhane; see dreams
Mo'i, a prophet and priest, 7
Mokapu peninsula, Ko'olaupoko, Oahu, 21
Mokoli'i islet, Ko'olaupoko, Oahu, 73
mokomoko; see games and sports
Mokuahole, the sea off Kalena, Maui, 79
Mokuaweoweo crater on Mauna Loa, Hawaii, 67
moku hale, 85, 96, 97, 106, 120, 121
Mokuhinia, a *mo'o,* 83
Mokuhinia pond, Waine'e, Lahaina, Maui, 83, 85 [site of Kamaluululele Park]
Mokulehua, a *kanawai akua,* 22
Mokulehua, tradition of, 51, 52
Mokuleia, Waialua, Oahu, 127
Mokupapa islet, Kalena, Kipahulu, Maui, 79
Moku'ula, Waine'e, Lahaina, Maui, 83
Molilele pali, Ka-'u, Hawaii, 41
mo'o, 59, 82-89
    forms of, 83

mo'o (continued)
    names of: see Hauwahine; Kalamainu'u; Kanekua'ana; Kihawahine; Laniwahine; Laukupu; Lonowahine; Mokuhinia; Walimanoanoa; Walinu'u
    offerings to, 59-60, 85-86
    transfiguration into, 85-86
Mo'okini heiau, Kohala, Hawaii, 41
Mo'opuakea, a prophet, 7
mua, 27

Na'alehua, Ka-'u, Hawaii, 88
naha chiefs, 4-5, 9-10
naha mating, 5, 21
Nahi'ena'ena, 5
Naho'aiku, 28
Nahoali'i, 28
Nakoaka'alahina, burial cave on Kauai, 38
Nakoloilani, a thunder god, 28, 30, 44, 66, 71
na kukulu o ka lani, 49
Nalanipipi'o, a chiefess, 4, 10, 22
Namakaohalawa, the channel entrance of Pu'uloa, 'Ewa, Oahu, 83, 84
Namakaokaha'i, 28, 66, 67
na paia ku a Kane, 49, 50, 51
Napaepae, a man of Lahaina, 88
Napeha pool, Halawa, 'Ewa, Oahu, 48
Napuoko, a chief of Honokohau, Hawaii, 122
Naula [Niula ?], a prophet, 7
Nawaiuolewa at Kahuku, Ko'olauloa, Oahu, 39
ni'aupi'o chiefs, 4-5, 9-10, 21
Ni'aupi'o Kolowalu, a *kanawai ali'i,* 11, 14
Niho'aikaulu, 28, 31, 120
Niula; see Naula
noa chief; see *noanoa* chief
noanoa chief (*noa* chief), 6
noho ana; see unions, *noho ana*
Nononui, a Lo chief, 5
Nu'a, 7, 28, 31
Nu'akea, 7, 28, 31
Nu'uanu, battle of, 17, 31
Nu'uanu, Oahu, 72

offerings
    for *'ana'ana* training, 120
    to appease the *'aumakua,* 29, 32-33
    for breaking of an oath, 13; see also *pikai*
    for the cutting of the Kalaipahoa trees, 130
    at death, 33
    for homeless souls, 48

offerings (continued)
    kaku'ai offerings, 64-65, 67, 71, 77, 85-86
    to Kalaipahoa, 136
    kuni offerings, 36
    mo'o offerings, 59-60, 96
    to Pua *ma*, 132
Oloku, Honolulu, Oahu, 40
Ololupe ('Olopue), 135
Olopana, a chief from Kahiki, 68
Olopio, 'Iao valley, Wailuku, Maui, 39
'Olopue; see Ololupe
omens
    'ailolo, 121
    at death, 35
    of god's approbation, 12
    of the *kahuna lau nahelehele*, 100
    kuni, 126
'o'o ihe; see games and sports
'O'okala cape, Hamakua, Hawaii, 6
'O'opuloa, Hamakualoa, Maui, 69
'Opelunuikauha'alilo, child of Pele, 68
Owa, 47; see Milu, realm of
owls as *'aumakua* forms, 87, 88

Pa'akakanilea [Pa'akanilea], a chief, 5
[Pa'akanilea]; see Pa'akakanilea
Pa'ako, Honua'ula, Maui, 78
Pa'ao, 7, 41
pa'ao'ao
    ailments, 101-102, 114-115
    remedies, 102-103, 106
pahe'e; see games and sports
pahelehele; see games and sports
pahi'uhi'u sorcery, 131
Pailolo channel, between Maui and Molokai, 88
Pakapakakaua, a Lo chief, 5
Pala'au, Molokai, 131
Palaha, a *kahuna lapa'au*, 111-112
Paliloaali'i, a *kanawai ali'i*, 11
Pali-o-Kaka'e, 'Iao valley, Wailuku, Maui, 39
Pamano, 90, 91
Paoakalani, a Lo chief, 5
Papa (Haumea), 3, 25
Papa'a, 88
Papa'aea, Hamakualoa, Maui, 69, 70
papa ali'i, chiefly class, 7
papa chiefs, 5, 9
Papaholahola, a *kanawai ali'i*, 11
papa hulihonua, 8, 27, 47
Papa'i, Kea'au, Puna, Hawaii, 15, 16
papa 'ili'ili, 98, 108, 109

papa kahuna pule, 7; see also priesthood orders
papa kanaka, mankind, 8
papa kaula, 7; see also prophets (*kaula*)
papa kauwa, outcasts, 8-9
papa ku'ialua, 8
Papaluana, Kipahulu, Maui, 41
Papamau, a *kanawai akua*, 14
Papio, a chiefess, 73
Paukukalo, Wailuku, Maui, 83, 85
Paukukaula, a *kanawai akua*, 14, 22
Paumakua, 68, 91
Paunau, Lahaina, Maui
    a *pu'uhonua* land, 19
Pe'aleihuluomanu, 14
Pehu (Kapehu), a shark, 73, 76, 79, 133
Pele (Honuamea), 28, 31, 50, 65, 66, 67, 68
    kanawai of, 14, 22
pele (volcanic manifestations), 64-69, 87, 89
    transfiguration into, 64-66
Peleioholani, 22, 54, 74, 131
Pelham, Dr. John; see Pili, Dr.
"pig-eating" battle on Kauai, 17
pikai, 35, 114; see also purification
Pikele'ula, a *kanawai ali'i*, 11
Pili, Dr. (Dr. John Pelham), 41-43
Piliwale, a Lo chief, 5
Piliwale spring, Molokai, 131-132
pi'o chiefs, 4-5, 9-10, 18, 21, 22
pit of Pele, *ka lua o Pele*, 50, 60, 64-66, 67;
    see also Kilauea Crater
Pohaku o Kane, 32-33, 58, 96
Pohaku'oki'aina (Pohaku Palaha), Maui, 39
Pohaku Palaha (Pohaku'oki'aina), Maui, 39
Pohukaina, burial cave on Oahu, 38
Polipoli, Napoko, Maui
    a *pu'uhonua* land, 19
Polou, 39 [now a place name in Keana, Ko'olauloa, Oahu]
Po'okapu, a man of Hana, 81
Po'omuku (William Stevens), 88
prayers, 103, 107, 114
    'ana'ana, 119, 121, 135, 136, 138, 139
    names of; see *pule*
    see also chants and prayers, texts of
priesthood orders, 4, 7, 12, 99
priests; see *papa kahuna pule*
prophecies, 7, 37, 54; see also *kuni*, ceremonies
prophets (*kaula*), 7, 47, 48, 54-55
    of Pele, 65
    of thunder gods, 69, 71, 72
    of shark gods, 75

Pua, the sorcery god, 132; see Pua *ma*, legend of
Pua *ma*
    forms of, 132
    houses for, 132, 135, 137
    legend of, 131-132
    names of: see Kahili'opua; Kaho'owaha; Ka'onohiokala; Kapo (Kauluimaunaloa); Keawenuikauohilo; Kuamu; Pua
    remedies against, 138-139; see also treatments, against magic and sorcery
Pu'ali, a *kahuna kuni*, 122
puaniu house; see *hale puaniu*
Pueo, 51, 52
Puheke, father of Palaha, 111-112
Puhene, a man of Molokai, 133
pu'ili; see games and sports
Pu'iwa, Nu'uanu, Oahu, 38
pule, names of
    'ana'ana, 120, 123
    ho'ola'a, 128
    ho'omana'o, 107
    ho'omaika'i, 107
    kahoahoa, 28, 65
    kahoahoa 'aumakua, 39
    kahoahoa kupapa'u, 39
    kaholo, 123, 125-126, 140
    kala (*kalahala*), 139
    kanaenae, 48
    o kini Kailua, 120
    Kumuhonua, 107
    kuni, 123
    'umi, 123, 126, 139, 140
    uweke, 139
Puna'aikoa'e, 89
Punalu'u, Ka-'u, Hawaii, 41
Punia; see Puniaiki
Puniaiki (Punia), 76, 91
punishments
    by *'aumakua* forms, 75, 87-88, 90, 95; see also *ma'i 'aumakua*
    for concealing *kauwa* ancestry, 9
    for practicing death-dealing magic, 37, 123, 125, 130; see also *kuni*
    for stealing, 37
    under (introduced) law, 38, 42
    for violations of chiefs' kapus or *kanawai*, 5, 9, 10, 11, 14
    for violations of gods' kapus or *kanawai*, 11, 12, 29, 72, 75, 81
Pu'oa'oaka, battle of, 43
purification, 27, 32-33, 35, 114

Pu'ua, a *kanawai ali'i*, 11
Pu'uho'owale, Lahaina, Maui, 133
pu'uhonua, 17-19, 32, 33
pu'uhonua of Honaunau, 18
pu'uhonua lands, 17-19
Pu'uiki in Hana, Maui, 72
Pu'ukapolei, plain at; see Kaupe'a
pu'u kaua, 17, 18
Pu'ukoamakai'a, a *kanawai akua*, 14, 72; see also mark [birthmark] of Kaho'ali'i
Pu'ukohola heiau, Kawaihae, Hawaii, 15, 16
Pu'uloa, 'Ewa, Oahu, 49, 73, 83, 89
Pu'umane'one'o, Maui, 40
Pu'uwepa burial cave, Kohala, Hawaii, 41
Puwalu, a chief, 6

remedies (medicines), 97, 98
    'ea, 103
    pa'ao'ao, 102-103
    plants and substances used as, 103, 104, 106, 109-110, 138, 141
    sea water used as, 113
    see treatments, medical
Restoration Day, 88
revelations; see visions
rituals and ceremonies
    'ailolo, 121
    kuni (*kuni make*), 36, 120, 121-122, 126, 139
    kuni ola, 126, 139
    Makahiki, 21
    at *Pohaku o Kane*, 32-33
    of priesthood order of Holoa'e, 7
    of priesthood order of Kuali'i, 7
    see also heiau(s), ceremonies and rituals
ritual periods, 11-12, 13, 21, 77

sacrifices
    human, 12
    of *kauwa*, 8
    see also *moepu'u*
sharks, 73, 74
    'aumakua forms, 73-81
    attacks by, 75-76, 78, 78-79
    as guides or protectors, 74-75, 82
    names of: see Ka'ahupahau; Kalahiki; Kamohoali'i; Kanakaokai; Kanehunamoku; Kaneikokala; Ka'uhuhu; Kuhaimoana; Kupiapia; Laukahi'u; Moanaliha; Mikololou; Pehu (Kapehu); 'Unihokahi
    transfiguration into, 76-78

sickness; see illness
signs
>of thunder gods; see marks [birthmarks]
>of transfigured bodies, 79
>>shark forms, 77, 79
>>in thunder, 71
>>*pele,* 65
sins, 37, 52
sorcery (*hana 'ino*), 131
>counteracting of, 138-140
>gods of; see Pua ma
>kinds of, 131, 133, 138, 140, 141
>spread of, 132-133, 134-135, 137
>see *kalaipahoa*
spirits
>expulsion of, 138
>possession by, 53-55
>possession by transfigured, 79-80, 86
sports; see games and sports
Stevens, William (Po'omuku), 88
Stone of Kane; see *Pohaku o Kane*
symptoms of illnesses (diseases), 102, 104, 108, 109

tapas, names of, 12, 21, 54, 59, 77, 80, 86, 96, 97, 114
tattooing, 70
thunder and lightning *'aumakua,* 69-72
training (instruction)
>*'ana'ana,* 120-121
>kahuna professions (general), 27
>medical (*haha*), 106-109
transfiguration; see *kaku'ai*
treatments, medical
>for childbearing, 99, 100
>lancing, 106
>against magic and sorcery, 122, 138-140, 141
>for *pehu* [edema], 112; see *kaikea, kaiku, waikea, waiki*
>see also remedies (medicines)

Ua'alakawai, a *kanawai ali'i,* 11
'Ualapu'e, Molokai, 133
Uhana, Lanai, 49
'uhinipili (*'unihipili*); see *akua 'unihipili*
Uko'a fishpond at Kawailoa, Waialua, Oahu, 82, 84
>the strange fishes of, 84
Uli (Uliiuka), *'aumakua* of *'ana'ana,* 119, 123, 127
>epithets of, 123

Uli (Uliwahine), 28, 31
Uliikai, 119, 123
Uliiuka; see Uli
'Ulu genealogy, 91
ulu hale, 106
Uluka'a, an *'aumakua* realm, 50, 73
Ulumaheihei Hoapili, a chief and priest, 7, 17, 41, 70, 85
ulu 'ohi'a, 21
'ulu o Leiwalo, 47, 48, 49, 52
umauma; see games and sports
'Umi-a-Liloa, 4, 6, 12
'Umiamaka, 43, 44
umu loa (*imu loa*), 122, 139
'unihipili (*'uhinipili*); see *akua 'unihipili*
'Unihokahi, a shark, 73-74
unions, 4-6, 21, 22
>*ho'ao* marriages, 4, 25-26
>*noho ana,* 26
unu; see *unuunu ho'oulu 'ai*
unuunu ho'oulu 'ai (*unu*), 33

visions, 55-56, 75; see also *kahoaka*
volcanic manifestations; see *pele*

Wahiawa, Oahu, 5, 119
Waia, a husband of Papa (Haumea), 25
Wai'ale'ale, Maui, 39
Waialua, Oahu, 3, 39, 48, 80, 81, 88, 122, 127
Wai'anae, Oahu, 89
waihau heiau, 59, 83, 86, 96
Waihe'e, Maui, 100
Wahieloa, 41
Waikane, Ko'olaupoko, Oahu
>a *pu'uhonua* land, 18
waikea treatment, 110, 111
Waikele, 'Ewa, Oahu, 122
waiki treatments, 110-111
Waikiki, Honolulu, Oahu, 20, 40, 73, 74, 85
Waikolu, Molokai, 129
Wailoa, a husband of Papa (Haumea), 25
Wailua, Puna, Kauai
>a *pu'uhonua* land, 17
Wailuku, Maui, 73
Waimea, Hawaii, 41-42, 43
Waimea, Kauai, 122
Wainanali'i fishpond, North Kona, Hawaii [site of lava bed called Kani-ku], 67
Waine'e, Lahaina, Maui, 83

Waiohonua, Hana, Maui, 81
Waipahu, 'Ewa, Oahu, 38, 122
Waipu, Kaupo, Maui, 39
Waipukua, Waihe'e, Maui
    a *pu'uhonua* land, 19
Waiu, Kaupo, Maui, 39
Waiuli, burial pit, Maui, 39, 40
Waiuli, hill on Maui, 39

Wakea, 3, 11, 12, 21, 25, 48, 63, 67, 89, 119
Walimanoanoa, a *mo'o* goddess, 28, 31, 67, 85
Walinu'u, a *mo'o* goddess, 28, 31, 67, 85
Wao'ala, Waialua, Oahu, 80
wohi chiefs, 5, 9-10
wohi kapu, 22